Other Books by Jean Fritz

AND THEN WHAT HAPPENED, PAUL REVERE?

CAN'T YOU MAKE THEM BEHAVE,
 KING GEORGE?

GEORGE WASHINGTON'S BREAKFAST

SHH! WE'RE WRITING THE CONSTITUTION

WHAT'S THE BIG IDEA, BEN FRANKLIN?

WHERE DO YOU THINK YOU'RE GOING,
 CHRISTOPHER COLUMBUS?

WHERE WAS PATRICK HENRY ON THE
 29TH OF MAY?

WHY DON'T YOU GET A HORSE, SAM ADAMS?

WILL YOU SIGN HERE, JOHN HANCOCK?

Can't You Make Them Behave, King George?

by Jean Fritz

pictures by Tomie de Paola

PAPERSTAR

G. P. Putnam's Sons

The Putnam & Grosset Group

Printed on recycled paper

Library of Congress Cataloging-in-Publication Data
Fritz, Jean. Can't you make them behave, King George?
Summary: A biography of George the Third, King of Great Britain
at the time of the American Revolution. I. George III,
King of Great Britain, 1738-1820—Juvenile literature.
I. dePaola, Thomas Anthony. II. Title
DA506.A2F74   1976   941.07'3'0924 [B] 75-33722
ISBN 0-399-23304-0 (hardcover)
20 19 18 17 16 15 14 13
PaperStar ISBN 0-698-11402-7 (paperback)
10 9 8 7 6 5 4

To Margaret Swart
—*J.F.*

For Margot Tomes
—*T. de P.*

Before King George the Third was either king or the Third, he was just plain George, a bashful boy who blushed easily. His toes turned in when he walked, and his teachers nagged him about being lazy. Now, of course, as everyone knows, a king should not blush or turn in his toes or be lazy, but George didn't think much about being a king. His grandfather, George the Second, was king at the moment, and when he died, George's father, Frederick, would be king. And not until Frederick died would George have to worry about his turn.

So he went on blushing and turning in his toes. He daydreamed and sometimes drew pictures on the margins of his school papers. Once after a scolding he put tar on a teacher's seat so that when the teacher sat down, he had a hard time getting up.

GEORGE!

Then suddenly on March 20, 1751, when George was 12 years old, his father died. And George, instead of being just plain George, was George, Prince of Wales. The next king. What was more, everyone expected George to start behaving like the next king. *Right now.*

"Take your elbows off the table, George," his mother would say. "Be a *king!*

"Don't gobble your food, George. Do you want to look like your Uncle Cumberland?

"Stand up straight, George. Kings don't slouch."

He was surrounded by private tutors, who from morning to night gave him arithmetic problems to solve, history lessons to learn, Latin passages to translate. They told him to turn out his toes, to speak up, to keep still, to be a man, to get to work. Sometimes George sulked under so much instruction. Once after a particularly hard Latin passage written by an old Roman named Caesar, George wrote on his paper: "Mr. Caesar, I wish you would go to the devil." But for the most part he tried to do what he was told. He paid particular attention to his favorite tutor, Lord Bute, who seemed to know all the rules for the king business. And since he was going to have to be king, George decided that when the time came, he would be a good one. He would be a father to his people.

The time came on October 25, 1760, when George was 22 years old. His grandfather died, and suddenly there was George, all by himself, the new king. The first thing he did was to gallop off to see Lord Bute and check the rules. If he was going to be a good king, he wanted to start off right.

And he did. He even looked like a king—tall, auburn-haired, with well-shaped legs and toes going the right direction. (Occasionally he had pimples, people noticed, but never more than one or two at a time.) When he made a speech, he stood straight and spoke in a strong voice. At parties he didn't just stare at

RULE ONE...

the floor, as his grandfather had done, he mixed with his company, and he didn't just hold out his hand for ladies to kiss, he kissed the ladies.

John Hancock, who was visiting London, wrote back to America: The new king was good-natured and well liked.

GOOD EVENING, MY DEAR.

But of course, what a king needed was a queen, and George the Third refused to be crowned until he had a queen to be crowned with him. He sent scouts scurrying to Europe to find out what princesses were available. There turned out to be seven princesses.

One princess was fond of philosophy, and the king said he didn't want that. One was too young; two were stubborn; one had a grandfather who had married a druggist's daughter; one had a mother who had been in jail. The king said no to all of them. At the bottom of the list was 16-year-old Princess Charlotte of Mecklenburg (a state in north Germany). Princess Charlotte had rather a large mouth, but otherwise the king could find nothing wrong with her. So he said yes, and she said yes, and he made the plans.

First, the king sent for the princess' measurements. Then he supervised the making of her wedding dress. It was to be a silver and white gown with a mantle of violet velvet lined with ermine and fastened on one shoulder with a bunch of pearls. He ordered a diamond tiara, and he had the royal yacht repainted and renamed the *Charlotte*. He picked out 11 bridesmaids and ordered their clothes. Indeed there was no detail that the king did not see to, even though in the midst of preparations, he came down with chicken pox.

Meanwhile, Princess Charlotte, who didn't want to leave home at all, picked all the herbs in her private herb garden and all the flowers in her private flower garden, and she gave them away to the poor. She practiced playing "God Save the King" on her harpsichord and learned to sing the words. Since she didn't speak English, this was not easy, but she practiced and practiced. She even practiced on the royal yacht crossing the North Sea when everyone else in her party was too seasick to sit up.

15

Princess Charlotte and King George met at 3 in the afternoon of September 8, 1761, and they were married at 9 the same evening. The princess' wedding dress fit all right, but the king had counted too much on that bunch of pearls. The ermine mantle was so heavy that she had a hard time keeping the dress on her shoulders. But she said, "I do," and he said, "I do." Then they went to the palace, and Charlotte sang and played "God Save the King" for the royal family.

Now for the crowning. On September 22, King George and Queen Charlotte rode in sedan chairs to Westminster Abbey to be crowned by the Archbishop of Canterbury. At the beginning of the ceremony the archbishop cried out, "I here present unto you George, the undoubted king of the realm." Everyone in the abbey shouted, "God save the king!" Then the archbishop turned to all four points of the compass—north, south, east, west—and each time presented George, the undoubted king. Each time the people responded, "God save the king!"

George and Charlotte put on the royal robes, received the royal regalia, made the promises they had to make, and finally the coronation was over. George had a crown on his head and felt like a real king. Not only father to the thousands of people who were cheering outside the abbey, but a father to all the people in his whole empire, including the men, women, and children in faraway America.

Indeed King George was feeling so good that he seemed hardly to mind the things that went wrong at his coronation banquet.

First were the candles. Lord Talbot, the king's chief steward, thought how clever it would be if suddenly all the 2,000 candles in the banquet hall could light up at the same time just as the king, queen, and the guests came into the room. So he had the candles connected with a string of flax fuses, and when the people entered, he lighted the flax and the candles burst into flame just as he had planned. What he had not planned was that the burning flax would turn into thousands of sparks and shower down on the heads of those present. (The ladies screamed, but no one was hurt.)

Then the chairs. Lord Talbot forgot to provide chairs for the king and queen, and since no one could sit down until the king and queen did, there was a great deal of standing about until the proper chairs were found. And when at last people could sit, there were not enough tables for them to sit at. No table for the Lord Mayor of London and the aldermen. So they were moved to the table reserved for the Knights of the Bath, and the Knights of the Bath were crowded in among the law lords. Then because Lord Talbot thought he would be clever and save money, there wasn't enough food to go around. When some barons complained, Lord Talbot asked them if they wanted to fight.

Worst of all was the horse ceremony. Lord Talbot was supposed to ride his horse into the banquet hall and up to the king and queen to pay his official respects. In preparing for the ceremony, Lord Talbot thought how clever it would be if his horse, instead of turning around, would back away from the king and queen. For days he trained his horse to walk backward, and at the banquet that was just what it did. But instead of walking forward to the king and queen and *then* backing away, the horse backed its rear end right up to the king and queen.

Anyway, mistakes or not, George the Third was king, and now what? Well, he had to be a good king. So he set about following the rules.

A king, his mother told him, should not be fat. So he tried not to eat much. Fresh fruit and sauerkraut were his favorite foods. (Sometimes his guests thought he didn't want them to be fat either. Once a friend reported that after a whole day of hunting with the king, of galloping and leaping, of being popped into ditches and jerked over gates, what do you think the king offered him? A little barley water!)

Next, a king must be moral. So at once King George issued a royal proclamation against the use of bad language.

Furthermore, a king should not break promises. Once King George was thrown from a horse and was so black and blue that his doctors wanted to keep him in bed. But he had promised to go to the theater that night. So up he got and off he went. A promise was a promise, he said.

And of course, a king should have heirs. This took a little longer, but over the years King George and Queen Charlotte had 15 children: George, Frederick, William, Charlotte, Edward, Augusta, Elizabeth, Ernest, Augustus, Adolphus, Mary, Sophia, Octavius, Alfred, and Amelia. Once a week the family walked in pairs around the garden so the public could view them. (Princess Augusta hated this.)

Another rule was that a king should be orderly. This was not hard for George; he loved order—everything in its proper place, everyone at his own work. He liked to walk around the countryside and see that even the land was doing its job. (He didn't like mountains. Useless things, he called them.)

And he was exact. If he said dinner was at eight, he meant *exactly* at eight. When he measured the height of the princes, he measured it to a sixteenth of an inch. When he dated a letter, he included not only the day and the year, but the hour and the minute that he started writing.

In addition, a king should be careful of money. So instead of having satin or velvet curtains around his bed, King George made do with plain white cotton ones. He refused to have a rug on his bedroom floor (it would be unmanly, he said), and except on public occasions he dressed plainly. He personally inspected the kitchen to make sure that there was no waste, and in order to cut down on the number of servants, he had the queen's hairdresser serve meals.

Of course, concerned as he was about household costs, the king was also concerned about government costs, and when George came to the throne, the government was costing a great deal. England had been fighting a long and expensive war, and when it was over, the question was how to pay the bills. Finally, a government official suggested that one way to raise money was to tax Americans.

"What a good idea!" King George said. After all, the French and Indian part of the war had been fought on American soil for the benefit of Americans, so why shouldn't they help pay for it? The fact that Americans had also spent money and lost men in the war didn't seem important. Nor did the fact that Americans had always managed their own money up to now. They were English subjects, weren't they? Didn't English subjects have to obey the English government? So in 1765 a stamp tax was laid on certain printed items in America.

King George was amazed that Americans objected. He was flabbergasted that they claimed he had no *right* to tax them. Just because they had no say in the matter. Just because they had no representatives in the English government. What was more, Americans refused to pay. If they agreed to one tax, they said, what would come next? A window tax? A tax on fireplaces?

Now King George believed that above all a king should be firm, but the government had the vote, and in the end it voted to repeal the tax. Still, King George was pleased about one thing: The government stood firm on England's *right* to tax the colonies. And in 1767 the government tried again. This time the tax was on lead, tea, paint, and a number of items England sold to America. Part of the money from this tax was to be used to support an English army to keep order in America; part was to pay governors and judges previously under the control of the colonies. Who could object to that? King George asked.

The Americans did. They hated the whole business so much, especially the English soldiers stationed in their midst, that even when the other taxes were repealed and only the tea tax remained, they would not put up with it. When tea arrived in Boston, they dumped it into Boston Harbor.

When he heard this news, King George felt more like a father than he ever had in his life. A father with a family of very, very disobedient children. And of course, he must punish them. So he closed the port of Boston and took away the right of Massachusetts to govern itself.

Firm, firm, firm. From now on he would be firm. After the Battle of Lexington and the Battle of Bunker Hill, King George said he felt strong as a lion. People would soon see, he said, that Americans would back down, meek as lambs.

Instead, on July 4, 1776, Americans declared their independence. Naturally King George was annoyed. But he wasn't worried. How could children, however rebellious, succeed against a firm father? How could a few colonies hold out against a powerful empire? He'd just send a few more regiments over and then watch the Americans come around! It never occurred to George the Third that he might not be right. "I wish nothing but good," he once said, "therefore everyone who does not agree with me is a traitor or a scoundrel."

For a while King George had every reason to feel confident. The English troops captured New York, and when George heard this, he said one more battle and it would be over. When he was told that his troops had marched into Philadelphia, he ran into the queen's room. "I have beat them!" he shouted. "Beat all the Americans!"

But he hadn't beaten them. The fighting went on, and meanwhile, George the Third had to go about the business of being a king. He put his seal on official papers, gave out medals and titles, memorized the name of every ship in the navy, tasted the food sent to the troops, checked on who was spending what, and for hours on end he listened to people talk.

Indeed, being a king, especially a good king, was often boring. He couldn't even drop a glove without half the palace, it seemed, stooping to pick it up and arguing about who should have the honor of returning it. "Never mind the honor," the king once said. "Never mind, never mind. Just give me my glove. What? what? what? Yes, you all picked it up, yes, yes, yes, all, all, all—you all picked it up." (King George had a habit of talking rapidly and repeating himself so that his talk often sounded like a gobble.)

But as king, he did have a few advantages. He was, for instance, the most prayed-for man in the empire. Naturally it was pleasant to think of the heavy traffic of prayers ascending on his behalf every Sunday morning. From every country church and every city cathedral in every corner of the kingdom. (But not in America. There the preachers gave up praying for him when the Punishment started.) The king was also the most toasted man. No party (except in America) began without all the people present raising their glasses and wishing the king a long life. (The king wished it, too.) And he had the biggest birthday celebration. Each year on June 4 all his subjects (except in America, of course) celebrated his birthday with parades and banquets and speeches and gunfire and fireworks.

All those prayers and toasts and fireworks were not to be sneezed at. Still, there were times when George wanted to forget about being a king. Fortunately he had hobbies to turn to. For one thing, he made metal buttons (he loved turning a lathe). He wrote articles on farming and signed himself "Ralph Richardson" which was the name of one of his shepherds. He played backgammon with the officers of the royal household, and he collected ship models, coins, clocks, and watches. (He had a four-sided clock that even showed the tides.) He played the flute and harpsichord, hunted, and studied the stars in his private observatory. And for the queen's special amusement, he maintained a zoo, which consisted of one elephant and one zebra.

But always in the end he had to go back to being a king. Back to the problem of America. This was the way he thought of America. A problem. King George did not really think of the Revolutionary War as a *war* until the fall of 1777, when 5,000 English soldiers surrendered to the Americans at Saratoga.

How could such a thing happen? the king asked. Hadn't he been told, even by an ex-governor of Massachusetts, that Americans would give up? That only a small number of Americans were really against him? And how could he, a peace-loving king, find himself in an honest-to-goodness war with his own colonies? He tried to console himself. He was a good king, he said. Good kings deserve to win. So this must be a temporary setback. All he had to do was to show the world that he wasn't the least bit worried. So that night after hearing about the defeat, King George went to a court party and spent the evening telling stupid jokes and laughing so uproariously that his Prime Minister, Lord North, had to take him aside and try to quiet him down.

The war dragged on. France, impressed with the victory at Saratoga, joined the war on America's side. There were people in England now who wanted to stop fighting, but not George. No, no, no. Never, never. No independence. No peace without honor. If one group of English colonies got away, what would happen to the others? What would be left of the empire?

But no matter how he showed himself in public, privately George was depressed. The world was not staying settled, everything in place, the way he liked it. Not only was America acting up, but there were difficulties in England as well. Riots even. And George's own family was misbehaving. Two of his brothers were involved in scandals, and George's son, the Prince of Wales, was so contrary he deliberately arrived for meals as much as an hour late although he *knew* that the king wanted everyone to be *exactly* on time.

On November 25, 1781, the news reached London that the English army under General Cornwallis had surrendered at Yorktown to General Washington. When Lord North heard this, he threw up his arms. "It's all over!" he said.

But the king said nothing was over. They still had ships, hadn't they? (He named them.) They still had officers. (He had learned their names, too.) They still had troops. They still had guns and gunpowder.

King George set his lips firmly and wrote a letter to the Secretary of State for America. This defeat, he said, should not make the smallest difference in their plans. Still, King George was so upset that when he dated the letter, he forgot to record the hour and the minute of the writing.

Two days later the king addressed the government. "I prohibit you from thinking of peace," he thundered.

But the government did think of peace, and eventually the government voted for it.

So now what? King George couldn't fight the war all by himself. He couldn't chop off the heads of all those who had voted for peace. Kings didn't do that anymore. He could, of course, abdicate—quit the king business altogether. For a time he thought seriously of this. He even drafted an announcement of his abdication, but then he put it away in his desk. He was so *used* to being a king. So when the time came for him to sign the peace proclamation, he signed. As soon as he had finished, he jumped on his horse and took a hard gallop away from the palace. When the time came to announce in public the separation of the two countries and the independence of America, he swallowed hard and announced. Afterward he asked a friend if he had spoken loudly enough.

As long as he lived, King George had nightmares about the loss of the American colonies. It certainly hadn't been his fault, he said. *He* hadn't done anything wrong. He had just wanted to teach Americans a lesson. Give them all bloody noses—that's what he'd wanted.

Page 9 George wrote his wish for "Mr. Caesar" in French: You can see in his original scrawl just how disgusted he was.

Page 31 Americans also contended that if they had been *asked* (instead of being forced) to raise money for England, they would have done so as they had done on previous occasions.

In King George's day the king was a "constitutional monarch." He had lost the enormous powers that a king had once had and had to abide by the vote of the government. On the other hand, unlike present kings, he took an active and leading role in the government.

Page 32 Many Americans disapproved of the Boston Tea Party. They were willing to pay for the lost tea, but when instead the king punished them so severely, they became more united against him.

Page 47 In 1788 when the king was 50 years old, he became violently ill of a disease that has since been diagnosed as porphyria. One of the symptoms of the disease is that one's mind is affected, but in those days people thought that the king had simply gone mad. He recovered from his first attack but in later years suffered again. For the last ten years of his life he was a wretched-looking figure dressed in a purple bathrobe with wild white hair and a wild white beard. He died in 1820 at the age of 82.

THE

EVERYTHING
KIDS'
GIANT

BOOK OF JOKES, RIDDLES, AND BRAIN TEASERS

Michael Dahl, Kathi Wagner, Aubrey Wagner, and Aileen Weintraub

adamsmedia
Avon, Massachusetts

PUBLISHER Karen Cooper

DIRECTOR OF ACQUISITIONS AND INNOVATION Paula Munier

MANAGING EDITOR, EVERYTHING® SERIES Lisa Laing

COPY CHIEF Casey Ebert

ACQUISITIONS EDITOR Katrina Schroeder

SENIOR DEVELOPMENT EDITOR Brett Palana-Shanahan

ASSOCIATE DEVELOPMENT EDITOR Hillary Thompson

EDITORIAL ASSISTANT Ross Weisman

EVERYTHING® SERIES COVER DESIGNER Erin Alexander

LAYOUT DESIGNERS Colleen Cunningham, Elisabeth Lariviere, Ashley Vierra, Denise Wallace

An Everything® Series Book.
Everything® and everything.com® are registered trademarks of F+W Media, Inc.

Published by Adams Media, a division of F+W Media, Inc.
57 Littlefield Street, Avon, MA 02322. U.S.A.
www.adamsmedia.com

Contains material adapted and abridged from *The Everything® Kids' Joke Book* by Michael Dahl, copyright © 2001 by F+W Media, Inc., ISBN 10: 1-58062-686-6, ISBN 13: 978-1-58062-686-6; *The Everything® Kids' Knock Knock Book* by Aileen Weintraub, copyright © 2004 by F+W Media, Inc., ISBN 10: 1-59337-127-6, ISBN-13: 978-1-59337-127-2; *The Everything® Kids' Riddles & Brain Teasers Book* by Kathi Wagner and Aubrey Wagner, copyright © 2004 by F+W Media, Inc., ISBN 10: 1-59337-036-9, ISBN-13: 978-1-59337-036-7.

ISBN 10: 1-4405-0633-7
ISBN 13: 978-1-4405-0633-8
eISBN 10: 1-4405-0634-5
eISBN 13: 978-1-4405-0634-5

Printed by RR Donnelley, Harrisonburg, VA, US

10 9 8 7 6 5 4 3 2 1

August 2010

Interior illustrations by Kurt Dobler and Barry Littmann. Puzzles by Beth L. Blair.

This book is available at quantity discounts for bulk purchases.
For information, please call 1-800-289-0963.

Visit the entire Everything® series at *www.everything.com*

contents

PART ONE: JOKES • 1

iii

Part One

JOKES

HUMANS ARE THE ONLY CREATURES on this planet who laugh. Oh sure, hyenas make a funny bark that may sound like a laugh. Grade B movies and sitcoms show chimpanzees and dolphins laughing at their silly human costars. But people are the only animals that giggle, chuckle, titter, guffaw, belly laugh, chortle, and yuck. Have you ever known a hamster who snickers at an elephant joke? Or a Rottweiler who appreciates a well-thrown custard pie in his face? Didn't think so.

Besides loving to laugh, we also like making other people laugh. Who hasn't enjoyed being the center of attention, even if only for a few seconds, after you've told a truly terrific joke? Well, this book has tons of them—jokes, howlers, groaners, puns, witty retorts, and practical gags.

One more thing. This book is not to be read in the silence of your bedroom or favorite hiding place. Carry it with you at all times, read it out loud, underline the best parts, dog-ear the pages, share the jokes with all your friends.

Read, laugh, and be more funny!

MONSTER MANIA

What kind of dog does Dracula have as a pet?
A bloodhound.

What is the Mummy's favorite music?
Wrap.

Why did King Kong climb to the top of the Empire State Building?
He was too big to use the elevator.

What sport do vampires like to watch?
Bat-minton.

Why are most mummies vain and conceited?
They're all wrapped up in themselves.

Why did the dragon cough during the day?
Because he smoked knights.

Why is Frankenstein such a good gardener?
He has a green thumb.

Did you hear about the old vampire who kept his teeth in the freezer?
He gave his victims frostbite.

The little vampire could never gain weight.
His eating was all in vein.

Why does the mad scientist like to eat a hot dog with a glass of beer?
It's a frank and stein.

Did you hear about the zombie hairdresser?
Each day she dyed on the job.

Why did the cheerleading squad move into the haunted house?
Because it's got spirit!

Where does Godzilla sleep?
Anywhere he wants to!

Jokes

What do you get when you cross a ghost with a firecracker?
Bamboo!

Did you hear about the two vampires who raced one another?
It was neck and neck.

Why are cannibals so popular?
I don't know, but they always have lots of friends for lunch!

What did one casket say to the other casket?
"Is that you coffin?"

. . . .

Hole In One

Fill in the missing letters in the words below. Then, copy the letter from each word into the box with the same number. When you're finished, you'll get the answer to this riddle: What did the witch use to fix her broken jack-o'-lantern? **HINT:** Be careful! Sometimes more than one letter can finish a word. Be sure each letter makes sense in the final answer.

> What did the witch use to fix her broken jack-o'-lantern?

She used a

1	2	3	4	5	6	7

8	9	10	11	12

1. __UPPY
2. J__MP
3. LU__P
4. HAP__Y
5. SHAR__
6. SM__LE
7. SA__D
8. SLOP__Y
9. S__D
10. __UNA
11. __HURCH
12. C__INA

3

What's Dracula's least favorite food?
A steak. It goes right through him and leaves a nasty case of heartburn.

How many dead people are in the graveyard?
All of them!

SICKOS

What do beekeepers get?
Hives.

What do airline pilots get?
Flu.

What do computer geeks get?
Slipped discs.

If athletes get athlete's foot, what do astronauts get?
Missile toe.

What do firefighters get?
Water on the knee.

What do workers at McDonald's get?
Fallen arches.

What do carpenters get?
Hangnail.

What do roofers get?
Shingles.

What do spies get?
See-sickness.

What do basketball players get?
Hooping cough.

What do watchmakers get?
All wound up!

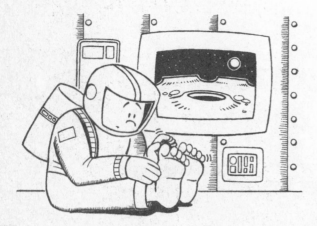

WHAT'S GNU?

Mona: I had trouble with my horse yesterday. I wanted to go in one direction, and he wanted to go in another.
Sam: So how did you decide?
Mona: He tossed me for it.

Sam: I think my pet duck is broken.

Mona: Broken?
Sam: Yeah, he has a quack in him.
Mona: What's worse than a giraffe with a sore throat?
Sam: A centipede with athlete's foot.

Sam: I'd like to buy a bird.
Store Clerk: How about a talking mynah?
Sam: Sounds great!
Store Clerk: This one here is very talented. She can talk in seven languages, sing *The Star-Spangled Banner*, and recite the Gettysburg Address.
Sam: Never mind that. Is she tender?

Rich Snob: I don't like your bird, young man.
Sam: Why not?
Rich Snob: Because every time I walk by, it says, "Cheap! Cheap!"

Why did the hen slide her eggs down the hill?
She loved playing with the children.

How much fur can you get from a skunk?
As fur as you possibly can!

Jokin' Around

Fowl Definitions

From the Dictionary for Bird-Brains

Hatchet—What a chicken does with its eggs.

Information—How geese fly.

Foul ball—An egg.

Crow bar—Where birds like to drink and hang out.

5

How do you spell mousetrap with only three letters?
    C-A-T

Mona: What kind of pet can you stand on?
Sam: A car-pet.

Mona: What kind of pet makes the loudest noise?
Sam: A trum-pet.

Mona: What kind of pet can help you write letters?
Sam: The alpha-pet.

Alex: Why is that dachshund sitting in the sun?
Amy: Because his owners like hot dogs.

Do you know how to raise rabbits?
    Yes, by the scruff of their necks.

Sam: Wow! It's raining cats and dogs.

Mona: How can you tell?
Sam: I just stepped in a poodle.

Sam: Have you ever seen a fish bowl?
Mona: Sure, lots of times.
Sam: How do they get their fins into those little holes?

Father Kangaroo: Why are you scratching?
Mother Kangaroo: The kids are eating crackers in bed again.

Sam: Can you name four members of the cat family?
Mona: Papa Cat, Mama Cat, and two kittens.

Mona: How did the pig write his name?
Sam: He used an *oink*-pen.

What did the leopard say after dinner?
    "That hit just the right spots."

Sam: Hey! Your dog bit my ankle.
Mona: Sorry, but that's as high as he can reach.

Mona: How do you keep a wild elephant from charging?
Sam: Take away his credit card.

Why Oh Why?

Pick up words as the chicken walks from **START** to **END**. Write each word down in the order in which the chicken finds them, and you'll end up with the answer to this riddle:

Why did the chicken cross the playground?

1	2	3	4	5	6

Write the answer here.

7

Why does a flamingo stand up on one leg?
Because if he pulled the other one up he'd fall over.

Mona: My pony sounds funny.
Sam: That's because he's a little hoarse.

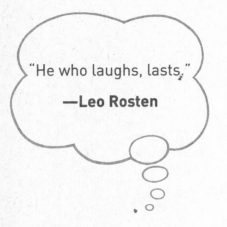

"He who laughs, lasts."

—**Leo Rosten**

Mona: Why do hummingbirds hum?
Sam: They don't know the words.

What did the little kid say when he saw the peacock?
"Look, Ma, the chicken's in bloom!"

Sam: I haven't seen your pet chicken lately.
Mona: Well, this week she's been laying low.

Words to Know

Punch line: the part of the joke that gets the laugh

The animal doctor is always busy as a bee! Take a gander at a few of his patients:

The leopard is seeing spots,
The kangaroo is feeling jumpy,
The goldfish is flushed,
The chameleon is looking green,
The woodpecker caught a bug,
The baby duckling has been getting a little down lately,
And the bullfrog is afraid he's going to croak!

CRAZY COLORS (OR HUE MUST BE NUTS!)

What color is a marriage?
Wed.

What color is an echo?
YELL-oohhhhhhh!

What color is a ghost?
Boo

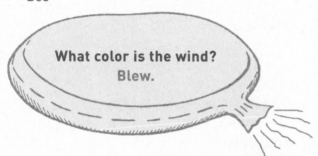

What color is the wind?
Blew.

What color is a baby ghost?
Baby boo.

What color is a kitten's meow?
Purr-ple.

What color is a soccer score?
Goaled!

What color is a police investigation?
Copper.

What color is a witch's potion?
Bracken brew.

COMPUTER WONKS

Why did the computer geek sell his cat?
He was afraid it would eat his mouse.

How do you contact Hercules by computer?
Send him he-mail.

What has a video screen, a keyboard, six legs, and plugs into the wall?
A computer bug.

What do computer geeks eat for dessert?
Apple pie a la modem.

Did you hear about the geek who almost drowned?
He was surfing the Web and got bumped off.

9

Jokin' Around

Totally Buggy

Computer Viruses to Watch Out For:

The Disney Virus
The screen starts acting Goofy.

The Titanic Virus
Everything goes down.

The Diet Virus
The computer quits after just one byte.

The Las Vegas Virus
Users have to turn in their chips.

The Divorce Virus
Your motherboard stops talking to your data.

Nerd: Why is my computer screen all wet?
Dweeb: I was trying to send e-mail, but the stamps kept sliding off!

Did you hear about the guy who flunked technical college?
   He can only operate nincomputers.

Nerd: How many bytes are in your software program?
Dweeb: I'll let you know as soon as I've finished eating it.

Mother: Having trouble with your computer, son?
Karl: My PC says it can't see my printer.
Mother: I'm not surprised. Look how messy your room is!

Nerd: Do you have a cursor on your computer?
Dweeb: I'll say! You should just hear the words my dad uses when the computer goes down!

Nerd: What's wrong with your keyboard?
Dweeb: Myspacebarseemstobestuck.

You heard about the computer scientist who spends half his time directing the town's orchestra?
   He's a semi-conductor.

"Of course I know how to copy disks . . . Where's the Xerox machine?"

If at first you don't succeed . . . call it version 1.0.

What was the world's first computer?
An Apple. Eve gave one to Adam.

What are the three main parts of a printer?
The power cord, the jammed paper tray, and the blinking light.

"My computer is almost human."
"What do you mean?"
"When it makes a mistake, it blames it on another computer."

I had a rotten day at work today. My computer broke down and I had to think all day long.

TOM AND TINA SWIFTIES

"Look at the cute pony," said Tina a little hoarsely.

"I can't remember what groceries I need," said Tom listlessly.

"Is it time to turn the pancakes?" asked Tina flippantly.

"Look at that scroungy old dog," Tom muttered.

"Who cut the cheese?" asked Tina sharply.

"I'd gladly give you a thousand dollars," said Tom grandly.

"My pet bird is sick," said Tina illegally.

"Let's set up camp," said Tom intently.

"I'll make the fire," Tina bellowed.

"I got the lowest grade in my cooking class," said Tom degradedly.

"We're all out of pumpernickel bread," said Tina wryly.

11

"Why can't we go bowling?" Tom bawled.

"I finished taking my shower," said Tina dryly.

"Give me another strawberry cake," Tom retorted.

"These oysters are all mine!" said Tina shellfishly.

"Keep them! I prefer other seafood," said Tom crabbily.

"I love arithmetic," Tina added.

"And I love correcting my mistakes," Tom remarked.

"That's my gold mine," Tina claimed.

"But it used to be mine!" Tom exclaimed.

DIDJA HEAR?

Didja hear about the police officer who arrested the young cat?
He saw the kitty litter.

Didja hear about the baby girl who wanted to play basketball?
She had trouble dribbling.

Didja hear about the taxicab driver who lost his job?
He was driving away all his customers.

Didja hear about the pet shop owner who couldn't get sell his porcupine?
He was stuck with it.

Didja hear about the cannibal who ate his mother's sister?
He was an aunt-eater.

Didja hear about the woman who'd buy anything that was marked down?
She came home with an elevator.

Didja hear about the sailor who was kicked off the submarine?
He liked sleeping with the windows open.

Picto-Laugh #1

A pictograph is a very simple drawing of something funny. Can you guess what this little picto-laugh is showing? **HINT:** Think about something itsy-bitsy!

Say What?

Figure out where to put each of the scrambled letters. They all fit in spaces under their own columns. When you fill in the grid, you will have the answer to the following riddle: Didja hear about the piano tuner who was arrested at the aquarium?

Didja hear about the piano tuner who was arrested at the aquarium?

• •

Didja hear about the rubber man from the circus who was killed in an auto wreck?

He died in his own arms.

Didja hear about the lady who stopped feeding the pigeons?

The birds revolted and formed a coo.

Didja hear about the kitten that loves to play with a piece of string?

After a while he has a ball.

LARRY AND LUNA

Luna: My poor cat doesn't have a nose!
Larry: How does she smell?
Luna: Terrible!

Luna: I must be sick. I'm seeing spots.
Larry: Have you seen a doctor?
Luna: No, just spots.

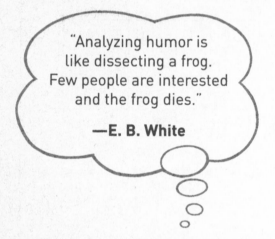

"Analyzing humor is like dissecting a frog. Few people are interested and the frog dies."

—E. B. White

Luna: Why is it better to buy a thermometer in the winter?
Larry: Because in summer they go up!

Luna: My candy bar is missing.
Larry: That's too bad, because it tasted delicious.

Luna: What's the last thing you take off before you go to bed?
Larry: My feet off the floor.

Larry: How many feet are in a yard?
Luna: That depends on how many people are standing in it.

Luna: How many seconds are in a year?
Larry: Twelve.
Luna: Only twelve! Are you sure?
Larry: Yeah, the second of January, the second of February . . .

Luna: I can tell the future.
Larry: Really?
Luna: Yes. I can tell you what the score of a soccer game is before it even starts.
Larry: What is it?
Luna: Nothing to nothing.

Larry: What's the best thing to put in a pie?

Luna: Your teeth!

Luna: Do you know how long the world's longest nose was?
Larry: Eleven inches.
Luna: That's not very long.
Larry: If it was any longer it would be a foot.

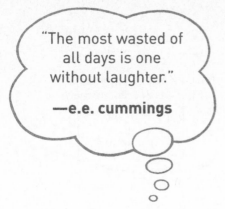

"The most wasted of all days is one without laughter."

—e.e. cummings

Larry: Did I tell you my mom's been in the hospital for years?
Luna: Wow! She must really be sick.
Larry: Nah, she's a doctor.

Luna: I just got back from the beauty shop.
Larry: It was closed, huh?

Larry: There's something wrong with that pizza I ate.
Luna: How do you know?
Larry: Inside information.

Larry: How do you keep a skunk from smelling?
Luna: Plug his nose!

Luna: Is there any tapioca pudding on the menu?
Waiter: There was, but I wiped it off.

Larry: Why are you scratching yourself?
Luna: Because I'm the only person who knows where it itches.

Larry: What did you think of the Grand Canyon?
Luna: It was just gorges!

Luna: Who was that on the phone?
Larry: Some joker. He said, "It's long-distance from Japan," and I said, "It sure is!" and hung up.

Larry: Boy! My diet must be working.
Luna: Why do you say that?
Larry: I can finally see the numbers on the bathroom scale.

Larry: I'm on a new diet. I only eat food that swims.
Luna: That sounds great! Fish is very healthy for you.
Larry: Yuck, forget fish! Do you realize how much trouble I'm having teaching a cow to dog-paddle?

Larry: Do you believe in astrology?
Luna: No, it's just a lot of Taurus.

SCHOOL JOKES

Alex: Teacher! Teacher! Jimmy just swallowed four quarters!
Teacher: Now, why would he do that?
Alex: It's his lunch money.

Alex: Teacher! Teacher! Now, Jimmy swallowed all his pennies. And it's your fault!
Teacher: Why is it my fault?
Alex: You told him he needed more sense.

Teacher: You need to study harder, Alex. Why, when I was your age, I could recite all the presidents' names by heart.
Amy: Yeah, but there were only two or three back then.

Teacher: Where are all the kings and queens of England crowned?
Amy: On the tops of their heads.

Teacher: Give me a sentence using the word "gladiator."
Alex: The lion ate my bossy Aunt Mimi, and I'm glad he ate her!

Teacher: Correct this sentence: "Aliens is in the classroom."
Alex: Forget the sentence, Teach! Run for your life!

Teacher: Tell me how you'd use the word "rhythm" in a sentence.
Alex: My older brother is going to the movies, and I want to go rhythm.

Teacher: Where can you find the Red Sea?
Amy: Usually on my report card.

Teacher: Let's do a simple math lesson. How many fingers do you have?
Alex: Ten.
Teacher: And if three fingers were taken away, what would you have?
Alex: I would have to give up my saxophone lessons!

FUN FACT

BOGGLE BOX

In his bestselling book, *The BFG* (Big Friendly Giant), author Roald Dahl's giant hero has his own name for everything. For instance, a school is called a "boggle box."

If you've ever been to school—and who hasn't?—you'll know that the name fits!

HA, HA, HA!

HA, HA, HA!

HA, HA, HA!

Teacher: Name a creature that is very good at catching flies.
Amy: A baseball player in left field.

Teacher: Can you use the word "fascinate" in a sentence?
Alex: Yeah. My jacket has ten buttons, but I can only fasten eight.

Teacher: Can anyone tell me what a myth is?
Amy: A female moth.

Mother: Explain this "D" on your test, dear.
Amy: I'm having trouble with my Is.
Mother: You need new glasses?
Amy: No, I can't spell "Mississippi"!

Teacher: Did you wake up grouchy this morning, young man?
Alex: No, Dad and I let her sleep.

Teacher: Who was Joan of Arc?
Alex: Noah's wife.

Alex: Why are kindergarten teachers so optimistic?
Amy: Cuz every day they try to make the little things count.

Teacher: How did you get so messy?
Amy: I had an inkling of what I wanted to write my report about. So I grabbed a pen and paper.
Teacher: And then?
Amy: Then my pen had an inkling all over my shirt!

Teacher: Tell me the name of the Prince of Wales.
Amy: Orca.

Mother: I don't think my child deserves a zero on this test.
Teacher: Neither do I, ma'am. But it's the lowest score I can give!

Teacher: Use the word "paradox" in a sentence.
Alex: The hunter shot a paradox flying over the lake.

Mother: Your teacher tells me you're at the bottom of the class.
Angie: Yeah, but they teach the same thing at both ends.

Teacher: Why were you late to school?
Amy: There are eight in my family, Teach, but the clock was only set for seven.

Mother: Why don't you like your new teacher, honey?
Amy: Because she told me to sit in the front row for the present. And then she never gave me any present!

Mother: Why did you have to stay after school today, Alex?
Alex: I flunked the test. I didn't know where the Appalachians were.
Mother: Well, next time remember where you put things, dear.

Teacher: That makes five times I've had to punish you this week, Darren. What do you have to say for yourself?
Darren: I'm glad it's Friday!

Alex: Would you yell at me for something I didn't do?
Teacher: Certainly not.
Alex: Good, because I didn't do my homework.

QUICKIES

One microbe ran into another microbe while swimming through a bloodstream.

"You don't look so hot," said the first microbe.

"I feel terrible," said the second microbe. "I think I'm coming down with penicillin."

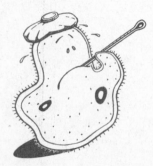

If we breathe oxygen during the day, what do we breathe at night?

Nitrogen.

"I think the cuckoo in my cuckoo clock is tired."
"That's silly!"
"No, it's not. You'd be tired too if you'd been running all night."

What's the hardest thing about falling out of bed?

The floor.

Sounds Funny To Me

Match each funny sound riddle to the correct picture punchline.

1. What goes "Z-Z-U-B, Z-Z-U-B, Z-Z-U-B"?
2. What goes "HOE, HOE, HOE"?
3. What goes "ABCDEFGHIJKLMNOPQRSTUVWXYZ —sluuuuurp"?

4. What goes "HA, HA, HA—thump"?
5. What goes "99 thump, 99 thump, 99 thump"?
6. What goes "tick-WOOF, tick-WOOF, tick-WOOF"?

What did the princess say while she waited for her photos to come back from the store?
   "Some day my prints will come!"

Terry: Why is the Mississippi River so rich?
Nick: Because it has two banks and it makes deposits all day long.

Why are you taking that hammer to bed?
   So I can get up at the crack of dawn!

What do you get for the man who has everything?
   A burglar alarm!

"Long distance? I'd like to place a call to Aberystwyth, Wales."
"Could you spell that please?"
"If I could spell it, I'd write!"

How do robots celebrate Mother's Day?
  They send a dozen red roses to the power company.

Judge: This is the last time I want to see you in my court! Do you realize that for the last twenty years, I've seen you in here at least once a month?
Crook: Sorry, your Honor. But it's not my fault that you haven't been promoted.

Karl: Boy, am I mad at my brother!
Trent: What did he do?
Karl: I let him ride my new bicycle, and I told him to treat it as if it were his own.
Trent: So?
Karl: He sold it.

Molar: Hey, why are you getting all dressed up?
Wisdom Tooth: The dentist is taking me out tonight.

"You're very healthy," said the doctor. "You should live to be eighty."
"But, I am eighty!" said the patient.
"See? What did I tell you?"

A young fellow was walking through an unfamiliar part of town late at night. Two muggers jumped out from the shadows and dragged him to the ground. The young guy put up quite a fight, but eventually the two thugs overpowered him.

  One of the muggers grabbed the man's wallet, looked inside, and then threw it down in disgust.

  "You put up all that fight for just a measly two bucks?" said the mugger.

  The fellow answered, "Shucks, no. I was afraid you were gonna find the three hundred dollars I hid in my shoe."

What's the hottest day of the week?
  Fry day.

What's the unhappiest day of the week?
  Sadder day.

What's the driest day of the week?
  Thirst day.

"Could you fix the volume on my car horn?"
"Is it broken?"
"No, but my brakes are."

Darren: Every time I have a cup of coffee, I get a sharp pain in my right eye. What should I do, Doctor?
Doctor: Take the spoon of out your cup.

Mother: Jenny, have you finished filling up the salt shakers yet?
Jenny: No, Mom. It's hard pushing the salt through those tiny holes.

Trent: Is there a place where I can catch the 1:30 bus to town?
Danny: That depends on how fast you can run. It left ten minutes ago.

A father saw his son out in the backyard cleaning their homemade swing, a rubber tire hanging by a rope from a tree branch. The son was hosing it down, wiping it off, dusting out the inside. The puzzled father went outside and said, "Son, I thought you were playing on the golf course with your friends this afternoon." "I was," replied the boy. "But the golf instructor said I needed to improve my swing."

Perry: Officer! Somebody stole my car!
Police Officer: Did you see who did it?
Perry: No, but I got the license number.

Two women met at a laundromat. As they talked, the first woman said, "I have five children." The other woman said, "That sounds nice. I wish I had five children." "Don't you have any children?" asked the first woman. "Yeah, ten!" said the second.

Jokin' Around

Eye to Eye

Make this statement to a friend: "I can put this sheet of paper down on the floor, and I'll bet we can both stand on it, but you won't be able to touch me." Your friend will be eager to take such an easy bet. Lay the sheet of paper down in a doorway. Shut the door carefully so that the two ends of the sheet stick out on either side. Voila! You and your friend will be able to stand on the sheet on opposite sides of the door. But neither of you can touch the other person. Bet won!

Tip: This trick works even better with an extra long sheet of paper.

21

OUTTA THIS WORLD

Why are astronauts always so clean?
Because they take meteor showers.

Which tastes better, a comet or an asteroid?
An asteroid, because it's meteor.

How is a comet like the dog Wishbone?
They're both stars with tails.

What planet goes up in the summer and down in the winter?
Mercury.

Where do astronauts eat?
The lunch-pad.

How do astronauts keep their rockets free from dust?
They drive through the vacuum of outer space.

What is at the center of Jupiter?
The letter "I."

Why couldn't the astronauts land on the moon?
Because it was full.

Why did the cowboy want to buy a satellite?
So he could watch where he was going when it got dark.

Did you hear about the astronomer who got knocked out?
He's seeing stars.

Where can you see new stars?
In Hollywood.

Astronaut: What's the difference between a Martian burp and a sandstorm?
Astronut: Sandstorms don't glow in the dark.

Alien: I was born on the planet Neptune.
Scientist: That's amazing! Which part?
Alien: All of me.

Astronaut: What are you digging in your pockets for?
Astronut: You said we'd be landing this thing at a meteor, and most parking meteors only take quarters.

Did you hear about the young girl who plans to be an astronaut?
Her teacher says she's taking up space!

Did you hear about the Martian who flew to Earth to buy a brand new car for his family? He told the car salesman, "I want the body green, the wheels green, the interior green, and the windows tinted green." The salesman said, "No problem." After the Martian ordered his new car, he made an interplanetary long-distance call to his wife to tell her the good news. "That's terrific, honey," said his wife. "But what color is it?" "Flesh tones," said the Martian.

Did you hear about that new restaurant on the moon? Great food, but no atmosphere.

What's the only Irish constellation?
   Orion.

"Sir, do you believe in UFOs?"
"No comet."

Two Venusians landed in front of a busy stoplight.
The first one said, "She's cute. I saw her first."
The second one said, "Yeah, but I'm the one she winked at."

What do astronauts take for a headache?
   Space capsules.

"I just got back from the Dog Star."
"Sirius?"

If astronauts are so smart, why do they count backwards?

Scientist: Your mission is to land on the Sun.
Astronaut: Are you nuts? I'll burn up!
Scientist: That's why you're going at night.

Two Martians landed their spacecraft in a quiet stretch of countryside.
   "I think this must be a human cemetery," said the first Martian. "See that marker over there? It's a gravestone. And it gives the human's age, too—one hundred and two."
   "What was his name?" asked the second Martian.
   "Miles to Milwaukee."

PROFESSOR FRUITCAKE

Did you hear about the mad scientist who married the Amish woman?

He drove her buggy.

Did you hear about the mad scientist who worked for the woman peanut farmer?

He made her nuts.

Did you hear about the mad scientist who trained the Olympic diver?

He sent him off the deep end.

Did you hear about the mad scientist who worked with the bungee jumper?

He pushed him over the edge.

Did you hear about the poor little baby who stayed with the mad scientist?

It went ga-ga.

Did you hear about the rocket experts who hired the mad scientist?

They went ballistic.

HINKY-PINKYS

What's a phony serpent?

A fake snake.

What do you call a chubby dog?

A round hound.

What's a big dance in a cemetery?

A grave rave.

What's a purple gorilla?

A grape ape.

What do phantoms eat for breakfast?

Ghost toast.

What's a frightening pet bird?

A scary canary.

What's a glove for a small cat?

A kitten mitten.

What's a happy-go-lucky Thanksgiving bird?

A perky turkey.

What do you call a frog whose car broke down?

A towed toad.

Hink Pink Kriss Kross

The answers to these Hink Pinks are two rhyming words of one syllable each. Fill each answer into the numbered Kriss Kross grid. Surprise—you've got one done!

ACROSS

3 happy boy
4 a fruity drink at noon
6 a cooking vessel that's not cool
8 a counterfeit reptile
10 a musical piece that's not short
11 home of a small rodent
12 large amount of fake hair
13 enjoyable joke that makes you groan

DOWN

1 a sick dollar
2 football players yelling together
3 great group of marching musicians
5 a chilly place to swim
7 skinny female monarch
9 large branch

3 across: G L A D L A D

Who works at a school for monsters?
A creature teacher.

What do you call a tired tent?
A sleepy teepee.

Who's the spooky leader of a church?
A sinister minister.

What's do you call a magician who works with reptiles?
A lizard wizard.

What's a fish who works in the operating room?
A sturgeon surgeon.

What do you call your crazy best friend?
A nutty buddy.

What do you call your pet pooch that got caught in the rain?
A soggy doggy.

What do you call a parent with six crying babies?
A diaper wiper!

What do you call Her Royal Highness's denim pants?
The Queen's jeans.

What do you call that dumb little guy who flies around and shoots arrows on Valentine's Day?
Stupid Cupid.

What's reddish yellow and helps a door swing back and forth?
An orange door hinge.

RING THE DOORBELL! (KNOCK KNOCK JOKES)

Knock knock.
Who's there?
Sarah.
Sarah who?
Sarah a doctor in the house?

Knock knock.
Who's there?
Dwayne.
Dwayne who?
Dwayne the bathtub, I'm dwowning!

Knock knock.
Who's there?
Amos.

Amos who?
A mosquito bit me!

Knock knock.
Who's there?
Annie.
Annie who?
Annie bit me again!

Knock knock.
Who's there?
Wendy.
Wendy who?
Wendy you want to go to the movies?

Knock knock.
Who's there?
Juicy.
Juicy who?
Juicy who threw that snowball at me?

Knock knock.
Who's there?
Phillip.
Phillip who?
Phillip my bag with candy! It's Halloween!

"In the end, everything is a gag."

—Charlie Chaplin

Knock knock.
Who's there?
Arthur.
Arthur who?
Arthur any cookies left?

Knock knock.
Who's there?
Iris.
Iris who?
I received a package in the mail.

Knock knock.
Who's there?
Sharon.
Sharon who?
Sharon share alike.

Knock knock.
Who's there?
Hugh.
Hugh who?
Yoo-hoo to you, too!

Knock knock.
Who's there?
Wilfred.
Wilfred who?
Will Fred come out and play today?

Knock knock.
Who's there?
Rita.
Rita who?
Rita good book lately?

Knock knock.
Who's there?
Boo.
Boo who?
Why are you crying?

Knock knock.
Who's there?
William.
William who?
William make me dinner if I stop knocking?

Knock knock.
Who's there?
Ira.
Ira who?
Ira member you, why don't you remember me?

Knock knock.
Who's there?
Upton.
Upton who?
Upton now it's been pretty quiet around here.

Knock knock.
Who's there?
Olive.
Olive who?
Olive you, do you love me?

Knock knock.
Who's there?
LaToya.
LaToya who?
LaToya store's open, let's go shopping!

Knock knock.
Who's there?
Hutch.
Hutch who?
Gesundheit!

Knock knock.
Who's there?
Dude.
Dude who?
Dude-doo is all over my front yard. Will you please watch your puppy!

Knock knock.
Who's there?
Champ.
Champ who?
Champoo the dog, he's got fleas!

Jokin' Around

Three Blind Mice

Look at the dice below:

Challenge your friends to take three dice, place one on a table or napkin, and balance the other two on top, side by side. First, show them how it's done. Your friends will not be able to reproduce the trick! No matter how hard they try, their top two dice will always fall off the bottom one.

How did you do it?

Spit. (No, not now!) That's the secret of the trick: spit. During the setup of the trick, while no one is paying attention to your hands, lick one of your fingertips. Then touch one of the die faces. A tiny amount of saliva will hold the two dice together, especially if you hold the dice tightly together for a second or two.

Tip: It's important to place the top two dice with the 2 and the 4 showing. Why? Because then the facing sides become the 1s on each die. The faces with 1s provide more surface area to hold your secret saliva.

When you hand the dice to your opponent, wipe off the tell-tale "glue" without drawing attention. Use your hands to rub off the spit or push the dice across the tablecloth or napkin.

Knock knock.
Who's there?
Banana.
Banana who?
Knock knock.
Who's there?
Banana.
Banana who?
Knock knock.
Who's there?
Banana.
Banana who?
Knock knock.
Who's there?
Orange.
Orange who?
Orange you glad I stopped saying banana?

Knock knock.
Who's there?
Edith.
Edith who?
Edith thick joothy hamburger for thupper.

Knock knock.
Who's there?
Tank.
Tank who?
You're very welcome.

Knock knock.
Who's there?
Toodle.
Toodle who?
Ta-ta!

Knock knock.
Who's there?
Hope.
Hope who?
Hopen the door and let me in!

Knock knock.
Who's there?
Donnelly.
Donnelly who?
Donnelly've me out
here in the dark!

Knock knock.
Who's there?
A little old lady.
A little old lady who?
I didn't know you could yodel.

Knock knock.
Who's there?
Chester.
Chester who?
Chester little kid.

Knock knock.
Who's there?
Aubrey.
Aubrey who?
Aubrey quiet!

Knock knock.
Who's there?
Skid.
Skid who?
Forget it! I'm staying right here.

Knock knock.
Who's there?
Juan.
Juan who?
Juan to buy some candy for the school band?

Picto-Laugh #2

A pictograph is a very simple drawing of something funny. Can you guess what this little picto-laugh is showing? **HINT:** Think about something slow on something fast!

Knock knock.
Who's there?
Alex.
Alex who?
Alex some more soda pop, please.

Knock knock.
Who's there?
Pete.
Pete who?
Pizza's here!

Knock knock.
Who's there?
Theophilus.
Theophilus who?
The awfullest storm I've ever seen out here!

Knock knock.
Who's there?
Ash.
Ash who?
Ash sure could use some help out in the garden.

Knock knock.
Who's there?
Giovanni.
Giovanni who?
Giovanni extra topping on that?

Knock knock.
Who's there?
Wanda.
Wanda who?
Wanda be a millionaire?

Knock knock.
Who's there?
Yah.
Yah who?
I didn't know you were a cowboy.

Knock knock.
Who's there?
Matthew.
Matthew who?
Matthew a thilly queth-tion?

Knock knock.
Who's there?
Isabelle.
Isabelle who?
Isabelle working, or should I just keep knocking?

Knock knock.
Who's there?
Oswald.
Oswald who?
Oswald my bubble gum!

Knock knock.
Who's there?
Howard.
Howard who?
Howard you like to step outside?

Knock knock.
Who's there?
Howie.
Howie who?
I'm fine, thanks, how are you?

Knock knock.
Who's there?
Ivan.
Ivan who?
Ivan idea you know who this is.

Knock knock.
Who's there?
Tasha.
Tasha who?
Tasha soccer ball out and let's play!

Knock knock. Who's there?
Dewey. Dewey who?
Dewey have to listen to any
more knock knock jokes?

JURASSIC PORK

Why are the dinosaurs extinct?
They smelled so bad.

What do you say when you want your dinosaur to move faster?
"Pronto, saurus!"

Why don't you ever let a tyrannosaur drive your car?
Because a tyrannosaurus rex.

Why are meteors better than toilet paper?
Because one meteor was able to wipe out all the dinosaurs in the world.

Why did the caveman always show up at the party first?
He was Early Man.

What do you call the first man who discovered fire?
Toast.

What did the cavewoman say when she found bugs crawling under a rock?
"Dinner's ready!"

What do you call the remains of a woolly mammoth?
A fuzzle.

What do you call a dinosaur stuck in a glacier?
A fossicle.

What do you get when you cross a dinosaur with a pig?
Jurassic Pork.

Why did the dinosaur cross the road?
Chickens hadn't evolved yet.

Knock knock.
Who's there?
Iguanodon.
Iguanodon who?
Iguanodon town to see the dinosaur exhibit.

Then there was the caveboy who invented the wheel. He told his buddies to keep it a secret. "Don't tell my dad," he said. "Or he'll make me invent the garage."

What do pterodactyls have that no other creature has?
  Little pterodactyls.

What toys did cavekids play with?
  Tricera-tops.

A full-grown stegosaurus can grow up to how many feet?
  Just the four.

The world's first glacier was spotted by a caveman with good ice sight.

Cavepeople invented the world's first music by rolling boulders down a hill. They called it rock-and-roll.

Teacher: Why were there no humans alive during the dinosaur age?
Alex: Because it was Pre-Stork times.

Jokin' Around

Double or Nothing

Tell a friend or an adult that you will be able to double their money without buying anything, going on the Stock Exchange, or using a computer. Then ask them for a dollar bill.
  Simply fold the bill in half and say, "There! I doubled your money!"

Did you hear about the cavewoman who found a saber-toothed tiger trapped in a block of ice? She quickly built a fire and melted the ice, releasing the dangerous creature. After the tiger carried off her husband, her neighbors asked her why she had done it. "I made a terrible mistake," she said. "I thought I thawed a pussycat!"

GROSS!

A man is racing to the bathroom, a second man is leaving it, and a third man is still inside. Can you guess their nationalities?

Russian, Finnish, and European.

What did Mother say to Father when their baby boy fell down the stairs?

"Oh, look, honey! Our little boy is taking his first twenty-three steps!"

Mother: Why did you put a frog in your sister's bed?
Jimmy: I couldn't find a snake.

What's worse than finding a worm in your apple?

Finding half a worm.

"Waiter! There's a cockroach in my salad!"
"Please don't shout, sir. Or else the other customers will be asking for one, too!"

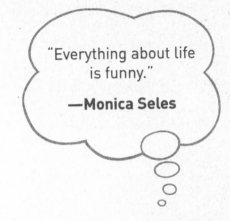

"Everything about life is funny."

—Monica Seles

Teacher: Oh dear! I've lost another pupil.
Principal: How did that happen?
Teacher: My glass eye flew out the window while I was driving.

Did you hear about the poor girl who swallowed the thermometer?

She's dying by degrees.

What's the difference between a saloon and an elephant's burp?

One is a bar room, and the other is a bar-OOOOM!

Do you remember when you lost your baby teeth?

Yeah, and was I surprised my dad could hit a baseball that hard!

"A train smashed into my bicycle, and I didn't even get hurt."
"Why not?"
"My brother Dave was riding it."

How do you keep a rooster from crowing on Sunday morning?

Make rooster stew Saturday night.

Why doesn't your sister like eating dill pickles?

She keeps getting her head stuck in the jar.

"That bully down the street just broke my finger!"
"Gosh, how did he do that?"
"He hit me in the nose."

Did you hear about the new principal who's been keeping the boys on their toes?

He raised all the urinals six inches.

How was King Henry VIII different from normal husbands?

He married his wives first, and axed them after.

There was a young monk of Siberia
Who of fasting grew wearia and wearia,
Till one day with a yell
He escaped from his cell
And devoured the Father Superia.

HOW'S BUSINESS?

Astronomer: It's looking up.

Submarine pilot: It has its ups and downs.

Oil rigger: Boring.

Tree doctor: Knot Two bad.

Carpenter: It's leveling off.

Surgeon: I always get a lot out of my patients.

Roofer: Customers are sliding off.

Boat racer: Sails are dropping.

Minister: Prophets are increasingly read.

Farmer: The field keeps growing.

Air traffic controller: Can't come, plane!

Model: The figures aren't all in yet.

Aerobics instructor: I'm reducing the bottom line.

> "When humor goes, there goes civilization."
>
> **—Erma Bombeck**

Beekeeper: Business is humming.

Car mechanic: Planning to re-tire.

Pizza chef: Making dough hand over fist.

Miner: Roughly carving out a living.

Highway worker: A bit bumpy.

Ballet dancer: Keeps me on my toes.

Teacher: Sorry, but that's classified information!

Jokin' Around

The Money Drop, or The Buck Doesn't Stop Here

Take out a crisp 1-dollar bill and hold it in your right hand. Let it hang down from your thumb and forefinger. Place the fingers and thumb of your left hand loosely around the bill without touching it. Let go of the bill with your right hand and catch it in your left hand. Don't grab it until the right hand has completely let go.

Show this little movement to your friends and bet them they can't catch the bill.

Again, hold the bill in your right hand. Let them (one at a time, of course) place their left hand loosely around the hanging bill. Tell them to catch the bill after you let go. Say, "If you can catch the falling bill, it's yours to keep."

They can't do it!

Why? In the time it takes your friends' eyeballs to register that the bill is falling, and for their brain to send out a second message to their hands telling them to grab, the bill has already dropped from their grasp. Gravity works too fast in this case, faster than human reflexes.

The reason you are able to catch the bill is because your brain knows when you are about to release the bill. Your friends, however, don't have that "insider" information.

Tips: The bill should be crisp. If it is not new, fold a crease in the bill lengthwise.

Instruct your friends not to grab the bill until they see you let go.

After practicing this trick, try it with a 10- or 20-dollar bill (if you dare!).

HAVING A BALL

What has 18 legs, spits, and catches flies?
A baseball team.

Why did the football coach rip apart the pay telephone?
He was trying to get his quarterback.

> "The great comics and comedians have been the ones who dared to mix comedy with tragedy."
> **—Robin Tyler**
>
> (Who does Tyler think are great comics? Charlie Chaplin, Carol Burnett, Lily Tomlin, and Richard Pryor.)

Which football team travels with the most luggage?
The Packers.

What dessert should basketball players never eat?
Turnovers.

Which college team has the tallest players?
O-HIGH-O State.

Fullback: I'm sick, Coach. The doctor says I can't play football.
Coach: I don't need a doctor to tell me that!

Why is bowling cheaper than playing golf?
Because in bowling, no matter how badly you play, you can never lose the ball!

"What do you call your dad when he water skis in the winter?"
"A Popsicle."
"What does your mom call him?"
"Crazy!"

"Did you hear about the scuba diver who heard music underwater?"
"Was it a singing fish?"
"No, a coral group."

A college star fullback played with his team for 12 years!
He could run and tackle—he just couldn't pass.

What do you call a basketball player's pet chicken?
A personal fowl.

What do you get when a soccer player kicks a duck?

Someone who foots the bill.

Did you hear about the football coach who got his teeth knocked out?

He was showing a new player how to kick the ball. He held it on the ground and said, "Now when I nod my head, kick it!"

Golfer: Young man, why do you keep looking at your watch?

Caddie: This isn't a watch. It's a compass!

Did you hear about the billionaire who bought his kid 10 new golf clubs?

Each of them comes with a swimming pool and a private parking lot.

What is the quietest sport in the world?

Bowling. You can hear a pin drop.

What's the noisiest sport in the world?

Tennis. There's always a racket on the court.

Why is a baseball stadium such a cool place to be?

It's full of fans!

Did you hear about the quarterback who beat up his receiver every morning?

The quarterback gets up at six, and the receiver gets up at seven.

Golfer: Boy, the traps on this golf course are sure annoying.

Pro: I'll say, so would you please shut yours?

I heard there was a baseball team that won without ever putting a man on base.

Yeah, it was an all-girl team!

Angry Golfer: You must be the world's worst caddy!

Caddy: Oh no, that would be too much of a coincidence.

"There are two things the golf pro will not eat for breakfast."

"Really, what are they?"

"Lunch and dinner."

Why didn't the golfer wear his new shoes on the course today?

Because yesterday he got a hole in one.

Little Rosie was telling her friend about all the places her family had lived. "We must have lived in ten different towns since I was a baby." Her friend was impressed and asked, "Is your dad a minister or in the Army?" "Neither," said Rosie, "he's a football coach."

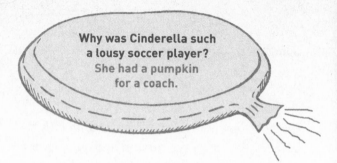

Why was Cinderella such a lousy soccer player? She had a pumpkin for a coach.

A fellow took his younger brother to the golf course with his pals. The younger boy thought he'd play his first game. He watched all the older boys tee off, and then stepped up to hit the ball.
"ONE!" he yelled, as he swung at the ball.
    His brother rolled his eyes and said, "Why didn't you yell 'Fore' like the rest of us?"
    The boy said, "You aim at whichever hole you want, I'm trying to hit the first one."

A mother brought her daughter to the golf course for the first time.
"What are those guys doing over there?" she asked her mother.
"They're checking out the sand traps."
"Cool, let's go see if they caught any."

Caddie: Here's a lost ball I found out on the course.
Boss: How do you know it was lost?
Caddie: Because they were still looking for it when I left.

Golfer: Any idea how I could cut about ten strokes off my game?
Caddie: Yeah, quit on the seventeenth hole.

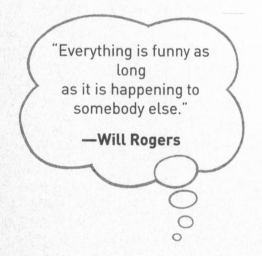

"Everything is funny as long
as it is happening to somebody else."

—**Will Rogers**

VIDEO QUIPS (PUNNY NAMES)

Car Wars
directed by Otto Mobile

Cliff Hanger
directed by Ben Dover and Hugo First

I Was a Teenage Werewolf
directed by Anita Shave

Under the Bleachers
directed by Seymour Butts

Summer Vacation
directed by Sandy Beech

Explode!
directed by Adam Bomm

The Fortune Teller
directed by Horace Cope

Escape from New York
directed by Willy Makit

Escape from New York, Part Two
directed by Betty Will

Saved by the Bell
directed by Justin Tyme

Jokin' Around

The Expanding Envelope

Tell your friends that you can walk through an envelope. That's right! Through an envelope. No one will believe you, but that's never stopped you before.

First, seal your envelope. Next, using scissors, carefully cut the envelope along the lines shown below. Cut into the body of the envelope and the sides . . . NOT the ends.

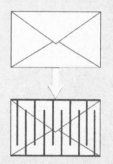

You will be able to carefully unfold your cut envelope into a much larger hoop. Step through the hoop. See, you've done it again!

Seeing Dead People
directed by Freyda Thudark

Who Wants To be a Zillionaire?
directed by Sherwood B. Nice.

The Pizza Guy
directed by Ann Chovey

Scary Movie
directed by Hans Archer Throte

Incredible Airplane Crashes!
directed by Isaac DeMye Stumick

Rock-and-Roll Prom
directed by Tristan Shout

The Last Video Game
directed by Joyce Tick

King of Comedy
directed by Shirley U. Jest

Lost Treasure
directed by Barry Deep

The Ghost Screams at Midnight
directed by Waylon Mone

Night of the Cat Burglar
directed by Jimmy DeLock

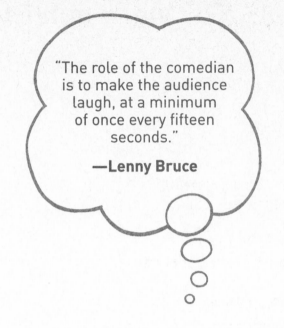

"The role of the comedian is to make the audience laugh, at a minimum of once every fifteen seconds."

—Lenny Bruce

Dinosaur Park
directed by Tara Dacktill

Revenge of the Mad Cow
directed by I. C. Hanz

Chickens Run
directed by Iona Farm

Return of the Zombies
directed by Doug Moregraves

All Those Dogs!
directed by Hunter and Juan del Mayshuns

GAGS AND GIGGLES

The dim-witted terrorist was sent out to blow up a car. He burned his lips on the exhaust pipe.

Two boys went to the movies. After the film had already started, they both got up and walked to the concession stand for some popcorn and soda pop. When they walked back into the darkened theater, one of the boys said to a man sitting on the aisle, "Excuse me, sir, but did we step on your toes on the way out?"

"You certainly did," said the man.

The boy turned to his friend and said, "Okay, this is our row."

There was the poor shoe salesman who had pulled out half of his stock, trying to find the perfect shoe for a young girl.

Words to Know

Gag: a laugh-provoking remark, trick, or prank

"Do you mind if I sit and rest a moment?" he asked her. "Your feet are killing me."

A snooty young woman was put off by a man begging for money.

"Are you satisfied walking the streets like this and asking for handouts?"

"No, ma'am," said the beggar. "I wish I could use a car."

Harry and his friends went deer hunting one fall. The first morning they all split up and disappeared into the woods. After lunch, Harry spotted one of his friends coming out of the woods.

"Where's the rest of the guys?" asked Harry, excitedly.

"They're at the cabin," said his friend.

"All of them?" asked Harry.

"Yeah, all of them."

"Are you sure?"

"Yes, Harry, I'm sure," said his friend. "Why do you keep asking?"

Harry had a big smile. "Boy, is that a relief. That means I shot a deer!"

Once the flood was over, Noah opened up the Ark and released all the animals back onto dry land. After the last animal had bounded off to freedom, Noah trudged wearily inside the ship to start the long chore of cleaning up. To his surprise, he noticed two snakes coiled up in a corner.

"Why are you two still here?" asked Noah.

One of the snakes answered, "Well, sir, you told us to go forth and multiply."

"Yes, indeed," said Noah.

"We can't multiply," said the snake. "We're adders."

A vampire took a vacation on a cruise ship. The headwaiter asked if he'd like to check out their menu.

"No thanks," said the vampire. "But do you have a passenger list?"

Gretchen: Why are you feeding your chickens boiled water?
Karl: I want them to lay boiled eggs.

Max: There's just one thing that would make you look even better than you do now.
Dot: What's that?
Max: Distance.

Did you hear about the knothead who fell down the elevator shaft?
When he gained consciousness he yelled,
"I said UP!"

Rosie: Do you think my painting is any good?
Bill: In a way.
Rosie: What kind of way?
Bill: Away off.

A fellow walks into a hotel and asks for a room.

"We don't have any rooms," said the clerk. "We're full up."

"But I've been to every other hotel in this town," said the man. "They're all full. Are you sure you don't have any room somewhere?"

"I already told you," said the clerk. "No available room."

The man thought a moment then said, "If I were the president of the United States would you have a room for me?"

"Yes," said the clerk. "*If* you were the president."

"Well, give me *his* room, then," said the man, "Because he's not coming."

Did you hear about the rich kid whose father told him, "Son, I'm sorry, but tomorrow I need the limousine and chauffeur for work."

"But, Pop," said the kid, "how will I get to school?"

"Like every other normal kid in America," said the father. "You'll take a cab."

A prisoner on his way to the electric chair was asked if he had any last requests.

"I'd like some strawberries," says the prisoner.

"Strawberries?" says the guard. "They're not in season for six months yet."

The prisoner says, "Fine. I'll wait."

"We saw the Grand Canyon in ten days."
"That's a long vacation."
"Yeah, it took us five days to drive through and another five to refold the maps."

How did they measure hail before golf balls were invented?

"Are you sure you've ridden a horse before?"
"Oh yes."
"Then what kind of saddle would you like? With a horn or without?"
"I'll take the one without a horn. I doubt if I'll run into much traffic."

You heard what Noah told his son when they went fishing?

"Easy on the bait, son, we only have two worms."

A newspaper reporter was interviewing a gnarled, wrinkled, white-haired farmer as he sat quietly rocking on his front porch.

"Sir," said the reporter. "I'd like to know the secret of your long life."

"Well, son," replied the farmer. "I drink a gallon of whisky, smoke ten cigars, and stay out partying every night of the week."

"That's amazing," said the reporter. "And how old are you?"

"Twenty-six."

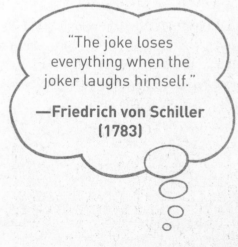

"The joke loses everything when the joker laughs himself."

—**Friedrich von Schiller (1783)**

Jokin' Around

Bottom's Up

Bet your friends or family that you can drink from a soda pop can without opening it or tampering with it in any way. They'll think you're nuts! But you can prove them wrong.

Take a soda pop can and then turn it over. All aluminum pop cans have a slight indentation on the bottom. You can easily fill this indentation with water (or with pop from a different can). You'll be able to sip your drink from the can's bottom without opening it or tampering with it.

Tip: When making the bet, be sure to tell them that you will "drink *from* a can" and not "drink *out* of a can." The words are important. Say the wrong thing and your friends and family can trip you up, and you'll be forced to eat—or drink—your own words!

Mother: Honey, ask the butcher if he has calf's tongue.
Jimmy: Why ask? I'll just wait until he opens his mouth and look.

Mother (looking at the meat display): Jimmy, can you tell if the butcher has pickled pig's feet?
Jimmy: No, I can't. He's wearing shoes.

"Did you hear the news? They rescued a man from the swamp this morning whose foot was bitten off by an alligator!"
"Which one?"
"Who knows? All alligators look the same."

Have you heard about that new dog food?
  It tastes like a mail carrier.

A rookie cop got bawled out by his sergeant after working his first stakeout.
  "How could you let that crook escape?" yelled the sergeant. "I told you to keep an eye on all the exits."
  "I did, Sarge. He must have gone out one of the entrances."

Did you hear about the weirdo who went to see a movie at the drive-in theater called
  Closed for Repairs?

THE WORLD'S SEVEN BEST LIMERICKS

There was a young lady named Bright
Whose speed was much faster than light.
She went out one day
In a relative way
And came back on the previous night.

There was a young fellow of Crete
Who was so exceedingly neat,
When he got out of bed
He stood on his head
To make sure of not soiling his feet.

There was a young lady of Niger
Who smiled as she rode on a tiger.
They returned from the ride
With the lady inside
And the smile on the face of the tiger.

The bottle of perfume that Willie sent
Was highly displeasing to Millicent.
Her thanks were so cold
That they quarreled, I'm told,
'Bout that silly scent Willie sent Millicent.

Words to Know

Limerick: a light or humorous verse with a specific rhythm and rhyme scheme

A flea and a fly in a flue
Were imprisoned so what could they do?
Said the fly, "Let us flee,"
Said the flea, "Let us fly,"
So they flew through a flaw in the flue.

A certain young man named Bill Beebee
Was in love with a lady named Phoebe
"But," he said, "we must see
What the clerical fee be
Before Phoebe be Phoebe Beebee."

There once was a maid from Japan
Whose limericks never would scan.
When they questioned her why,
She replied, "Because I
Like to squeeze as many syllables into the concluding line of the limerick as I possibly can."

FUN FACT

BRIEFLY FUNNY

Limericks have been making people laugh for over a hundred years. But funny stuff can always be improved on. Comic poet Ogden Nash invented a streamlined, or mini version, of the Limerick called the **Limick**.

An outlaw from Spain
Fled to Paris by train
Where he jumped in the river—
They found him in-Seine.

A fellow from Hutton's,
The grandest of gluttons,
Makes room for dessert
By popping his buttons.

It's Rhyme Time

Add the missing letter in each of the following words to make a group of words that all rhyme. Now choose the three words that will correctly finish the limerick below. BE CAREFUL! Sometimes more than one letter can be used to make a word. If you can't find three words in your list that fit in the limerick, go back to the word list and try making other words.

B__Y   FR__

D__E   __YE

PI__   WH__

T__Y   __RY

There was a young boy
who asked,"_____
Can't I look in my ear
with my_____?
If I put my mind to it,
I'm sure I could do it,
But I'll never know till
I_____!"

SIGNS ON THE DOTTY LINE

Signs found hanging on the doors of . . .

An Astronaut: OUT TO LAUNCH
A fencing instructor: OUT TO LUNGE
A nuclear Scientist: GONE FISSION
A music Teacher: GONE CHOPIN, BE BACH SOON
A dance instructor: BACK IN A MINUET
A car mechanic: ON A BRAKE
A chiropractor: BE RIGHT, BACK!
A surgeon: JUST CUT OUT
A dog trainer: WILL RETURN IN FIVE MINUTES. SIT. STAY.
A nudist colony: WE'RE NEVER CLOTHED
A dentist: OPEN WIDE

Bye Bye

Which sign did the eye doctor leave on her door when she went on vacation?

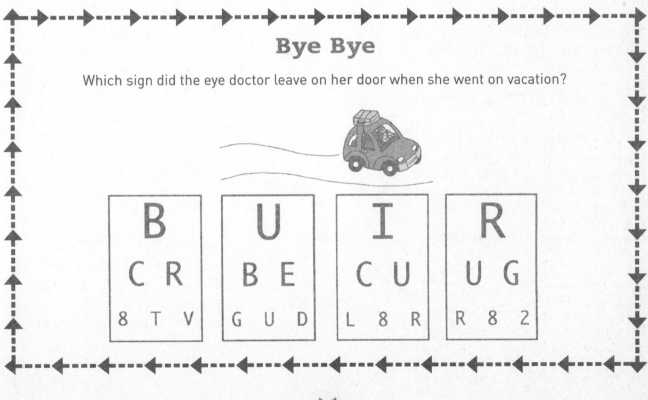

B	U	I	R
C R	B E	C U	U G
8 T V	G U D	L 8 R	R 8 2

LAUGHING STOCK

"Does your family own a cat?"

"No, why?"

"I thought I heard it meowing last night."

"That's just our dog. He's been listening to foreign language tapes."

Jenny: Doctor, I have a problem. I love Bermuda shorts.

Doctor: Lots of people love Bermuda shorts.

Jenny: With mustard and relish?

"I got a role in the new *Tarzan* movie. Boy, you should have seen all the crazy animals we had to work with."

"Were you the star?"

"No, but when the lion got loose and chased the cast, I was the leading man!"

"The best humor is the most obvious. When the audience has to stop and think too hard about a punchline, the punch is lost."

—Thom Melcher

Harold and Stanley were brothers. Harold went on a business trip and asked Stanley to look after his pet kitten. The first night of his trip, Harold phoned his brother and asked how little Buttons was doing.

"Buttons is dead," said Stanley, flatly.

Harold was appalled. "Stanley! That's no way to tell me bad news."

"How should I have told you?" asked Stanley.

"Break it to me gently," said Harold. "Little by little. You could have said that Buttons was up on the roof. Then say you had to call the fire department. Then say the ladder wasn't long enough. Then tell me that Buttons tried to jump. And then you could have said he was in the hospital. And that he was growing weaker and weaker. That he stopped eating. Then, eventually, you could have told me that poor Buttons died."

"Sorry," said Stanley. "I'll know better next time."

"All right," said Harold. "By the way, how's Mom?"

"Well, she's up on the roof."

A miser won the lottery with a ticket he bought—$1,000,000! But he still seemed depressed. "What's wrong?" asked his neighbor. The miser sighed and said, "When I think of the dollar I *wasted* buying this other lottery ticket."

Joey: Yuck! This is the worst tasting apple pie I ever had!
Waiter: What does it taste like?
Joey: Glue!
Waiter: Then that's the pumpkin pie. The apple pie tastes like mud.

Mother: Billy, what is all that grass doing sticking out of your pockets?
Billy: The worms in there have to eat something, don't they?

Troop Leader: Do you know how to make a fire with just two sticks?
Cub Scout: Yes, sir. As long as one of the sticks is a match.

My poor sister had an awful time of it. First she got arthritis and rheumatism. And after that she got appendicitis, tonsillitis, and then pneumonia. They even had to give her hypodermics. Whew! I didn't think she'd ever make it through that spelling contest!

Five-year-old Kevin came running down the stairs, wailing and weeping. "What ever is the matter?" asked his mother. "I was upstairs with Daddy," said Kevin. "He was putting up pictures. And he hit his thumb with the hammer." The mother grinned. "That's all right, honey. Your daddy is a grown-up man. He doesn't let something like that worry him. And you shouldn't either. You should have just laughed." Then Kevin sobbed, "I did!"

My doctor believes in shock therapy. That's why he sends me his bill!

"Excuse me, could you tell me the fastest way to get to the hospital?"
"Stand in traffic."

"I was thinking of attending the time-management workshop."
"When does it start?'
"Oh, fivish, sixish."

"A person without a sense of humor is like a wagon without springs—jolted by every pebble in the road."

—Henry Ward Beecher

51

A man walked into an antique store. It was filled with beautiful furniture, fine old paintings, and housewares of silver and crystal. Nothing caught his eye. As he turned to leave, however, he noticed the owner's cat licking milk out of a delicate china saucer. The man knew at a glance that the saucer was priceless, and he figured the stupid owner didn't realize what a treasure was sitting just beneath his nose.

The man casually struck up a conversation with the owner.

"Nice cat you got there."

"Thanks," said the owner. "He's a good cat, but I never seem to have enough time for him."

"Hmmm, would you be interested in selling him?" asked the man.

"Sure, if you're serious," said the owner. "You can have him for five bucks."

"Deal."

The man paid his five dollars, then picked up the cat and headed toward the door. "Oh, by the way," said the man, turning around. "You probably wouldn't mind if I just took that old milk saucer would you? The cat seems to like it."

"Are you kidding?" grinned the man. "That saucer has helped me sell seventy cats in the last month!"

"I'm on that new Japanese diet."
"How does that work?"
"You're only allowed to use one chopstick."

A doctor walks into a hospital room and stands next to the bed of his patient.

"Mister Cooper, I have some good news and some bad news."

"What is it, Doc?"

"The bad news is that we have to amputate both your feet."

"That's horrible! What's the good news?"

"The patient in the next bed wants to buy your shoes."

Picto-Laugh #3

A pictograph is a very simple drawing of something funny. Can you guess what this little picto-laugh is showing? **HINT:** Think about Mexican hats and exercise!

First Scientist: I discovered the perfect cure for dandruff.
Second Scientist: What is it?
First Scientist: Baldness.

Years ago, a huge ship was passing through a thick fog. Suddenly, up ahead, it saw a bright and unexpected light. The ship signaled: "Veer off!"

The reply: "You veer off!"

The captain of the ship became furious. He told his signal man, "Tell that idiot to veer off! Doesn't he realize this battleship is heading his way?"

The signal man obeyed the command and then waited for a reply.

"Well, what did he say?" asked the angry captain.

The signal man answered, "Well, sir, he says, 'Don't you realize this lighthouse is heading *your* way?'"

Harold got a summer job painting yellow stripes down the middle of the highway. The first day he did an excellent job and painted a strip a mile long. But the second day he painted only half a mile. And the third day Harold painted even less.

Finally, his angry boss told him, "Harold, you're slacking off! Each day you paint less and less."

Harold replied, "I know. But each day it gets longer and longer to walk back to that bucket!"

Love to Laugh

A good joke can make you laugh out loud or quietly to yourself. See if you can fill in five different kinds of laughs. We left a couple of L-A-U-G-H-S to help you.

"I don't have a penny to my name."
"Are you gonna get a job?"
"No, I'm gonna change my name."

Did you hear about the elephant hunter who hurt his back?
He was carrying decoys.

A miser walks into a dentist's office and asks the dentist how much he charges for pulling a tooth.
"Thirty bucks," said the dentist.
"Here's five," said the miser. "Just loosen it a little."

A young girl entered the courthouse and registered for a name change.

"What's your name now?" asked the clerk.

"Betty Stinks," said the girl.

The clerk laughed for almost a full minute. "I can understand why you'd want to change it," the clerk finally said. "What are you changing it to?"

"Elizabeth Stinks."

First Fisher: Is this a good lake for fish?

Second Fisher: It must be. I can't get any of them to come out.

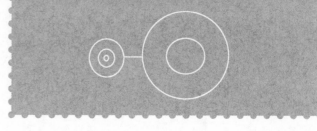

Picto-Laugh #4

A pictograph is a very simple drawing of something funny. Can you guess what this little picto-laugh is showing? HINT: Think about Mexican hats and breakfast!

"I want to see Dr. Braun."

"He's not here at the moment. But I'm sure Dr. Wilson could help you."

"I don't want Dr. Wilson. I want Dr. Braun."

"Then you'll just have to wait."

"Fine. How long?"

"Two weeks. Dr. Braun just left on his vacation."

A mother raced into a doctor's office, pulling her son along behind her. "Tell me, Doctor," she said, "can a ten-year-old boy take out a person's appendix?"

"Don't be ridiculous," said the doctor. "Of course not."

"See, Jimmy? You heard the doctor. Now go put that right back!"

Two cars, driving from opposite directions, met in the middle of a narrow bridge that was wide enough to let only one car pass at a time.

The first motorist rolled down his window, stuck his head out, and yelled, "I never back up for jerks!"

The second driver put his car in reverse and yelled, "That's all right. I always do!"

Jimmy: This is the slowest train I've ever been on! Conductor, can't you run any faster?

Conductor: Sure I can. But I have to stay on the train.

Larry: Why don't we fall off the earth and go shooting through space?
Perry: The law of gravity.
Larry: Then what did we do before that law was passed?

A young girl walked into a clothing store with her mother. "I'd like to try on that dress in the window," she said.

"Well, young lady," said the clerk, "we'd prefer that you use one of our dressing rooms."

Jimmy: How's your new job on the construction site?
Derek: Awful! After one week, I'm through with it!
Jimmy: What for?
Derek: Lots of reasons. The constant complaining, the laziness, the sloppiness, the bad language. They just wouldn't put up with it anymore!

It's Joke Time!

Draw a line from each riddle to the clock that shows the correct answer.
HINT: It helps to read the time on each clock aloud.

What time is it when five tigers are chasing you?

What time is it when you have a toothache?

What time is it when baseball teams have a tie score?

What time is the same backward or forward?

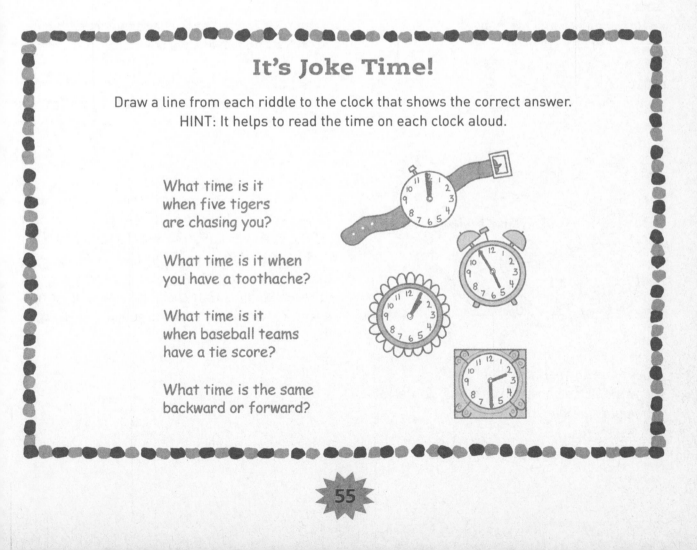

55

PUNDEMONIUM

I heard on the news that a nuclear scientist accidentally ate some uranium, and now he has atomic ache!

"How's your sister coming along with her new jigsaw puzzle?"
"She can't figure it out. I'm afraid she's going to pieces."

Did you hear they fired the cross-eyed school teacher?
He couldn't control his pupils.

Did you hear about the lobster that bought a new car?
It was a crustacean wagon.

Words to Know

Pun: the humorous use of a word in such a way as to suggest two or more of its meanings or the meaning of another word with a similar sound

Doctor: Have your eyes ever been checked?
Kyle: No, they've always been blue.

What did one Moroccan boy say to the other?
"I can't remember your name, but your fez is familiar."

A misshapen ogre made his living by ringing the bells at a famous cathedral in France. One day the ogre lost his footing on the roof of the cathedral and plummeted 200 feet to his death in the courtyard below. Two priests rushed to the ogre's side. The first priest asked, "Is that the Hunchback of Notre Dame?" The second priest replied, "No, but he's a dead ringer."

"Does your brother have a job?"
"He works at the hospital as a night orderly."
"Oh, a pan-handler, huh?"

Tyler: My dad is so strong, he can hold up several cars at once using one hand.
Brian: What does he do?
Tyler: He's a policeman.
Brian: Big deal! My dad is a lot stronger. He can hold up an entire bank by just handing a little note to the teller.

What's the best way to avoid falling hair?
   Jump out of the way!

Dottie was having trouble learning her directions, especially the difference between north and south. So her mother tried a little quiz. "Dottie, if you were standing with your back to the east, and your face to the west, what would be on your right hand?"
Dottie said, "Four fingers and a thumb."

Teacher: My goodness, Amy! You've been burping all morning.
Amy: It must have been those belchin' waffles I ate for breakfast.

Matty: We learned today that people who live north of the Arctic Circle eat whale meat and blubber.
Mary: I'd blubber too if that's all I had to eat.

Mom: Amy, what are you doing home from school so early?
Amy: The teacher asked me how far I could count, so I counted all the way home.

"My aunt always nagged my uncle to buy her a Jaguar."
"Did he ever get one?"
"Yeah, then it ate her up!"

Circus Clown: How do you like your new job?
Trapeze Artist: I'm finally getting the hang of things.

How do you measure a dog's temperature?
   By *pedigrees.*

Some know-it-all once said that the pun was the lowest form of humor. Then a modern comic added, "unless you happen to make it yourself!"

I feel sorry for the two lighthouse keepers.
Their marriage is on the rocks.

Young earthworm: This dirt tastes terrible.
Mother earthworm: I don't understand. It was fresh ground this morning.

You heard about the glass blower who inhaled?
He got a pane in his stomach.

What did the Cub Scout say when he fixed the horn on his bike?
Beep repaired!

Why does your dog go round and round before he lies down?
He's a self-winding watchdog.

A music store was robbed last night. The burglar broke in, stole a drum, and beat it!

Why is that woolly sheep scratching itself?
Because it has fleece.

"Comedy is the new rock-and-roll."
—Janet Street-Porter

Teacher: Alex, why are you brushing your teeth during class?
Alex: I want to be ready for the oral exam.

Did you hear about the two silkworms who had a race?
They ended in a tie.

That movie was terrible. I've seen a better film on dirty teeth.

Why did the bank robber flee to the nudist colony?
That's where he had his hide out.

What do you see when the smog clears in southern California?
U.C.L.A.

What part of a car is responsible for causing the most accidents?
The nut located behind the wheel.

CLUELESS KIDS

They think that . . .

An octopus is a cat with eight paws.
A polygon is a parrot who flew from its
   cage.
An amoeba is a small prison, because it
   only has one cell.
Peanut butter is a baby billy goat.
Shell-shock is when you accidentally drop
   an egg.

"Doctor, can you help me? I keep thinking I'm a packet of biscuits."
"Biscuits? Oh, you mean those little square packets you crumble up for your soup?"
"Yes, exactly."
"Then you must be crackers!"

Picto-Laugh #5

A pictograph is a very simple drawing of something funny. Can you guess what this little picto-laugh is showing? **HINT:** Think about the color pink!

"You look awful, Stanley. Flu?"
"Yeah, and crashed!"

I read that Tibet is the noisiest place on earth.
   Everywhere you look it's Yak, Yak, Yak!

Did you hear about the Siamese twins who went to Prague for major surgery?
   They came out as separate Czechs.

"This report card should be underwater!"
"Because it's so wet?"
"No, because it's below "C" level!"

What happened to the origami store that used to be on the corner?
   It folded.

An inexperienced hunter was deep in the woods and kept following a set of tracks—until the train ran him over!

Fill Me In

Color in all the shapes with exactly three sides to find the answer to this riddle: Why did Silly Billy throw a stick of butter out the window?

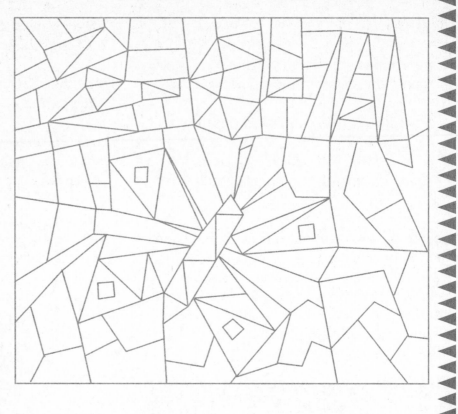

Why did Silly Billy throw a stick of butter out of the window?

Karl: Darn, I left my watch back up on that hill.
Ben: Should we go up and get it?
Karl: Nah, it'll run down by itself.

Gretchen: Every morning my dog and I go for a tramp in the woods.
Heather: Sounds delightful.
Gretchen: Yes, but the tramp is getting real tired of it.

At a fancy hotel, a man walks in and asks the desk clerk, "Do you take children?"

"No sir," replied the clerk. "Only checks and American Express."

The farmer came in from the barn and said to his wife:

"I shot the cow."

"Was he a mad cow?"

"Let's just say he wasn't too happy about it."

A once-famous rock star told her friend, "The last time I made an appearance at that nightclub, I drew a line five blocks long."

Her friend asked, "Did they make you erase it?"

"I think I have a good head on my shoulders."
"You sure have a point there."

Why do you keep a sun lamp in your lunchbox?
It's a light lunch.

FUNNY BUSINESS

Did you realize that if 3M and Goodyear ever merged they could call themselves MMMGood?

And if Polygram Records, Warner Brothers, and Nabisco Crackers ever joined forces, they would be called Poly-Warner-Cracker.

A PUN-OPLY FOR PUN LOVERS

Here's an alphabetical list of old or obsolete words that all mean "pun." Some of these words are over 500 years old!

bull
carrawitchet
clinch
crotchet
figary
flim
jerk
liripoop
pundigrion
quarterquibble
quillet
quirk
sham
whim

If you always have a pun up your sleeve that you can't wait to try out on your friends, you are said to be "liripoopionated."

And if you pun way too much, your friends can accuse you of "quibble-ism."

NUTS FROM THE FAMILY TREE

Mother: What's the best way to discipline children?
Father: Start at the bottom.

Ashley: Everyone says I got my good looks from my father.
Jason: Oh, is he a plastic surgeon?

"My older brother thinks he's a chicken."
"You should take him to a doctor."
"Why? We need the eggs."

"We got a dog for my little brother."
"I wish my Dad would let me make a trade like that."

Mother: Darling, will you still love me when my hair is gray?
Father: Why not? I loved you through those five other colors.

At the airport, Mother turned to Father and said, "I sure wish we had brought the television with us."
"Why is that?" asked Father.
"Because I left the plane tickets on it."

Karl and Ben went out hunting. They were just bedding down in their tents one night when a huge snarling bear lumbered into their campsite. Karl quickly knelt down and started lacing up his sneakers.
"What good will that do?" shouted Ben. "You can't outrun a bear."
Karl replied, "I only have to outrun *you!*"

A very proud grandmother was walking through the park, pushing her two grandchildren in a stroller. A young woman walked by and said, "My, what fine looking little boys. They must be your grandsons." "Yes they are," said the grandmother. "How old are they?" asked the younger woman. "The lawyer is three and the doctor is two."

Jason: What's it like having a twin sister?
Megan: It's just like being an only child.
　　　Except twice.

"Mom, guess what? I won the election for class president!"
"Honestly?"
"Did you have to bring that up?"

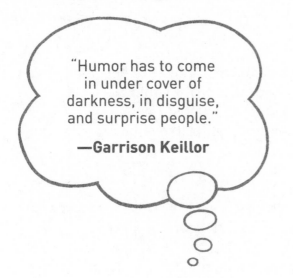

"Humor has to come in under cover of darkness, in disguise, and surprise people."

—Garrison Keillor

"Dad, where is yesterday's newspaper?"
"Your mother wrapped the garbage in it and threw it away."
"Darn, I wanted to see it."
"There wasn't much to see. Just some old egg cartons and dogfood cans and apple cores and . . ."

"My dad used to write for TV. He wrote *The Jeffersons*, *The Hughleys*, and *The PJ's*."
"Did they ever write back?"

"I can always tell when my big brother is lying."
"How's that?"
"He moves his lips."

"What are you having for dinner tonight?"
"Reruns."
"Reruns?"
"Yeah, leftover TV dinners."

"My brother made a right turn from the left lane and crashed into another car. The other driver jumped out and yelled at my brother. Why didn't you signal? he asked."
"What did your brother say?"
"He said, 'Why should I signal? I always turn here.'"

My Dad is a real pessimist. He just opened up a new Chinese restaurant and he only sells *misfortune* cookies.

"Doctor, my sister thinks she's an elevator. Can you help her?"
"Have her come up to my office."
"I would, but she doesn't stop at your floor."

"George Washington's parents were really thoughtful."
"What makes you say that?"
"They made sure their kid was born on a holiday."

Troy: Mom! Megan said I was dumb.
Mother: Megan, apologize to your brother!
Megan: Okay. I'm sorry you're dumb.

"My sister loves to eat."
"What's her favorite food?"
"Seconds."

Troy: Your piano playing stinks!
Megan: Well, for your information, that piece I was playing is very difficult.
Troy: Too bad it's not impossible.

"My brother is connected with the police."
"How's he connected?"
"With handcuffs."

Alex: My dad lost his wallet with over three hundred bucks in it.
Troy: Wow!
Alex: And he's offering a reward of twenty dollars to whoever finds it.
Troy: I'll give you thirty.

Three comedians were asked which is funnier: a witty line or someone slipping on a banana peel. Fran Lebowitz and Ellen DeGeneres both said that falling down is funnier. Lily Tomlin said it "depends on who's doing the slipping."

Amy: Dad, the landlord is here for the rent.
Father: Tell him I'm not home.
Amy: I can't lie like that!
Father: All right, I'll tell him myself.

Alex: Mom, I think it's time I got an allowance.
Mother: How about I give you double what I give your little brother, Matt?
Alex: But Matt gets zero allowance.
Mother: Okay, so I'll give you triple.

A young boy was telling his teacher all about the new addition to his family. "And every night," complained the boy, "little Kevin wakes everyone up with his crying."

"Well, he's just a wee little thing," said the teacher.

"No," said the boy. "He's a wee-wee thing. That's why he's crying."

Mother: Why did you kick your little brother in the stomach?
Jimmy: He turned around.

Teacher: How do you make antifreeze?
Rosie: Steal her blanket.

The real-estate agent told the family, "I'll be honest with you. This house has its good points as well as its bad points."

"What are the bad points?" asked the father.

"Just north of here is a toxic waste dump. And just south is a huge hog farm."

"What are the good points?" asked the mother.

"You can always tell which way the wind is blowing."

In the middle of a sweltering summer afternoon, the Thomas family was entertaining out-of-town guests. When supper was ready, the father asked the youngest son to say the blessing.

The boy whispered to his father, "But what do I say?"

The father replied, "Just say what you've heard me say before."

So the boy bowed his head and said in a loud voice, "Oh Lord, why in heaven's name did I ever invite these people on a hot day like today?"

Jimmy: My sister thinks I'm too nosy.
Troy: Did she tell you that?
Jimmy: No, that's what I read in her diary.

"What are you drawing, honey?"
"A picture of God."
"But no one knows what God looks like."
"They will when I'm finished with this."

"My brother has laryngitis, so he's talking with his hands."
"Is that why he's snapping his fingers?"
"Yeah, he has the hiccups."

Danny: Guess what, Dad? Mom backed the car out of the garage and ran right over my new bike.
Father: That'll teach you to leave it parked out on the front lawn.

"Young man, there were two cookies in the jar last night, and this morning there is only one. How do you explain that?"
"It was so dark, I guessed I missed it."

My mom gets carsickness every month—when she looks at the payment.

Mother: Rosie! Why did you fall in the mud puddle with your new dress on?
Rosie: There wasn't time to take it off.

Father: I think our son must get his brains from me.
Mother: Probably, because I still have all mine.

Matt: Dad! The dog just ate the pie Mom finished baking.
Father: That's all right, son, don't worry. We'll get you a new dog.

Did you hear about the nervous father who is pacing up and down in the hospital lobby, waiting to hear about the birth of his first child? Finally, after several hours, the nurse arrives. The father runs up to her and asks, "Nurse, tell me, is it a boy?" The nurse says calmly, "Well, the middle one is."

Mother: Boys, stop fighting! Who started this anyway?
Nick: Matt started it when he hit me back.

Aunt Missy: Do you know what an opera is, Rosie?
Rosie: Yeah, it's where someone gets stabbed and instead of bleeding they sing.

A grandmother took her little five-year-old grandson with her shopping. At one point in the store the little boy said loudly, "I have to go pee-pee." The grandmother shook her head and said, "No, dear. When you need to use the bathroom you say that you have *to whisper.* All right?"

That night the five-year-old woke up at midnight and toddled into his parents' bedroom. "Daddy," he said, tugging on his father's arm, "I have to whisper! I have to whisper!"

The father sleepily turned over on his side and said, "All right, son. Go ahead and whisper right in my ear."

Picto-Laugh #6

A pictograph is a very simple drawing of something funny. Can you guess what this little picto-laugh is showing? **HINT:** Think about a game of hide-n-seek!

"My sister ran the hundred-yard dash in five seconds."
"That's impossible! The world record isn't even eight seconds."
"She knows a short cut."

"Do you have to make so much noise when you eat?"
"Our teacher told us to start the day with a sound breakfast."

Ben: Why are you jumping up and down?
Karl: I just took some medicine, and the bottle said to shake well.

Rhyming Riddles

Draw a line to match each riddle
to the proper picture.

It keeps you nice and very neat—has lots of teeth, but cannot eat.

It runs all night, and runs all day, but never, ever runs away.

Sits on the table by your plate and cup—if it falls down, it might stick up.

Sometimes curly, some-times flat—it's over the head and under a hat.

"You sure take your car in for lots of repairs."
"I know, my dad is always braking it."

Mother: Why are you standing in front of the mirror with your eyes shut?
Melody: I want to see what I look like asleep.

"My dad only eats at the finest restaurants."
"How do you know that?"
"You should see our silverware."

Father: Go right up to your room and straighten it.
Jimmy: Is it crooked?

Jokin' Around

The Woman on the Bus

A woman was riding the bus downtown with her new baby.

A rude passenger sitting across the aisle took one look at the woman and her baby and said, "That's the ugliest baby I ever saw in my life. Looks just like a monkey." The woman was so upset that she quickly got off the bus at the very next stop. She walked over to a park bench, sat down, and started crying.

A young man walking by noticed the poor woman. "What's wrong?" he asked her. But the woman was too upset to tell him. It was a hot day out, so the man walked over to a convenience store and a few minutes later returned to the park bench.

The young man handed the woman a can of soda pop. "It's so hot out, I thought you might like this," he said. The woman gratefully accepted his offer. "Thank you very much," she said. Then the man reached into his pocket. "Here, take this," he said. "I bought a banana for your monkey, too."

"Why aren't you sharing your scooter with your little brother?"

"I am, Mom, half and half. I use it on the way down the hill, and he has it on the way up the hill."

Heather: I just finished giving my kitten a bath.
Tracy: Does she mind it?
Heather: No, she likes it. But afterwards it always takes me a while to get rid of the fur on my tongue.

Mother: What a dirty face! Your Aunt Missy won't kiss you like that.
Alex: That's what I figured.

Mother: What's your little brother yelling about?
Sandy: I don't know. I let him lick the beater after I made peanut butter fudge. Maybe I should have turned it off first.

A young boy, taking a vacation cruise with his parents, turned green with seasickness.

"Are you sure you don't want dinner, honey?" asked his mother.

The boy shook his head and replied, "Just throw it overboard, Mom, and save me the trip to the railing."

YOU KNOW YOU'RE A LOSER WHEN . . .

- ✔ Your ship comes in and you're at the train station.
- ✔ Your talking mynah bird says, "Who asked you?"

- ✔ Your twin forgets your birthday.
- ✔ Your parents attend PTA meetings under an assumed name.
- ✔ Your answering machine hangs up on you.

SPOONERISMS

The Reverend William Archibald Spooner (1844–1930) of Oxford University in England was famous for getting his tongue tied. Instead of saying "Our Lord is a loving shepherd," Spooner called him a "shoving leopard." Instead of sitting on a "stone bench," he'd relax on a "bone stench." Spoonerism is now the name we give a gag or phrase where the first letters of a word are exchanged for another. Below are some of the Reverend's sillier blunders.

- He whispered to a young man in an overcrowded church: "Excuse me, sir, but you're occupewing my pie. May I sew you to another sheet?"
- He told a tardy student: "You have hissed all my mystery lectures!"
- To a group of farmers, he started a speech by saying: "I have never before spoken to so many tons of soil."
- After performing a wedding ceremony, he then instructed the nervous groom: "It is kisstomary to cuss the bride."

Words to Know

Spoonerism: a phrase where the first letters of a word are exchanged for another

Here's a few more tongue stumblers:

"I need to buy a new can of oderarm deunderant."

"This fog is as thick as sea poop."

"Drinking lots of coffee always weeps me a cake."

"In New York Harbor, my uncle supervises all the bug totes."

"While I run into the shandy cop, would you keep your buy on my icicle?"

What's The Difference?

These riddles ask you to tell the difference between two things. The answer is always a pair of words. When you read the words one way, they describe the first thing in the riddle. When you switch the pair of words around, they describe the second thing! See if you can choose the correct pairs of words that will complete each riddle. Write your answers in the spaces provided. The first one has been half done for you!

1. What's the difference between a rain gutter and a clumsy baseball player?

   (One catches drops, and the other _____.)

2. What's the difference between a fake dollar bill and a crazy rabbit?

   (One is _____, and the other is a_____.)

3. What's the difference between a jail warden and a jeweler?

   (One _____, and the other _____.)

4. What's the difference between a sneaky student and a mouse?

   (One is a _____, and the other is a _____.)

5. What's the difference between a bowl of moldy lettuce and a depressing song?

   (One is a _____, and the other is a _____.)

6. What's the difference between a healthy rabbit and a bad joke?

   (One is a _____, and the other is only a _____.)

PAIRS TO CHOOSE FROM:

sells watches

cheesy eater

drops catches

bad salad

fit bunny

mad bunny

watches cells

sad ballad

bad money

easy cheater

bit funny

A SPOONERFUL OF TEA (A TRUE STORY)

The Reverend Spooner met a stranger while strolling through the university grounds one evening.

Spooner: Come to my place for tea tomorrow, young man. We're having a welcome party for the new math professor.
Stranger: But I am the new math professor.
Spooner: That's all right. Come anyway.

SPOONER'S BUG

Q: What spoonerism has become a common word that refers to something we see during the summer months?
A: Butterfly. The insect was once known as a *flutter-by*, named for its fluttery, delicate movement.

Comic Biography

Goldwyn Said It First

On the other side of the Atlantic Ocean, Americans have their own M.C., or Master of Confusion. His name is Sam Goldwyn (1882–1974), a hot-headed movie producer whose verbal blunders have passed into legend.

Include me out.
I can answer your request in two words: Im-possible.
I'll give you a definite maybe.
Don't talk to me when I'm interrupting.
I never liked you, and I always will.
This new atom bomb is dynamite!
I don't pay any attention to him. I don't even ignore him.
Our comedies are not to be laughed at.
Anyone who goes to a psychiatrist ought to have his head examined.

NUN OF THAT

A new nun joined a special order where all the sisters had to take a vow of silence. Only two words were allowed each sister per year. After the first year, the Mother Superior asked the newest nun how things were going.

"Bad food," said the nun.

The next year the Mother Superior asked the nun the same question.

"Hard beds," said the nun.

At the end of the third year, the nun walked up to the Mother Superior and said, "I quit!"

"Well I'm not surprised," said the Mother Superior. "Ever since you got here you've done nothing but complain."

"That is the best—to laugh with someone because you think the same things are funny."

—**Gloria Vanderbilt**

Nun: Remember, young lady, we are in this world to help others.
Melody: Okay, but what are the others here for?

Quick Draw

These funny drawings show the names of three common things. Can you guess what each is?

WAY-OUT OUT WEST (COWBOY JOKES)

A cowboy was riding his horse one day when he accidentally got thrown off. The quick-thinking horse pulled the cowboy to a shady oasis, propped him up against a tree, and then galloped off for help. He soon returned with some folks from a neighboring town, including a doctor. The doctor and the others brought the cowboy into town and nursed him back to full health.

A week later, when the cowboy was telling his buddies at the saloon this story, one of them said, "That's the gol-dang smartest horse I ever heard tell of."

"Aw, he ain't that smart," said the cowboy. "The doctor he brung with him was a vet."

A cowboy bought a beautiful new horse. The salesman told him that the horse's former owner had been a famous preacher.

"This horse is very religious," said the salesman. "And he only responds to special commands. For instance, instead of saying Giddy-up, you say Praise the Lord. And instead of telling him to Whoa! you say Hallelujah. Got that?"

"Praise the Lord and Hallelujah," nodded the cowboy.

Weeks later, the cowboy was riding through unfamiliar territory. Gorges and cliffs fell hundreds of feet on either side of the trail. The cowboy wanted to stop and take a rest, but he confused the two words the salesman had taught him.

"Praise the Lord," the cowboy said, but the horse kept on galloping faster and faster. The cowboy saw that the trail up ahead ended in a dangerous cliff. He tugged and pulled at the reins even harder and yelled, "Praise the Lord! Praise the Lord!" but the horse continued to race toward the cliff.

All at once, the cowboy remembered the right word.

"Hallelujah!" he cried.

The horse immediately stopped, mere inches from the crumbling edge of the cliff.

The cowboy breathed a sigh of relief and pulled off his hat, wiping the dust from his eyes.

"Praise the Lord," he said.

Jokin' Around

Turtle Soup

Three little turtles, who lived in the same house together, were having Sunday dinner. They each sipped their own bowl of soup.

"This soup would sure taste better with some bread," said the first turtle.

"We're all out of bread," said the second turtle.

"Well, I'm not going to the store," said the third, and littlest, turtle. "If I go, you two will eat my soup."

The other two turtles promised him they would never touch his soup. "Go to the store and hurry back," said the first turtle. So the littlest turtle reluctantly walked out the door.

Minutes stretched into hours. Hours stretched into days. A week later, the turtles were still waiting for their friend to return from the store with the bread.

The first turtle said, "I don't think he's ever coming back. We might as well go ahead and have his soup."

Just then, the littlest turtle poked his head back inside the door. "See?" he said. "I knew if I left you guys would eat my dinner!"

MONEY IS ONLY PAPER

Tallulah Bankhead (1903–1968) was a flamboyant actress known for her generosity as well as for saying whatever popped into her head. Once when Tallulah was using a lady's bathroom, sitting in a stall, she realized there was no toilet paper.

She called over to the next stall, "Have you any toilet paper, darling?"

"No, I'm afraid not."

"Hmm, any tissue paper?"

"Sorry, no."

Tallulah paused and then asked calmly, "Have you two fives for a ten?"

A NUTTY CRIME

A judge had three young boys come before his bench.

The first boy said, "All I did, Your Honor, was break a window, wreck someone's bike, and throw peanuts in the lake."

The second boy said, "Me too, Your Honor. I only broke a small window, wrecked a friend's bike, and threw peanuts in the lake."

The third boy said, "All I did was break a window and wreck a bike."

The judge turned to the third boy and said, "Didn't you throw peanuts in the lake?"

The boy said, "I'm Peanuts."

MORE NUTS

A man walks into a fancy bar and orders a glass of wine. It's early evening and the bar has only a few customers.

The man hears a voice next to him say, "Nice tie." The man looks around, but there is no one sitting nearby. He figures he must be hearing things.

He takes a sip of wine and hears, "I like that suit you're wearing." Again, the man swivels around on his chair but sees no one.

Another sip of wine and the man hears, "That blue shirt really brings out your eyes."

"Okay!" says the man. "That does it! What's going on, and who keeps talking to me?"

The bartender, unfazed, looks over at the man and says, "It's just the peanuts, mister. They're complimentary."

FUN FACT

PRETTY FUNNY

Have you ever noticed how few handsome men or beautiful women are comedians? There are a few exceptions: Cary Grant, Carole Lombard, Tom Selleck, Cybill Shepherd, Julia-Louis Dreyfus. Woody Allen, the director of *Sleeper*, *Bullets Over Broadway*, *Bananas*, and *Annie Hall*, has his own theory. "Funny and pretty are opposites," he says. But the standup comic Mort Sahl has a different idea. He enjoyed telling jokes, he says, because to him "people always look better when they laugh."

Bruce Vilanch, the incredibly busy Hollywood writer, widely known for his stint as the big, blond funnyman on Hollywood Squares, shares this advice about writing comedy: "Rewriting is really what good writing is all about!" Asked if there is any subject he would not write a joke about, Vilanch replies: "My rule of thumb is, did anybody die? It's difficult to do a joke in which death is involved . . . it's just cruel."

CLASSIC ONE-LINERS

A one-liner is a joke that is told in one line or sentence. Or else several phrases are strung together and spoken without a break. For example: My room is so small . . .

I closed the door and the doorknob was in bed with me.

the mice are hunchbacked.

when I turn around, I'm next door.

I put the key in the keyhole and broke the window.

I have to go outside to change my mind.

when I stand up I'm on the second floor.

the ceiling gets dusted whenever I comb my hair.

Words to Know

One-liner: a joke that is told in one line or sentence

MORE ONE-LINERS

A mummy is an Egyptian who's pressed for time.

I saw a sign on the back of a truck: "Careful Passing. I Like to Chew Tobacco."

I'm a terrible cook. All the gingerbread boys I make are nearsighted so I've started using contact raisins.

What do you get if you cross a hill with an electric stove?
　A mountain range.

My mom went to the beauty salon and got a mud pack—for three days she looked great—then the mud fell off.

The standup comic Henny Youngman is called the King of the One-Liners. Rodney Dangerfield and Steven Wright are also terrific one-line jokesters. Here's one of Wright's loopy one-liners: "I live on a one-way, dead-end street. I don't know how I got there."

MEDICAL MARVELS

PUMP UP THE LAUGHTER

Did you know that by simply telling a joke you are exercising 72 different muscles in your neck, throat, mouth, and tongue? Laughing uses over 100 muscles. No wonder some people say they "laughed 'til they hurt." They just had a workout without even realizing it!

A JOKE A DAY KEEPS THE DOCTOR AWAY

Dr. Lee Berk of the Loma Linda School of Public Health in California discovered that laughing increases the body's antibodies and T cells, which help fight off infection and alien bacteria.

Dr. William Fry of Stanford University says that laughing 200 times will burn up the same amount of calories as 10 minutes on a rowing machine.

Does that make *Dumb and Dumber* a workout video?

FUNNY BONE

Your funny bone isn't actually a bone, it's a nerve—the ulnar nerve, in fact. This nerve is exposed as it travels over the medial condyle of the humerus, er, the bony knob at the end of your upper arm. Some clever (and unknown) medical student saw the punny resemblance between the words "humerus" and "humorous" and created the notion of the funny bone. Hitting your funny bone, however, is no laughing matter!

Comic Biography

Quick on Her Feet

Carol Burnett, the former queen of prime time comedy (1967–1979), was getting out of a taxicab in front of the TV studio. She accidentally slammed the door shut on her coat and the oblivious cabbie took off. Carol was forced to run along side in order not to be dragged off her feet. After running several blocks, she was finally rescued by a pedestrian who hailed the cab and brought the vehicle to a stop.

The cabbie, now realizing what had happened, jumped out of his car and ran to Carol's side. "Are you all right?" he asked.

"Fine," panted Carol. "But how much more do I owe you?"

TONGUE TWISTERS

Attempt to articulate these tricky tongue-tanglers quickly in triplicate.

Red leather, yellow leather.

Around the rugged rocks, the ragged rascal ran.

Rubber baby buggy-bumpers.

The sixth shiek's sixth sheep is sick.

The skunk sat on a stump, the skunk thunk the stump stunk, but the stump thunk the skunk stunk.

The clothes moth's mouth's closed.

She shall sell seashells.

How much wood would a woodchuck chuck if a woodchuck could chuck wood?

Bugs' black blood.

Eight apes ate eight apples.

Cool clean canned clams.

A stiff stack of thick steaks.

Toyboat, toyboat, toyboat.

IN THE BAG

A guy was trying to cross the border into the next country on his bicycle. Two suspicious-looking bags were tied to the back of the bike.

The border guards stopped him and said, "Hey, buddy, what's in the bags?"

"Sand," said the man.

The guards pulled off the two bags and examined them. They both contained only sand, just as the man said, so they waved him through the border.

This went on each week for six months. And each time the guards examined the bags they still found only sand.

One week the man stopped coming. One of the guards ran into the man downtown after work.

"Hey buddy," said the guard. "You sure had us going. We knew you were smuggling something."

The man just grinned.

"C'mon and tell me," whispered the guard. "I won't say anything. What were you smuggling?"

"Bicycles," said the man.

BURMA-SHAVE: THE UNKNOWN COMIC WITH AN EDGE

Years ago, when American families motored through the heartland on their way to a favorite vacation spot, they looked forward to reading the silly rhymes posted along the highways by the Burma-Shave company. Burma-Shave was a shaving cream for men, and the clever rhymes were posted—one line at a time—along highways and back roads all over the country. Kids and grownups tried to guess what the next rhyme would be before they drove past it. The highway poet remains anonymous, but here are a few of his, or her, best rhymes, broken up into separate lines as they appeared on separate signs along the way.

The whale
Put Jonah
Down the hatch
But coughed him up
Because he scratched.
Burma-Shave.

Does your husband
Misbehave
Grunt and rumble
Rant and rave?
Shoot the brute
Some Burma-Shave.

Ben
Met Anna
Made a hit
Neglected beard
Ben-Anna Split.
Burma-Shave.

THE NICKNAME GAME

Why do they call her Volleyball?
She's got plenty of bounce.

Why do they call him Birdseed?
He fits the bill.

Jokin' Around

Goin' Bowling

The family went bowling one night and brought seven-year-old Stevie for the first time. Along with the rest of the family, Stevie laced up his bowling shoes and then went to select a ball. Everyone else chose one, but Stevie could not make up his mind.

Ten minutes went by and finally Father said, "Stevie, just pick a ball. We don't have all night."

"But I can't!" wailed Stevie. "Every ball I pick up has holes in it!"

Why do they call her Icecube?
She's so cool.

Why do they call him Ace?
He's such a card.

Why do they call her Strawberry?
She's good in a jam.

Why do they call him Needles?
He's so sharp.

Why do they call her Sunny?
She's so bright.

Why do they call him Fingers?
You can always count on him.

Why do they call her Sugar?
She's so refined.

Why do they call him Fleece?
He's always on the lam.

Why do they call him Buck?
He's got a lot of cents.

Why do they call you Mushroom?
Because I'm a fun guy!

GOOFBALLS

Brother: How can you tell that elephants like to swim?
Sister: They always have their trunks on.

"Dad! There's a giant monster under my bed."
"Don't be silly. There's no such thing."
"Then how come I can touch the ceiling with my nose?"

Mother: Jimmy, your ear is bleeding!
Jimmy: I know, I accidentally bit it.
Mother: How could you bite your own ear?
Jimmy: I was standing on a chair.

Troy: Hey, what time does your new watch say?
Jimmy: It doesn't say anything. I have to look at it.
Troy: Don't be such a smart aleck!
Jimmy: Yeah? Well, what does yours say?
Troy: Tick, tick, tick, tick.

Why are the keys on this piano so yellow?
The elephant must have forgotten to brush.

Mother: You sent Jimmy down to the hardware store for some duct tape, right?
Father: Yes. But that was over an hour ago.
Mother: Well, he just phoned from the store and wants to know how big the duck is.

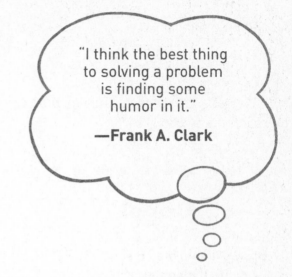

"I think the best thing to solving a problem is finding some humor in it."

—Frank A. Clark

Teacher: Does anyone know what it means to recycle?
Amy: That's when I have to ride my older sister's bicycle instead of getting a new one.

Store Manager: Ma'am, I've shown you every type of perfume we carry. Isn't there anything you'd like to buy?
Mother: Sorry, but your prices don't make any scents to me.

Troy: Our family just bought us one of those furry, Chinese dogs.
Jimmy: Chow?
Troy: No thanks, I just ate.

Jimmy: Well, *our* family bought one of those skinny greyhound types of dog.
Troy: Whippet?
Jimmy: Oh no! I only pet it.

Megan: I think our dog likes shopping.
Jason: How can you tell?
Megan: We just got back from the flea market, and he's itching to go back.

"I'm on the new seafood diet."
"Is it working?"
"Yeah, whenever I see food, I eat it!"

• • • • • • • • • • • • • •

Oops!

Draw a line to match each "OOPS!" to the proper picture.

OOPS! I'm stuck in the elevator door!

OOPS! My pigtails are too tight!

OOPS! I swallowed my spoon!

Jimmy: My mom says our kitchen floor is so clean we could eat off it.
Troy: Cool! At our house only the cat is allowed to do that!

"I hate that snobby Christina. Because of her I lost a hundred pounds."
"Wow! What did she do?"
"Stole my boyfriend."

"Doctor, my ear keeps ringing."
"You should get an unlisted ear."

What do you call a boomerang that doesn't come back?
   A stick.

"Bugs give me the creeps!"
"What about spiders?"
"No way! I don't even like looking at them."
"Then it's a good thing you didn't see that one crawl into your shoe."

Trent: Hey, Jimmy, why didn't you stick around for the second act of the school play last night?
Jimmy: Because on the program it said "Two Years Later" and I had to be home by nine.

"Can I have a dollar for a sandwich?"
"If you like, but it probably won't taste very good."

Didja hear about the farmer who bought a farm a mile long and an inch wide?
   He's raising spaghetti.

"This is the toughest sponge cake I ever ate."
"That's funny, the sponges I used were fresh."

The classroom was full of noisy and wild misbehaving students. The new teacher tried getting their attention, but the class continued to ignore him. Finally, in a last attempt to get the students to listen, the frustrated teacher shouted out: "Excuse me, people. But can anyone tell me what we use our ears for?" One boy remarked: "We mostly use our rears for sitting down on."

Karl: What was all that noise a moment ago?
Trent: That was me practicing my violin. Do you think I have a gift for playing?
Karl: No, but I'll give you one for stopping!

There's just one hard thing about parachute jumping.
   The ground.

"She sure gave you a dirty look."
"Who?"
"Mother Nature."

Teacher: What does it mean when the barometer is falling?
Trent: It means whoever nailed it up didn't do a good job.

Megan: I think my mom must be the strongest person in the world.
Troy: Why do you say that?
Megan: Because everyday she picks up my entire room using only her bare hands.

Jimmy: Mom! Amy fell down the stairs!
Mother: Don't worry, honey. The doctor's taking steps to treat her.

"Will this road take me to Bakersville?"
"No, you'll have to drive there yourself."

Why did the weirdo throw the clock out the window?
> *Only a weirdo would throw a clock out the window!*

Dad: Son, if you were out in the country, far from here, and only had a compass, how would you use it to find your way back?
Jimmy: Easy. I'd sell it for a few bucks and then buy a bus ticket home.

Troy: How much is that puppy?
Store Clerk: He's $50 or nothing.
Troy: Okay, I'll take him for nothing.

Neighbor: Young man, your cat was digging around in my garden!
Jimmy: I promise he'll never do that again.
Neighbor: How can you be so sure?
Jimmy: He was only burying your hamster he caught last night. But he's finished up by now.

"I can always tell when it's time for a snack."
"How?"
"My big hand is on the cookie jar and my little hand is inside."

When is it all right to belt a policeman?
> *When he gets in your car.*

Megan: What kind of fish is that, Mister?
Pet Store Owner: Crappie.
Megan: Really? He looks fine to me.

Jimmy: We got a brand new roof and it didn't cost us a cent!
Megan: Why not?
Jimmy: The carpenters told us it was on the house.

Where's the best place to find cows?
> *At a moo-see-'em.*

Jokes

Teacher: You have to be the most annoying student I ever had!
Alex: Do I have to be?

"Can you help me? I'm looking for the bus station."
"Is that thing lost again?!"

Father: Did you know the Anderson's dog can actually play video games?
Jimmy: He's not so smart. I played five games with him once, and he only won twice.

"Did you forget you were supposed to call me last night?"
"I don't remember."

"My sister never helps clean up the downstairs family room."
"Why not?"
"She says working in the basement is beneath her."

Amy: What kind of jeans are those?
Rosie: Guess.
Amy: I have no idea.
Rosie: I told you: Guess.
Amy: I simply asked what kind they are.
Rosie: Guess! Guess!
Amy: You don't have to be rude about it!

"Mom! You know that red light you just drove through? It's following us!"

Megan: Do you believe in ESP and seeing the future?
Wanda: Oh yes. In fact, my uncle had a terrible accident because he didn't pay attention to the signs.
Megan: Really?
Wanda: Yeah, especially the signs Stop and No Left Turn.

Two bank robbers were making their getaway in a stolen car.

"Turn around and see if the cops are following us," said Joe.

"But how can I tell if they're cops?" asked Bill.

"From their flashers," said Joe.

"Okay." So Bill turned and looked out the back window. "Yes, no, yes, no, yes, no . . ."

Jokin' Around

From the Loopy Library

What do the following books have in common?

Blood Clots
The Hermit on the Hill
The Frozen Airplane Propeller
Wanda Always Stays Home

They never "circulate."

"The doctor said I should drink my medicine after a warm bath."
"And did you?"
"I'm not finished drinking the warm bath yet!"

"That cat just hissed at me!"
"Better watch out."
"But you told me your cat was friendly."
"It is, but that's not my cat."

Trent: Down at the bus stop, everyone is hunting for a few quarters some guy dropped.
Karl: I suppose you were looking around, too.
Trent: No, I was just standing there with my foot on the quarters.

Teacher: Do you believe in sharing, Alex?
Alex: Yes, ma'am.
Teacher: What's something you share with your brother?
Alex: Our parents.

"The doctor said I should take these pills on an empty stomach."
"That's right."
"But they keep getting stuck in my belly-button."

Mother: Jimmy, will you please sit up straighter?
Jimmy: If I sat up any straighter I'd be standing.

WATT'S THE PROBLEM? (LIGHT BULB JOKES)

How many grandmothers does it take to change a light bulb?

Three. One to change it, one to powder it, and one to diaper it.

How many graduate students does it take to change a light bulb?

Ten. One to change the bulb and nine to write long, boring papers about it.

How many psychiatrists does it take to change a light bulb?

One. But the light bulb has really got to want to change.

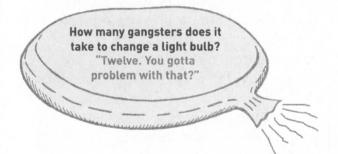

How many gangsters does it take to change a light bulb?
"Twelve. You gotta problem with that?"

How many Martians does it take to change a light bulb?

"What's a light bulb?"

How many cranky old men does it take to change a light bulb?

"Why change the light bulb? Everybody liked the old light bulb!"

How many wizards does it take to change a light bulb?

Depends on what you want the light bulb to change into.

How many undertakers does it take to change a light bulb?

None. They like their light bulbs dead.

How many seabirds does it take to change a light bulb?

About four or five terns ought to do the trick.

Picto-Laugh #7

A pictograph is a very simple drawing of something funny. Can you guess what this little picto-laugh is showing? **HINT:** Think about a bug on wheels!

87

ANYTHING FOR A LAUGH

Teacher: Jimmy, I hope I didn't see you copying Amy's test paper.
Jimmy: Boy, I hope you didn't either!

Midge and Amy went to a county fair and found one of those old-fashioned fortune-telling weight machines. Amy got on first. When the card popped out, Midge read, "It says here that you are clever, beautiful, and charming." "Really?" said Amy. "Yeah," said Midge. "And it has your weight wrong, too."

Meghan: My mom complains about everything! She bought me two new T-shirts, a red one and a yellow one, and I put on the red one for school yesterday. At breakfast my mom says, "So what's wrong with the yellow one?"

Mother: Did you take a bath today?
Kyle: Why, is one missing?

Stranger: You catching any fish, kid?
Alex: Yes, sir! I caught at least twelve big ones.
Stranger: Do you know who I am? I'm the local fishing warden.
Alex: Do you know who *I* am? I'm the biggest liar in the county.

Mother: Your hair is starting to get wavy.
Father: Really?
Mother: Yes, it's waving goodbye!

Lisa: Whenever I'm down in the dumps, I get a new pair of shoes.
Midge: I thought that's where you got them.

Midge: I'm on a new diet and exercise program. Every morning after breakfast I go horseback riding.
Amy: Is it working?
Midge: So far the horse has lost ten pounds.

Melody: I think our neighbor Mrs. Johnson must be upset about something. She hasn't been over to visit for weeks.
Father: Find out what happened, and next time she comes over we'll try it again.

Larry: I've never had a problem with backseat driving, and I've been driving for over fifteen years.
Luna: What kind of car do you drive?
Larry: A hearse.

Amy: The dog bit me in a very painful spot.
Rosie: Where'd he bite you?
Amy: In the backyard!

Gretchen: How does Old MacDonald spell "farm"?
Heather: E. I. E. I. O.

Troy: Excuse me, are you the head doctor here?
Doctor: No, I'm the foot doctor.

Thom: At my job I have a hundred men under me.
Kurt: Where do you work?
Thom: The cemetery.
Kurt: Well, at *my* job everyone looks up to me.
Thom: What do you do?
Kurt: I'm a kindergarten teacher.

Teacher: What is a light year?
Melody: A year with very little homework.

Rosie: What kind of fish are you frying?
Mother: Smelt.
Rosie: I sure can. But what kind of fish is it?

Doctor: Young man, you're going to need a flu shot.
Matt: Will it hurt?
Doctor: I'll be fine, but thanks for asking.

Jimmy: Where were you born?
Derek: On Rivers Avenue.
Jimmy: You're lucky you weren't run over by a bus!

Jokin' Around

Jiggy Geography

Parasites are people from Paris

Peruse are people from Peru

Maracas are people from Morocco

Canyons are people from Kenya

Goblets are people from Turkey

Teacher: Do you know what we call the person who delivers children?
Melody: She's called Mom. She delivers me to school, to my girlfriends' houses, to the mall, to soccer practice . . .

Trent: That sure is cool exercise equipment.
Matt: Thanks, I got it at the gym.
Trent: Did they have a sale?
Matt: No, they had a sign that said Free Weights.

Heather: You should see my new watch. It's rust-proof, dustproof, shockproof, waterproof, and never needs batteries.
Gretchen: Cool, let's see it.
Heather: I lost it. So if you should see it, let me know!

Jimmy: My older brother Dave crashed his car into a tree going forty miles an hour.
Troy: Wow! I didn't know trees could move that fast!

Geo-Giggles

Here are the names of six states. Put them in the correct blanks to make three silly state riddles.
HINT: The pictures will give you a clue!

NEW JERSEY

TENNESSEE

DELAWARE

MARYLAND

ARKANSAS

IDAHO

What did

_____?

She wore her

_____!

What did

_____?

She saw what

_____!

What did

_____?

She hoed her

_____!

ELEPHANT JOKES

No one knows how or why, but about 40 years ago elephant jokes stampeded onto the scene and became extremely popular. Here are a few samples of loopy, sometimes bizarre, pachyderm humor:

Can an elephant jump higher than a house?
Of course. Houses can't jump at all.

Why do elephants lie on their back?
They like to trip low-flying birds with their feet.

Why did the elephants quit their job at the factory? They were tired of working for peanuts.

What did Jane say when she saw the elephants coming over the hill?
"Here come the elephants!"

What did Tarzan say?
"Here come the grapes!" He was color blind.

What do you get when you cross an elephant with peanut butter?
A pachyderm that sticks to the roof of your mouth.

What's the difference between an elephant and a grape?
Grapes are purple.

Picto-Laugh #8

A pictograph is a very simple drawing of something funny. Can you guess what this little picto-laugh is showing? **HINT:** Think about broken elevators!

91

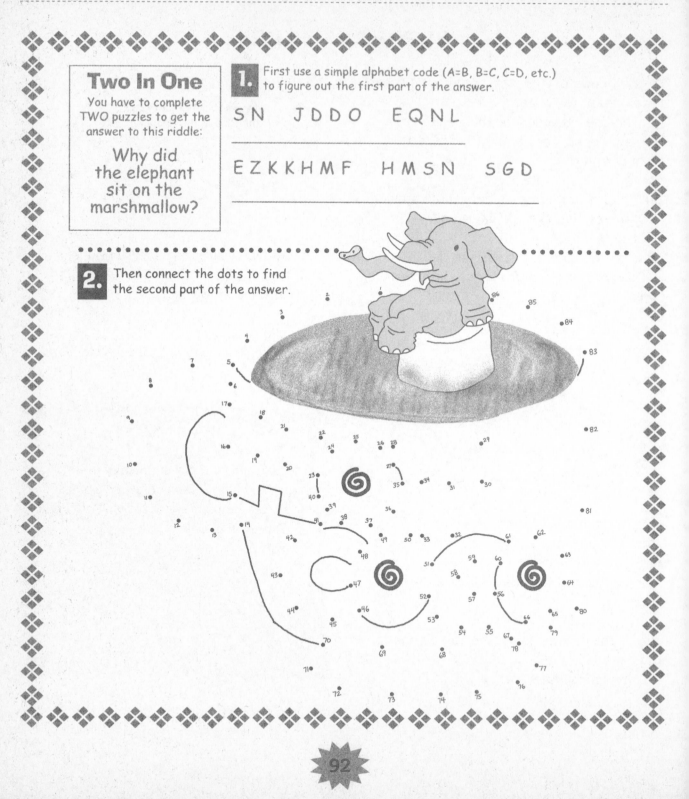

Two In One

You have to complete TWO puzzles to get the answer to this riddle:

Why did the elephant sit on the marshmallow?

1. First use a simple alphabet code (A=B, B=C, C=D, etc.) to figure out the first part of the answer.

SN   JDDO   EQNL

_____

EZKKHMF   HMSN   SGD

_____

2. Then connect the dots to find the second part of the answer.

How do you get down off an elephant?
You don't get down off an elephant. You get down off a duck.

How do you catch an elephant?
Hide in the bushes and act like a peanut.

How do you get the wrinkles out of an elephant's skin?
Take him out of the dryer as soon as it stops.

Why don't elephants smoke?
Their butts are too big to set in the ashtrays.

Why are elephants easier to find in Alabama?
Because in Alabama you'll find Tuscaloosa (tusks are looser).

What weighs 2000 pounds, has big ears, tusks, and two trunks?
An elephant going on vacation.

What's big and gray and goes up and down, up and down?
An elephant bungee jumping.

Elemorphant

Can you turn an elephant into a peanut in three steps? Start with the word ELEPHANT. In each step, you can do only one of the following things—delete a group of letters, add a letter, or change one letter into another. Remember, you have to end up with PEANUT in Step 3! **HINT:** Keep track of the letters on the lines provided.

ELEPHANT

1. _____
2. _____
3. _____

Jay Leno was once asked to name a comedian's most important tool. "A tape recorder!" he replied. Not to record the comedian, but to record the audience. Leno urges new comedians to listen and relisten to their live performances and note when the audience laughed, when they didn't laugh, if the jokes were fast enough, loud enough, smart enough. Armed with this new information, a budding comedian can delete the bad jokes, sharpen up the better ones, and make the next gig even funnier.

Part Two

KNOCK KNOCK

CAN YOU THINK OF ANYTHING more inviting than a good knock-knock joke? Who can resist answering "who's there?" after hearing someone say "knock knock"? You'd be hard-pressed to find someone who doesn't love these jokes.

Knock-knocks are popular in every country where people speak English, including the United States, Canada, Great Britain, and Australia. That's because each knock-knock joke is a pun, or a play on words, and puns are more popular in English than they are in other languages.

So, what's the purpose of a knock-knock joke anyway? Well, that's easy! To make you laugh, of course! A good laugh can have many truly wonderful results. Laughter is a universal language that all humans share no matter where they live or how old they are. Laughter can connect people of all ages around the world. Did you know that babies start laughing when they're only two months old? That's so much earlier than speaking or even crawling. Babies know funny when they see or hear it. And so do the rest of us.

Another fabulous result of a good laugh is that it really is the best medicine. Laughter is a great cure when you're down in the dumps and just can't shake the blues. Even the experts agree: Laughter helps to keep us healthy and happy. Science shows us that laughter increases the amount of oxygen running through our blood, makes us relax, and helps us feel less nervous during stressful times. This is no secret. People have known this for centuries. Some people even make a living just getting others to laugh!

Back in the very old days, court jesters appeared before the king and queen just to amuse them. Today, comedians, clowns, actors, and actresses all work hard to come up with funny material to get a good laugh from their audiences. Sometimes people will go out of their way to find something that will make them laugh. They watch movies, go to the theater, and turn on the television set, all in the hopes of kicking back and seeing how funny life can be!

Laughter makes people happy, and we all know that everybody likes to be around happy people. So start chuckling, giggling, guffawing, or even rolling-on-the-floor belly laughing. Gather some friends and start your own hysterical society. This is a group that gets together to tell each other jokes, riddles, and rhymes, act silly, and just plain make each other laugh. Don't worry if no one's laughing right away. Laughter is contagious. Just start tee-heeing, ho-ho-ing, and ha-ha-ing, and everyone else will soon follow.

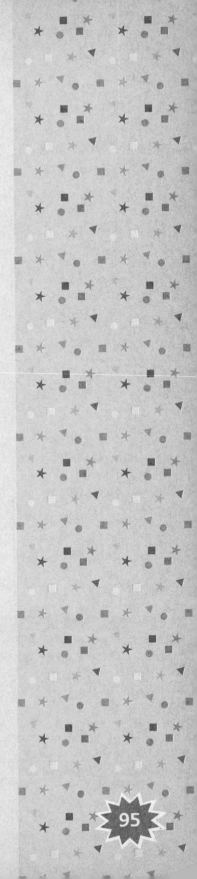

ONCE UPON A KNOCK KNOCK

Knock knock!
Who's there?
Erma.
Erma who?
Erma going tell you lots of knock-
    knock jokes!

Knock knock!
Who's there?
Heifer.
Heifer who?
Heifer dollar is better than none!

Knock knock!
Who's there?
Scold.
Scold who?
'Scold out!

Knock knock!
Who's there?
Lettuce.
Lettuce who?
Lettuce in and I'll tell you!

Knock knock!
Who's there?
Doug.
Doug who?
Doug-out is where the baseball play-
    ers sit!

I have a very big mouth, but
I never say a word. I
have a bank, but I don't
keep any money in it. I have a
bed, but I never get tired. I wave
at everybody, but I have
no hands. **What am I?**

A river

Knock knock!
Who's there?
Abe Lincoln.
Abe Lincoln who?
A-be Lincoln light on a Christmas tree!

Knock knock!
Who's there?
Barbie.
Barbie who?
Barbie Q chicken!

Knock knock!
Who's there?
Gumby.
Gumby who?
Gumby our guest for dinner!

FUN FACT

DON'T SWEAT IT

Did you know that there are more chickens than people in the world? That's because chickens can lay about 320 eggs each year. Also, did you know that chickens never sweat? They have to spread their wings and pant in order to keep cool.

TRY THIS

Crawly Caterpillars

Make caterpillars out of old toilet paper rolls! Wrap the toilet paper roll in color-ful construction paper (you can use tape or glue to make sure it sticks). Color squiggly designs on it. Cut up a pipe cleaner into six one-inch pieces. Glue or stick the pieces through the bottom of the caterpillar for legs. Now cut another pipe cleaner in half and bend the halves in the shape of antennae. Glue the anten-nae to the top of the caterpillar's head. Find a pompon and glue it on for a nose. Draw on some eyes. For extra big cater-pillars, use old paper towel rolls instead!

Knock knock!
Who's there?
Jude.
Jude who?
Jude the food, then swallowed it!

Knock knock!
Who's there?
Icy.
Icy who?
Icy a big monster under the bed!

Knock knock!
Who's there?
Window.
Window who?
Window we get to play something
    else?

Knock knock!
Who's there?
Agatha.
Agatha who?
Agatha chills when it's cold!

Knock knock!
Who's there?
Howell.
Howell who?
Howell do you know me?

Knock knock!
Who's there?
Genoa.
Genoa who?
Genoa good dentist?

Knock knock!
Who's there?
Cargo.
Cargo who?
Car-go vroom vroom!

Words to Know

Comedian: A man or a woman who makes a living by being funny. It is a comedian's job to tell jokes and get people giggling.

Knock knock!
Who's there?
Xavier.
Xavier who?
Xavier money in the bank!

Knock knock!
Who's there?
Ham.
Ham who?
Ham I going to see you again?

Knock knock!
Who's there?
Thelonius.
Thelonius who?
Thelonius night of the week!

Knock knock!
Who's there?
Watson.
Watson who?
Watson television?

Knock knock!
Who's there?
Lionel.
Lionel who?
Lionel eat you if he's hungry!

What's So Funny

HA HA HA

Knock knock!

Who's there?
Leaf.·
Leaf who?
Leaf me alone!

HA HA

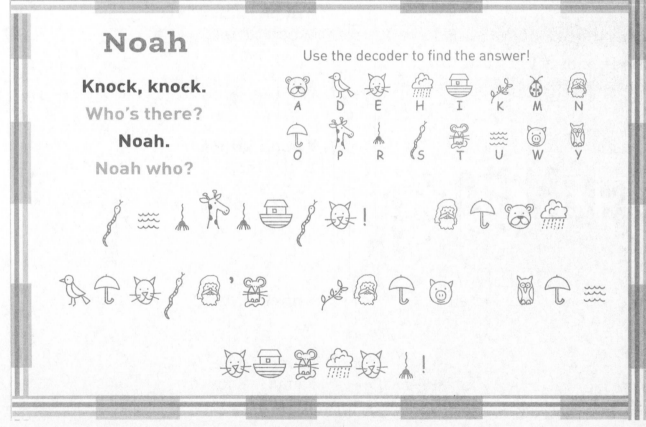

Noah

Knock, knock.
Who's there?
Noah.
Noah who?

Use the decoder to find the answer!

HA HA HA HA HA HA

Knock knock!

Who's there?
Court.
Court who?
Court of milk!

Knock knock!

Who's there?
Teresa.
Teresa who?
Teresa fly in my soup!

Knock knock!

Who's there?
Giza.
Giza who?
Giza nice man!

Knock knock!

Who's there?
Dishwasher.
Dishwasher who?
Dishwasher the way I always shpoke!

Knock knock!

Who's there?
Stopwatch.
Stopwatch who?
Stopwatch you're
   doing!

FUN FACT

ENGLISH ALL OVER

There are many countries that have English-speaking peo-ple. In many countries where English is not the first lan-guage, English is taught in schools. Did you know that there are more English-speaking people in China than there are in the United States?

Knock knock!

Who's there?
Founder.
Founder who?
Founder book in
   the library!

Knocked to Pieces

A knock-knock and its answer were put into the large grid, and then cut into eight pieces. See if you can figure out where each piece goes, and write the letters in their proper places. When you have filled in the grid correctly, you will be able to read the joke from left to right, and top to bottom.

HINT: The black boxes stand for the spaces between words. Careful—some pieces are turned or flipped!

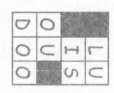

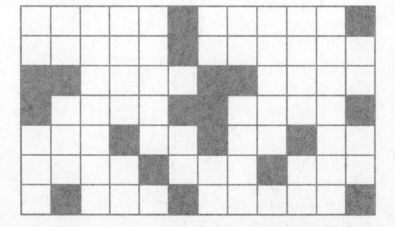

Say What?

To find the end to this knock-knock, cross out all letters that follow these rules:

- sound like the name of a vegetable
- come after "L" in the alphabet
- are tenth in the alphabet

When you are finished, read the remaining letters from left to right, and top to bottom.

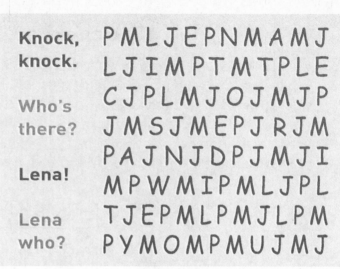

Knock, knock.

Who's there?

Lena!

Lena who?

```
P M L J E P N M A M J
L J I M P T M T P L E
C J P L M J O J M J P
J M S J M E P J R J M
P A J N J D P J M J I
M P W M I P M L J P L
T J E P M L P M J L P M
P Y M O M P M U J M J
```

I Can't Hear You

These two whispering girls may look the same, but see if you can find the ten differences between them.

HINT: It doesn't count that they are facing in different directions.

Knock knock!
Who's there?
Dewey.
Dewey who?
Dewey have to stay much longer?

Knock knock!
Who's there?
Samuel.
Samuel who?
Samuel like and Samuel won't!

Words to Know

Witty: Something that is clever or amusing. A witty statement will impress people or give them a good chuckle.

TRY THIS

Masked and Whiskered

Make a cat mask! Cut a paper plate in half, and use one half for your mask, so that the curved edge of the plate is at the top of the mask. Cut out two triangles for your eyes and a triangle for your nose. Glue three pipe cleaners on each side of the nose for whiskers. Cut ears out of construction paper and glue them on top. Then punch a hole through the sides of the mask and thread some yarn around it so you can tie it to your head. And don't forget to add decorations!

Knock knock!
Who's there?
Yoga.
Yoga who?
Yo-ga what it takes to be the best!

Knock knock!
Who's there?
Camel.
Camel who?
Camel get it, dinner's ready!

Knock knock!
Who's there?
Milton.
Milton who?
Milton snow turns to water!

Knock knock!
Who's there?
Freeze.
Freeze who?
Freeze a jolly good fella!

Knock knock!
Who's there?
Tex.
Tex who?
Tex two to tango!

Knock knock!
Who's there?
Aardvark.
Aardvark who?
Aardvark a million miles for you!

TRY THIS

Home Sweet Home

What could be sweeter than a house made of candy? Gather some soft candy such as gumdrops, marshmallows, and gummy shapes. Get a box of toothpicks and start building! Think of the candies as corners and toothpicks as edges, and build by sticking toothpicks through the candies to connect them. You can start with a triangle or square and keep building up. Just don't eat the whole house all at once!

Knock knock!
Who's there?
Fletcher.
Fletcher who?
Fletcher in or she'll break down the door!

Knock knock!
Who's there?
Vic.
Vic who?
Vic some flowers for me!

Knock knock!
Who's there?
Izzie.
Izzie who?
Izzie going to tell any more jokes?

Knock knock!
Who's there?
Sherwood.
Sherwood who?
Sherwood like some more pie!

Knock knock!
Who's there?
Bertha.
Bertha who?
Bertha-day party!

Knock knock!
Who's there?
Bacon.
Bacon who?
Bacon a cake for the party!

Knock knock!
Who's there?
Howl.
Howl who?
Howl I know if you're on your way over?

Knock knock!
Who's there?
Tail.
Tail who?
Tail all your friends about it!

Knock knock!
Who's there?
Adlai.
Adlai who?
Adlai my life on the line!

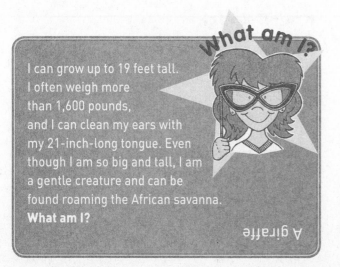

What am I?

I can grow up to 19 feet tall. I often weigh more than 1,600 pounds, and I can clean my ears with my 21-inch-long tongue. Even though I am so big and tall, I am a gentle creature and can be found roaming the African savanna. **What am I?**

A giraffe

105

Words to Know

Pun: A word or joke that is a play on words and may have two or more meanings. All knock-knock jokes are puns.

Knock knock!
Who's there?
Rabbit.
Rabbit who?
Rabbit up carefully, it's a present!

Knock knock!
Who's there?
House.
House who?
House it going?

Knock knock!
Who's there?
Maine.
Maine who?
Maine thing here is that we're all friends!

Knock knock!
Who's there?
Thermos.
Thermos who?
Thermos be another way!

Knock knock!
Who's there?
Statue.
Statue who?
Statue or is that someone else?

What's So Funny

Knock knock!
Who's there?
Wheel.
Wheel who?
Wheel stop coming over if we're not invited!

WHEN FUN COMES A KNOCKIN'

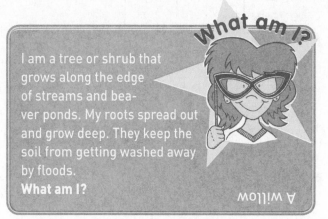

What am I?

I am a tree or shrub that grows along the edge of streams and beaver ponds. My roots spread out and grow deep. They keep the soil from getting washed away by floods.
What am I?

A willow

Knock knock!
Who's there?
Freddie.
Freddie who?
Freddie cat, Freddie cat!

Knock knock!
Who's there?
Eisenhower.
Eisenhower who?
Eisenhower late getting here!

Knock knock!
Who's there?
Ears.
Ears who?
Ears some more knock-knock jokes
    for you!

Knock knock!
Who's there?
Sheik.
Sheik who?
Sheik-speare was a famous poet!

Knock knock!
Who's there?
Feline.
Feline who?
Feline fine, and you?

Knock knock!
Who's there?
Tad.
Tad who?
Tad old black magic!

TRY THIS

A Quick Trick

Put an ice cube in a bowl of water. Lower a string on top of the ice cube. Sprinkle salt on top of the ice cube and the string. Then try to lift the ice cube with the string. The salt will melt just enough ice so the string will stick.

Knock knock!
Who's there?
Burma.
Burma who?
Burma hand on the stove!

Knock knock!
Who's there?
Ostrich.
Ostrich who?
Ostrich my arms up to the sky!

Knock knock!
Who's there?
Beagle.
Beagle who?
Beagle with lox!

Knock knock!
Who's there?
Lena.
Lena who?
Lena little closer, I have something to tell you!

Knock knock!
Who's there?
Pooch.
Pooch who?
Pooch your coat on!

Knock knock!
Who's there?
Hurley.
Hurley who?
Hurley to bed, Hurley to rise!

What's So Funny

Knock knock!

Who's there?
Weavish.
Weavish who?
Weavish you a very happy birthday!

Mix and Match

Write the number of the correct ending into the space by each knock knock. Choose from the list at the bottom of the page.

KNOCK, KNOCK.
Who's there?
BOO.
Boo who?

KNOCK, KNOCK.
Who's there?
CASH.
Cash who?

KNOCK, KNOCK.
Who's there?
COWS.
Cows who?

Who?

KNOCK, KNOCK.
Who's there?
ATCH.
Atch who?

KNOCK, KNOCK.
Who's there?
YOU.
You who?

KNOCK, KNOCK.
Who's there?
YA.
Ya who?

1. Don't cry — it's only a joke!
2. No they don't. Owls who!
3. I'm glad you're having a good time!
4. I always knew you were nuts!
5. Oh, I'm sorry you have a cold!
6. Who are you calling?

Knock knock!
Who's there?
Poker.
Poker who?
Poker and see if
she gets upset!

Knock knock!
Who's there?
Iran.
Iran who?
Iran as fast as I can!

Knock knock!
Who's there?
Justin.
Justin who?
Justin time for dinner!

Knock knock!
Who's there?
Omelet.
Omelet who?
Om-e-let stronger than you think!

Knock knock!
Who's there?
Megan.
Megan who?
Megan supper for you!

Knock knock!
Who's there?
Nicholas.
Nicholas who?
Nicholas equal to five cents!

Knock knock!
Who's there?
Havana.
Havana who?
Havan-a nice time!

Words to Know

Funnyman: A funnyman is just that, a man who is funny. Sometimes a comedian will be introduced to his audience with this title. One famous funnyman is Robin Williams. Of course, there are funnywomen too!

What's So Funny

HA HA HA

Knock knock!
Who's there?
Passover.
Passover who?
Passover that chapter, it's boring!

HA HA

Knock knock!
Who's there?
Shirley.
Shirley who?
Shirley you don't want
    to hear any more jokes!

Knock knock!
Who's there?
Miri.
Miri who?
Miri me and we'll spend the rest of
    our lives together!

Knock knock!
Who's there?
Uganda.
Uganda who?
Uganda keep getting away with this!

Knock knock!
Who's there?
Yachts.
Yachts who?
Yachts up with you?

Knock knock!
Who's there?
Irma.
Irma who?
Irma great student!

FUN FACT

A SMELLY SITUATION!

The power of smell is fascinating. This sense is very important to our survival. For example, it lets us know whether the food we're about to eat is fresh or spoiled. In all, the human nose can identify more than 10,000 different smells.

Knock knock!
Who's there?
Genoa.
Genoa who?
Genoa any new knock-knock jokes?

Knock knock!
Who's there?
Dent.
Dent who?
Dent be late!

Knock knock!
Who's there?
Gorilla.
Gorilla who?
Gorilla my dreams!

Knock knock!
Who's there?
Ya.
Ya who?
When did you become a cowboy?

Knock knock!
Who's there?
Berlin.
Berlin who?
Berlin' the water for some tea!

Knock knock!
Who's there?
Ayn.
Ayn who?
Ayn on my way!

Knock knock!
Who's there?
Nixon.
Nixon who?
Nixon stones will break my bones!

What am I?

I live underground in dry fields. I don't like to be around people at all. I'm very small, but I sure am tough and will defend my territory.
What am I?

A badger

Knock knock!
Who's there?
Detail.
Detail who?
De-tail on de rabbit is fluffy!

Knock knock!
Who's there?
Fodder.
Fodder who?
Fodder and I are going to the park!

Knock knock!
Who's there?
Fanta.
Fanta who?
Fanta Claus!

Knock knock!
Who's there?
Boo.
Boo who?
Don't cry, it's
    just a joke!

TRY THIS

Butterflies Welcome!

Make a butterfly garden. There are more than 10,000 types of butterflies in the world. They all flock to certain kinds of plants. If you have those plants in your garden, you'll surely see butterflies. Late spring or early summer is the best time to plant. Try milkweed for monarchs. Butterfly bush and butterfly weed also are great. See how many other butterfly plants you can find!

Knock knock!
Who's there?
Uruguay.
Uruguay who?
You go Uruguay, and I'll go mine!

Knock knock!
Who's there?
Affer.
Affer who?
Affer got!

113

Knock knock!
Who's there?
Hurda.
Hurda who?
Hurda my finger in the door!

Knock knock!
Who's there?
Costa.
Costa who?
Costa lot of money!

Knock knock!
Who's there?
Fiddle.
Fiddle who?
'Fiddle make you feel better, I'll tell
    you!

Knock knock!
Who's there?
Kook.
Kook who?
You sound like a cuckoo!

Knock knock!
Who's there?
Camilla.
Camilla who?
Camill-a little squirt!

Fifi is my
best
helper!

Please Fix That

The letters in each column go in the
squares directly below them, but not in the
same order! Black squares are for punctuation, and the spaces between the words.
When you have correctly filled in the grid,
you will have a silly answer from Mr. Fix It!

Knock, knock.
Who's there?
Poodle.
Poodle who?

	I	I				
	Q	O	L			
	I	O	R	A		
P	O	T	E	S	K	
S	O	T	T	L	O	
D	O	H	D	L	E	Y
L	T	U	A	T	E	N

114

What am I?

I come in different shapes and sizes. My color doesn't matter. I can be soft or hard. I am full of holes, yet I can hold water. **What am I?**

A sponge

Knock knock!
Who's there?
Dublin.
Dublin who?
Dublin the bus fare!

Knock knock!
Who's there?
Asthma.
Asthma who?
Asthma anything you want!

Knock knock!
Who's there?
Usher.
Usher who?
Usher wish we could do something
    else!

Knock knock!
Who's there?
Justice.
Justice who?
Just-ice time, but that's it!

Knock knock!
Who's there?
Ghana.
Ghana who?
Ghana dance all night!

Knock knock!
Who's there?
Sue.
Sue who?
Sue prize!

Knock knock!
Who's there?
Pear.
Pear who?
Pear of earrings!

115

What's So Funny

HA HA HA HA HA

Knock knock!

Who's there?
Bonn.
Bonn who?
Bonn on the
Fourth of July!

Knock knock!
Who's there?
Eclipse.
Eclipse who?
Eclipse my toenails!

Knock knock!
Who's there?
Udder.
Udder who?
Udder madness!

Knock knock!
Who's there?
Norway.
Norway who?
Norway am I leaving this house!

Knock knock!
Who's there?
Saul.
Saul who?
'Saul in the name of love!

Knock knock!
Who's there?
Wilma.
Wilma who?
Wilma lunch be ready soon?

Knock knock!
Who's there?
Parkway.
Parkway who?
Parkway over there!

FUN FACT

DON'T BOTHER TRYING!

Your elbow is a very important part of your body. It is the joint between the upper and lower arm. Your elbow allows your arm to bend. Without elbows, we would have a very hard time carrying out many basic tasks. But did you know that it is impossible to lick your own elbows? (I'll bet you tried to anyway!)

116

Hidden Helper

The answer to this joke is hidden in the letter grid. Use these clues to help figure it out:

- The answer starts in a corner.
- You read the answer in a logical order, one word after the other.
- You must add the punctuation.

Knock, knock.

Who's there?

E	R	L	L	E	B	R
P	E	B	R	O	O	O
A	L	N	E	K	D	O
I	L	L	G	O	R	D
R	B	O	N	R	U	E
M	E	E	N	B	O	H
A	N	H	A	S	Y	T

That's all I hear all day — knock, knock, knock!

Knock knock!
Who's there?
Alfie.
Alfie who?
Alfie horrible if you go!

Knock knock!
Who's there?
Walt.
Walt who?
Walt you don't know won't hurt you!

Knock knock!
Who's there?
Ewen.
Ewen who?
Ewen me could make great music!

Knock knock!
Who's there?
Amusing.
Amusing who?
Am-using my new joke book!

117

FUN FACT

HIP HIPPOS

A hippopotamus can run faster than a man. These huge creatures can weigh up to 8,000 pounds. To keep their skin moist in hot climates, hippos secrete a pink oil that some have mistaken for blood.

Knock knock!
Who's there?
Leslie.
Leslie who?
Leslie before anyone sees us!

Knock knock!
Who's there?
Aloha.
Aloha who?
Aloha you the rope!

Knock knock!
Who's there?
Shel.
Shel who?
Shel be coming 'round the mountain!

Knock knock!
Who's there?
Centaur.
Centaur who?
Cent-aur out for some more pizza!

Knock knock!
Who's there?
Aldus.
Aldus who?
Aldus fuss for nothing!

Knock knock!
Who's there?
Stella.
Stella who?
Stella nobody's home!

Knock knock!
Who's there?
Wayne.
Wayne who?
Wayne keeps falling on my head, so I bought an umbwella!

Knock knock!
Who's there?
Jack.
Jack who?
Jack of all trades!

Knock knock!
Who's there?
Locker.
Locker who?
Locker up for what she's done!

Knock knock!
Who's there?
Quack.
Quack who?
Quack another bad joke and I'm
    leaving!

Knock knock!
Who's there?
Jubilee.
Jubilee who?
Jubilee in magic?

Knock knock!
Who's there?
Farmer.
Farmer who?
Farmer birthday I'm getting a new
    bike!

Knock knock!
Who's there?
Diploma.
Diploma who?
Diploma came to fix the toilet!

What's So Funny

Knock knock!
Who's there?
Gabe.
Gabe who?
Gabe it everything
I got!

119

TIED UP IN KNOCK-KNOCKS

Knock knock!
Who's there?
Willy.
Willy who?
Willy call me before he comes over?

Knock knock!
Who's there?
Rover.
Rover who?
Rover hill, Rover dale!

Knock knock!
Who's there?
Vet.
Vet who?
Vet are you going to do today?

Knock knock!
Who's there?
Zany.
Zany who?
Zany body home?

Knock knock!
Who's there?
Figs.
Figs who?
Figs the chair, it broke!

Knock knock!
Who's there?
Thumb.
Thumb who?
Thumb body is at the door!

Knock knock!
Who's there?
Felix.
Felix who?
'Felix my ice cream, I'll be upset!

FUN FACT

AMAZING SNAILS

Snails are very interesting creatures, but most of the time we don't even notice them. That's because they are often underground, they move very slowly, and they don't make much noise. But did you know that many snails can lift things that weigh 10 times more than their bodies do? They also can sleep for three years at a time.

Knock knock!
Who's there?
Steven.
Steven who?
Steven the walls have ears!

Knock knock!
Who's there?
Emma.
Emma who?
Emma 'fraid I have to go home now!

Knock knock!
Who's there?
De Witt.
De Witt who?
De Witt now!

Knock knock!
Who's there?
Dozen.
Dozen who?
Dozen anyone know?

Knock knock!
Who's there?
Evelyn.
Evelyn who?
Evelyn comes full circle!

Knock knock!
Who's there?
Datsun.
Datsun who?
Datsun old one!

Knock knock!
Who's there?
Havana.
Havana who?
Havan-a great time, hope you are too!

What's So Funny

Knock knock!
Who's there?
Antilles.
Antilles who?
Antilles comes home,
we just have to wait!

HA HA HA HA HA

121

Knock knock!
Who's there?
Alfred.
Alfred who?
Alfred of monsters? Not me!

Knock knock!
Who's there?
Little old lady.
Little old lady who?
I didn't know you could yodel!

Money Making

It's easy to make coin rubbings. All you need is a bunch of coins, a blank piece of white paper, and a pencil. Place a coin under the paper. Then, tilt the pencil and rub the side of the lead back and forth along the front of the coin. The imprint of the coin will appear on the paper. You can then cut out the imprints and use them as play money.

Knock knock!
Who's there?
Pierre.
Pierre who?
Pierre through the telescope!

Knock knock!
Who's there?
Albert.
Albert who?
Al-bert you don't know who this is!

Knock knock!
Who's there?
Honda.
Honda who?
Honda road again!

Knock knock!
Who's there?
Oliver.
Oliver who?
Oliver 'nother
    cookie please!

Alli-OOPS!

Start at number 1 and connect the dots in order to find the answer to this joke. But be careful—you may not want to answer the door when you see who is knocking!

Knock, knock.

Who's there?

Alli.

Alli who?

Knock knock!
Who's there?
Gipper.
Gipper who?
Gipper a hand!

Words to Know

Hilarious: Something that makes you laugh so hard you can't control yourself. You just keep laughing and laughing. Anything or anyone can be hilarious!

How Polite!

Swim through the tank, collecting letters from **START** to **END**. They will spell the answer to this joke:

Knock, knock. **Who's there?** **Tank.** **Tank who?**

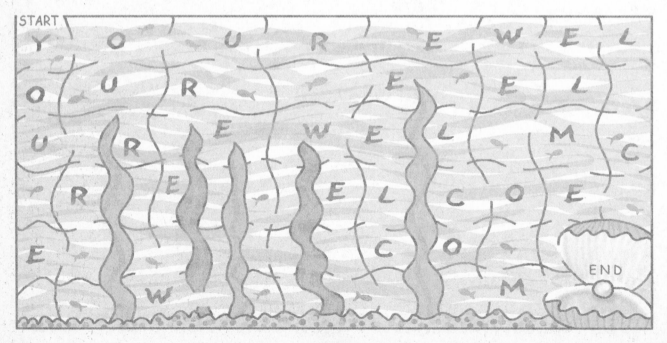

Knock knock!
Who's there?
Wendy.
Wendy who?
Wendy today, sunny tomorrow!

Knock knock!
Who's there?
Pencil.
Pencil who?
Pencil fall down if you
   don't buckle your belt!

Knock knock!
Who's there?
Boleyn.
Boleyn who?
Boleyn alley!

Knock knock!
Who's there?
Goat.
Goat who?
Goat to the door and answer it!

Knock knock!
Who's there?
Sadie.
Sadie who?
Sadie same thing over and over!

What am I?

I cannot be seen, and I cannot be felt. No one can hear me and I have no smell. I lie around stars, I fill empty holes, and I hide under hills.
What am I?

Darkness

Knock knock!
Who's there?
Germany.
Germany who?
Germany people are coming over?

Knock knock!
Who's there?
Waiter.
Waiter who?
Waiter minute!

Knock knock!
Who's there?
I-8.
I-8 who?
I-8 lunch at noon.
   When's dinner?

Knock knock!
Who's there?
Nan.
Nan who?
Nan that I know!

What's So Funny

Knock knock!

Who's there?
Max.
Max who?
Max-imum penalty
for the crime!

HA HA HA HA HA

FUN FACT

NO RHYME OR REASON

Everybody loves a good rhyming song. Though it's easy to rhyme almost every word in the English language, there are exceptions. You'd be hard-pressed to find a word in the English language that rhymes with "orange," "silver," or "purple." ("Burple" doesn't count!)

Knock knock!
Who's there?
Haydn.
Haydn who?
Haydn-go-seek is fun!

Knock knock!
Who's there?
Omar.
Omar who?
Omar goodness gracious!

Knock knock!
Who's there?
Sarah.
Sarah who?
'Sarah 'nother joke we can tell?

Knock knock!
Who's there?
Buster.
Buster who?
Bus-ter the park comes every hour!

Knock knock!
Who's there?
Thoreau.
Thoreau who?
Thoreau the ball!

Knock knock!
Who's there?
Hawaii.
Hawaii who?
I'm fine, Hawaii you?

It's Me!

Fill in the answers to the clues, one letter in each numbered space. Then transfer the letters to the boxes that have the same numbers. When all the boxes are filled in correctly, you will have the answer to this joke:

Knock, knock.

Who's there?

Shirley.

Shirley who?

A. __ __ __ __ __   Paper toys flown by strings.
   15 3 14 20 13

B. __ __ __ __ __ __   Between spring and winter.
   1 12 19 11 6 4

C. __ __ __   For what reason?
   25 2 8

D. __ __ __ __ __   Covered in wool.
   18 9 17 5 22

E. __ __ __ __   A person, place, or thing.
   16 24 10 23

F. __ __   Close to, or beside.
   21 7

1	2	3	4	5	6	7		8	9	10		11	12	13	14

15	16	17	18		19	20		21	22		23	24	25	!

127

What am I?

As I grow up I grow down. I travel in groups but stay close to my family. I love to swim, but when the weather turns cold, I fly away.
What am I?

A gosling (baby goose)

Knock knock!
Who's there?
Thistle.
Thistle who?
Thistle be the last time I tell you!

Knock knock!
Who's there?
Gwen.
Gwen who?
Gwen will I see you again?

Knock knock!
Who's there?
Tank.
Tank who?
Tank goodness you answered the door!

Knock knock!
Who's there?
Ozzie.
Ozzie who?
Oz-zie you later!

Knock knock!
Who's there?
Ireland.
Ireland who?
Ire-land you some money for lunch!

Knock knock!
Who's there?
Bertha.
Bertha who?
My Bertha-day's just around the corner!

Knock knock!
Who's there?
Fish.
Fish who?
Fish-us temper will get you nowhere!

Soap Suds Fun

Standing over the bathroom sink, rub a little bit of liquid soap between your hands. Wet your hands with just a drop of water. Then, keeping the tips of your fingers and palms together, slowly open the middle of your hands to form a tunnel. Gently blow through the tunnel in your hands, and huge bubbles should appear like magic.

Knock knock!
Who's there?
Anita.
Anita who?
Anita place to take a nap!

Knock knock!
Who's there?
Soup.
Soup who?
Soup-erman has special powers!

Knock knock!
Who's there?
Handel.
Handel who?
Handel with care!

Knock knock!
Who's there?
Abby.
Abby who?
Abby days are here again!

Knock knock!
Who's there?
Blue.
Blue who?
Blue your nose!

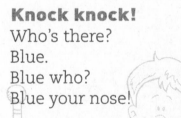

Knock knock!
Who's there?
Fido.
Fido who?
Fido I have to do everything?

Knock knock!
Who's there?
Distress.
Distress who?
Distress is the one I wore to the party!

Knock knock!
Who's there?
Carmen.
Carmen who?
Carmen get it!

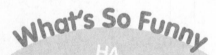

Knock knock!
Who's there?
Grimm.
Grimm who?
Grimm and bear it!

Knock knock!
Who's there?
Meow.
Meow who?
Take meow to the ball game!

Knock knock!
Who's there?
Xavier.
Xavier who?
Xavier breath!

Knock knock!
Who's there?
Taipei.
Taipei who?
Tai-pei letter and mail it!

What's So Funny

Knock knock!
Who's there?
Washer.
Washer who?
Washer don't know won't hurt you!

Knock knock!
Who's there?
Jimmy.
Jimmy who?
Jimmy your money, this is a stickup!

KNOCK-KNOCK YOUR SOCKS OFF

Knock knock!
Who's there?
Reuben.
Reuben who?
Reuben my eyes, I'm sleepy!

Knock knock!
Who's there?
Sausage.
Sausage who?
Sausage nice things in the shop!

Knock knock!
Who's there?
Rosina.
Rosina who?
Rosina garden is lovely!

Knock knock!
Who's there?
Kipper.
Kipper who?
Kipper eyes open for the signs!

Knock knock!
Who's there?
Pudding.
Pudding who?
Pudding your shoes on before your
   pants is a silly idea!

Knock knock!
Who's there?
Weed.
Weed who?
Weed better mow the lawn!

What am I?

I've got two really big front teeth that help me cut right through shrubs and even trees. I am known for building dams. These dams help slow down water and make deep pools where I love to splash around. **What am I?**

A beaver

Knock knock!
Who's there?
Nose.
Nose who?
Nose a lot of people!

Knock knock!
Who's there?
Fletcher.
Fletcher who?
Fletcher feet do the walking!

Knock knock!
Who's there?
Rufus.
Rufus who?
Rufus on fire!

Knock knock!
Who's there?
Stan.
Stan who?
Stan back, I'm coming through!

Knock knock!
Who's there?
F-2.
F-2 who?
F-2 go to the bathroom!

Knock knock!
Who's there?
Passion.
Passion who?
Just passion through!

Magnet Magic

Did you know that a powerful magnet can work through paper, cardboard, and even water? Impress your friends with this trick. Put a paper clip in a glass that's mostly filled with water. Tell your friends you can get the paper clip out of the water without getting wet. Then slide the magnet along the glass until it connects with the paper clip. Move the magnet and the paper clip up the glass and above the surface of the water, until you can reach in and grab the paper clip without getting your fingers wet.

Which Window?

Laura is visiting a friend who lives in an old apartment building. Use the clues to find out who will answer the door when Laura knock knocks!

- Laura's friend is not using the computer.
- The kid to the left of Laura's friend has a pet.
- Laura's friend does not know how to knit.
- Laura's friend has a window with curtains.

EXTRA FUN: Read the letters in the windows from bottom to top, and right to left. You will find the answer to this joke:

Knock, knock.

Who's there?

Juan.

Juan who?

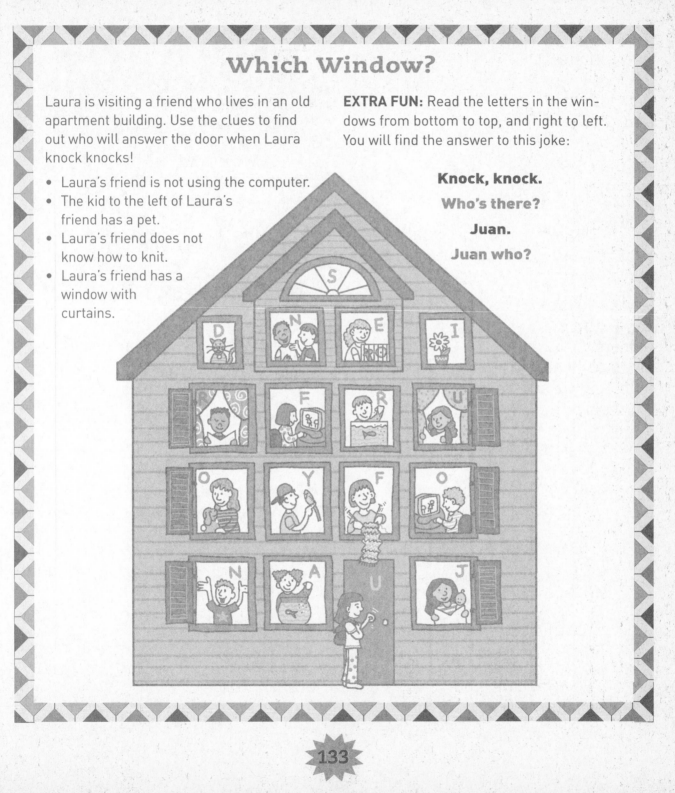

133

Knock knock!
Who's there?
Warrior.
Warrior who?
Warrior been?

Knock knock!
Who's there?
Square.
Square who?
Square are we going?

FUN FACT

SNEAKY CREATURES

There are 84 different types of chameleons on the planet. They have special cells in their skin that allow them to blend in with their surroundings. This way, it is hard for enemies to find them. But watch out—if a chameleon gets angry, it can turn bright red.

Knock knock!
Who's there?
Sincerely.
Sincerely who?
Sincerely, we still have time for breakfast!

Knock knock!
Who's there?
Diane.
Diane who?
Diane to get in the door!

Knock knock!
Who's there?
Yoda.
Yoda who?
Yoda greatest, baby!

Knock knock!
Who's there?
Oakham.
Oakham who?
Oakham all ye faithful!

Knock knock!
Who's there?
Goshen.
Goshen who?
Goshen's great for swimming!

134

Knock knock!
Who's there?
Eight ball.
Eight ball who?
Eight ball the food!

Knock knock!
Who's there?
Kismet.
Kismet who?
Kismet before anyone sees us!

Knock knock!
Who's there?
Rick.
Rick who?
Rick-ety bridge fell down!

Knock knock!
Who's there?
Sultan.
Sultan who?
Sultan pepper shakers!

Knock knock!
Who's there?
Cockadoodle.
Cockadoodle who?
Cockadoodle doo, not cockadoodle
  who!

Knock knock!
Who's there?
Mica.
Mica who?
Mi-ca is in the shop!

Words to Know

Comic Relief: A funny moment in a play or show that breaks up a very serious scene. Comic relief comes just in the nick of time when everything seems to be very tense and just too serious.

Knock knock!
Who's there?
Atch.
Atch who?
Bless you!

Knock knock!
Who's there?
Letter.
Letter who?
Letter ask us all she wants!

Knock knock!
Who's there?
Maude.
Maude who?
Maude in the U.S.A.!

Knock knock!
Who's there?
Comet.
Comet who?
Com-et a crime and you'll go to jail!

Knock knock!
Who's there?
Insect.
Insect who?
Insect your name here!

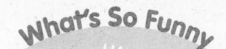

What's So Funny

Knock knock!

Who's there?
Bjorn.
Bjorn who?
Bjorn to run!

Knock knock!
Who's there?
Quebec.
Quebec who?
Quebec to the beginning!

Knock knock!
Who's there?
Amish.
Amish who?
Amish you, do you miss me?

Knock knock!
Who's there?
Ooze.
Ooze who?
Ooze in charge around here?

Knock knock!
Who's there?
Fajita.
Fajita who?
'Fajita 'nother thing, I'll be sick!

Knock knock!
Who's there?
Wilma.
Wilma who?
Wilma headache ever go away?

As I grow up I grow down. I travel in groups but stay close to my family. I love to swim, but when the weather turns cold, I fly away. **What am I?**

A kangaroo

Knock knock!
Who's there?
Minerva.
Minerva who?
Minerva-s wreck!

Knock knock!
Who's there?
Honeycomb.
Honeycomb who?
Honeycomb your
    hair, it's a mess!

Knock knock!
Who's there?
Dennis.
Dennis who?
Dennis is going to fix my toothache!

Knock knock!
Who's there?
Worm.
Worm who?
Worm yourself by the fireplace!

Knock knock!
Who's there?
Amir.
Amir who?
Amir so let me in!

Knock knock!
Who's there?
Les.
Les who?
Les go home!

Knock knock!
Who's there?
Ford.
Ford who?
Ford he's a jolly good fellow!

What's So Funny

Knock knock!

Who's there?
Isadore.
Isadore who?
Isadore open?

Half a Chance

This young lady only got half of her picture printed! Complete her portrait by copying the first half, square by square, into the empty grid.

Next, figure out which letter goes into each box, below. When you are finished, you will learn the second half of her name, too!

Knock, knock.
Who's there?
Alison.
Alison who?

E-4	Q-5	E+4	T-1	M+2	14

T+3	T-5	M+1	A+3	5	V-4	12	D-3	J+4	G-3

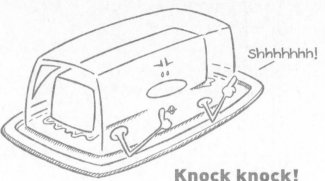

Shhhhhhh!

Knock knock!
Who's there?
Butter.
Butter who?
Butter if I keep it a secret!

Knock knock!
Who's there?
Dummy.
Dummy who?
Dummy a favor and be quiet!

Knock knock!
Who's there?
Tamara.
Tamara who?
Tamara is Thursday!

Knock knock!
Who's there?
Handsome.
Handsome who?
Handsome chips to me, I'm hungry!

Knock knock!
Who's there?
Luke.
Luke who?
Luke out, I'm going to tell another
knock-knock joke!

Knock knock!
Who's there?
Throat.
Throat who?
Throat out if it's rotten!

Knock knock!
Who's there?
Blue.
Blue who?
Blue away in the wind!

FUN FACT

SANDY CREATIONS

Those drinking glasses you have in the cabinet started out as sand on the beach! Hard to believe, but true. To make glass, sand is heated until it melts. Then the liquid is carefully shaped into glassware for you to drink your lemonade out of.

TRY THIS

An Optical Illusion

Take two magnifying glasses and hold them together, one on top of the other. Look closely at the words on an opened book through both lenses. Now, slowly pull the magnifying glasses toward you. Watch the words get bigger and bigger. If you keep pulling the magnifying glasses toward you, you'll see something strange happen. Suddenly, the words flip. This is because the lenses bent the light rays!

Knock knock!
Who's there?
Needle.
Needle who?
Needle little love in your life?

Knock knock!
Who's there?
Tom.
Tom who?
Tomcat ate your tongue?

Knock knock!
Who's there?
Woody.
Woody who?
Woody want from me?

Knock knock!
Who's there?
Quill.
Quill who?
Quill you marry me?

Knock knock!
Who's there?
Fanny.
Fanny who?
Fanny body home?

Knock knock!
Who's there?
Jeannette.
Jeannette who?
'Jeann-ette has a lot of holes in it!

Knock knock!
Who's there?
Harmony.
Harmony who?
Harmony more knock knocks do you
    want to hear?

Knock knock!
Who's there?
Dexter.
Dexter who?
Dexter halls with boughs of holly!

Knock knock!
Who's there?
Faith.
Faith who?
Faith the music!

TRY THIS

A Bugalicious Snack

Like insects? This snack is fun to make and even more fun to eat. You'll need some celery, peanut butter, and raisins. Put some peanut butter on the celery sticks, then place the raisins in the peanut butter. You now have ants on a log! Yummy!

Knock knock!
Who's there?
Al.
Al who?
Al be leaving soon!

Knock knock!
Who's there?
Thatcher.
Thatcher who?
Thatcher idea of a knock-knock joke?

Knock knock!
Who's there?
Israeli.
Israeli who?
Israeli nice of you to come over!

Words to Know

Shtick: A show-business word that means a comedian's routine. Most comedians have a certain type of act that they do much of the time. Comedians go on tour to do their shtick.

Rhyme Time

Can you use eight single-syllable words that rhyme with "knock" to describe the actions and things in this picture?

EXTRA FUN: Can you see two other things that can be described using two-syllable words that end in "-ock"?

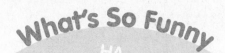

What's So Funny

Knock knock!

Who's there?
Kent.
Kent who?
Kent you tell?

Knock knock!
Who's there?
Goose.
Goose who?
You goose who! I already know!

Knock knock!
Who's there?
Hewlett.
Hewlett who?
Hewlett you in the house?

Knock knock!
Who's there?
Violet.
Violet who?
Violet a good meal go to waste?

Knock knock!
Who's there?
Spider.
Spider who?
'Spider everything, I'm still here!

Knock knock!
Who's there?
Elaine.
Elaine who?
Elaine on the highway is closed!

FUN FACT

IT'S ELECTRIC!

Humans aren't the only ones who know how to communicate with each other. Many animals have a way of communicating. Birds chirp, dogs bark, and cats meow. There are some fish out there that have a very interesting way of letting other sea creatures know what's on their minds. About 500 different species of fish use electricity to communicate. A banded knife fish, for example, may scare off an enemy by flashing on and off!

WHO'S THAT KNOCKIN'?

Knock knock!
Who's there?
Paris.
Paris who?
Paris the thought!

Knock knock!
Who's there?
Cash.
Cash who?
Cash whos are yummy!

Knock knock!
Who's there?
Ray.
Ray who?
Ray-ning all week long!

Knock knock!
Who's there?
Turner.
Turner who?
Turner 'round, quick!

Knock knock!
Who's there?
Eden.
Eden who?
Eden all the pudding!

Knock knock!
Who's there?
Homer.
Homer who?
Homer-run is great if
    you can hit one!

Knock knock!
Who's there?
Plato.
Plato who?
Plato mashed potatoes!

Words to Know

Punch line: A punch line has nothing to do with anyone punching. It is actually the funniest—or punchiest—part of a joke. Usually the punch line comes at the end of the joke. Ever listen to a long joke only to find out that the punch line wasn't so funny after all? That's no fun!

Crazy Criss-Cross

Unscramble each word and fit it into the numbered criss-cross grid.
When you are done, read down the shaded column to find the answer to this joke:

Knock, knock. **Who's there?** **Howie.** **Howie who?**

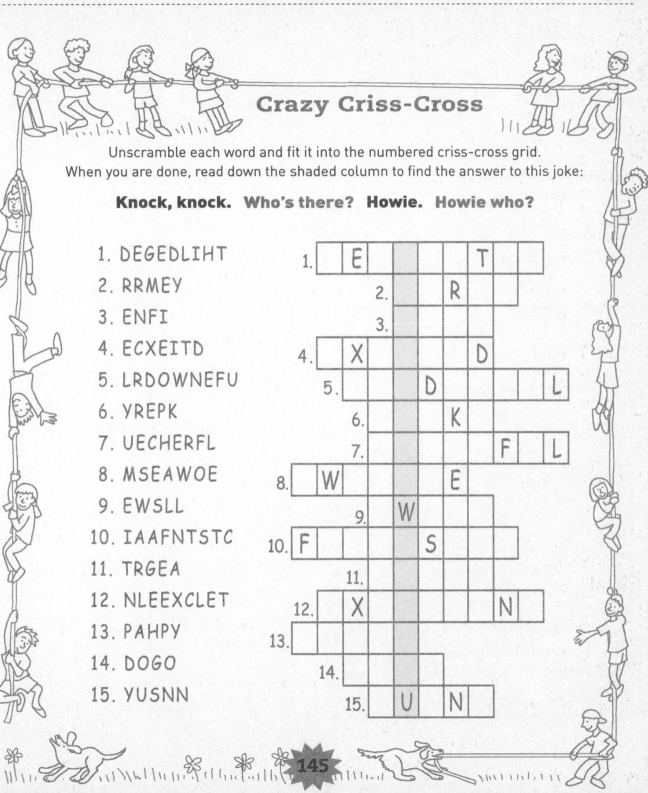

1. DEGEDLIHT
2. RRMEY
3. ENFI
4. ECXEITD
5. LRDOWNEFU
6. YREPK
7. UECHERFL
8. MSEAWOE
9. EWSLL
10. IAAFNTSTC
11. TRGEA
12. NLEEXCLET
13. PAHPY
14. DOGO
15. YUSNN

145

Knock knock!
Who's there?
Can't.
Can't who?
Can't elope!

Knock knock!
Who's there?
Noah.
Noah who?
Noah place to go!

Knock knock!
Who's there?
Warren.
Warren who?
Warren earth are you going?

Knock knock!
Who's there?
Salome.
Salome who?
Salome on a sandwich!

Knock knock!
Who's there?
Franz.
Franz who?
Franz, Romans, Countrymen!

Knock knock!
Who's there?
Wanda.
Wanda who?
Wanda off and you could get lost!

Knock knock!
Who's there?
Detour.
Detour who?
De-tour will take us to Spain!

What am I?

I collect acorns and bury them for cold weather. The problem is, I always forget where I've left them. Sometimes the acorns stay where I left them and grow into trees. I may be gray or black and I've got a bushy tail that makes me irresistible. **What am I?**

A squirrel

Knock knock!
Who's there?
Sandy.
Sandy who?
Sandy letter to your friend!

Knock knock!
Who's there?
Ina.
Ina who?
Ina few minutes I'm going to tell you
    another joke!

FUN FACT

KEEPING WARM

Ever wonder why certain
flowers close up at night?
They do this to stay warm.
New seeds come from the
inside of the flower. It's important
that these seeds are protected in
spring when nighttime can still be a
bit frosty.

Knock knock!
Who's there?
Viper.
Viper who?
Viper your face, it's dirty!

Knock knock!
Who's there?
Zaire.
Zaire who?
Zaire it goes!

Knock knock!
Who's there?
Canoe.
Canoe who?
Canoe come over
    for dinner?

Knock knock!
Who's there?
Munich.
Munich who?
Munich me happy!

Knock knock!
Who's there?
Grub.
Grub who?
Grub on and hold tight!

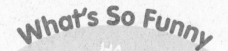

What's So Funny

HA HA HA HA HA HA

Knock knock!

Who's there?
Bette.
Bette who?
Bette your money
I'm right!

Knock knock!
Who's there?
Philip.
Philip who?
Philip the tub,
    I need a bath!

Knock knock!
Who's there?
Topic.
Topic who?
Topic a flower would be nice!

Knock Once

Knock, knock.   Who's there?

Beth.   Beth who?

Beth you can't   Beth you I can!
find the one
time the work
KNOCK is
spelled
correctly!

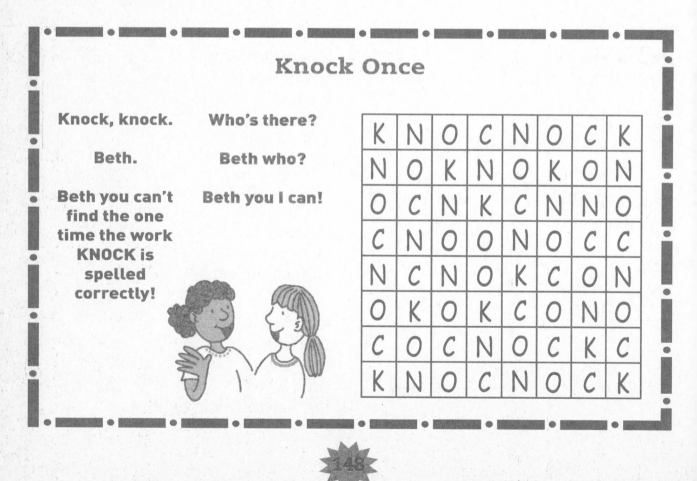

K	N	O	C	N	O	C	K
N	O	K	N	O	K	O	N
O	C	N	K	C	N	N	O
C	N	O	O	N	O	C	C
N	C	N	O	K	C	O	N
O	K	O	K	C	O	N	O
C	O	C	N	O	C	K	C
K	N	O	C	N	O	C	K

Words to Know

Jest: Not being serious. Sometimes a jest is a playful remark or a prank. In the Middle Ages, a jester was someone who worked at the king's court to entertain royalty.

Knock knock!
Who's there?
Nun.
Nun who?
Nun of your business!

Knock knock!
Who's there?
Earl.
Earl who?
Earl you can ask for!

Knock knock!
Who's there?
Macon.
Macon who?
Macon a sandwich!

Knock knock!
Who's there?
Hedda.
Hedda who?
Hedda 'nough, I'm leaving!

Knock knock!
Who's there?
Tail.
Tail who?
Tail everybody!

TRY THIS

A Tasty Experiment

Cut up an apple into four parts and put the slices on a plate. Squeeze lemon juice over two of the four slices and let stand for three hours. When you come back, see what happened. The slices with lemon juice didn't turn brown, but the others did. That's because chemicals in the air turn the apple brown, but other chemicals in the lemon juice stop that from happening.

Knock knock!
Who's there?
Accordion.
Accordion who?
Accordion to the
    weatherman
    it's going to rain!

Knock knock!
Who's there?
Nantucket.
Nantucket who?
Nantucket but she said she'd give it
    back!

Knock knock!
Who's there?
Egypt.
Egypt who?
Egypt you when he sold you a
    broken watch!

Knock knock!
Who's there?
Henrietta.
Henrietta who?
Henrietta bad apple!

Knock knock!
Who's there?
Cecil.
Cecil who?
Cecil-ly jokes are fun!

Knock knock!
Who's there?
UC.
UC who?
UC what I see!

Knock knock!
Who's there?
Pea.
Pea who?
Pea U, something smells!

what am I?

You may cut me, but I'll
grow back. I'm
green when I get
water and turn brown without it. People walk all over
me and sometimes they play
sports on me. **What am I?**

Grass

What's So Funny

HA HA HA HA HA

Knock knock!

Who's there?

Rita.

Rita who?

Rita book!

Knock knock!
Who's there?
Cohen.
Cohen who?
Cohen around the merry-go-round.

Knock knock!
Who's there?
Venice.
Venice who?
Venice dinner going to be ready?

Knock knock!
Who's there?
Van Gogh.
Van Gogh who?
Van Gogh and get me a cookie!

Knock knock!
Who's there?
Dots.
Dots who?
Dots not important!

Knock knock!
Who's there?
Ants.
Ants who?
Ants in your pants!

Knock knock!
Who's there?
Reed.
Reed who?
Reed a newspaper!

FUN FACT

IT'S NO COINCIDENCE

Ever notice that some eggs are brown and others are white? Believe it or not, there are many different types of chickens out there. Brown eggs come from red hens and white eggs usually come from White Leghorn chickens. But most amazing is that there are even chickens that lay blue eggs, the Auracana chickens!

Knock knock!
Who's there?
Moe.
Moe who?
Moe cake, please!

Knock knock!
Who's there?
Isabel.
Isabel who?
Isabel needed on the door?

Knock knock!
Who's there?
Gopher.
Gopher who?
Gopher a long walk!

In Motion

Take a piece of thin cardboard (for example, the side of a cereal box). Decorate it with a nature scene like a garden and a blue sky, or a seascape. Then make a little bird or a boat out of paper, something light that can move easily. Attach a paper clip to the bottom of your movable object. Put your object on the cardboard scene. Then get a magnet. You can move the small object around the cardboard by moving the magnet underneath the cardboard.

Knock knock!
Who's there?
CD.
CD who?
CD monkey in the cage!

Knock knock!
Who's there?
Weasel.
Weasel who?
Weasel while you work!

Knock knock!
Who's there?
Guitar.
Guitar who?
Guitar coats before we go outside!

152

Who Is It?

Collect the letters as you find your way through the maze from **START** to **END**. As you read them in order, they will spell the answer to this joke:

Knock, knock.

Who's there?

Handsome.

Handsome who?

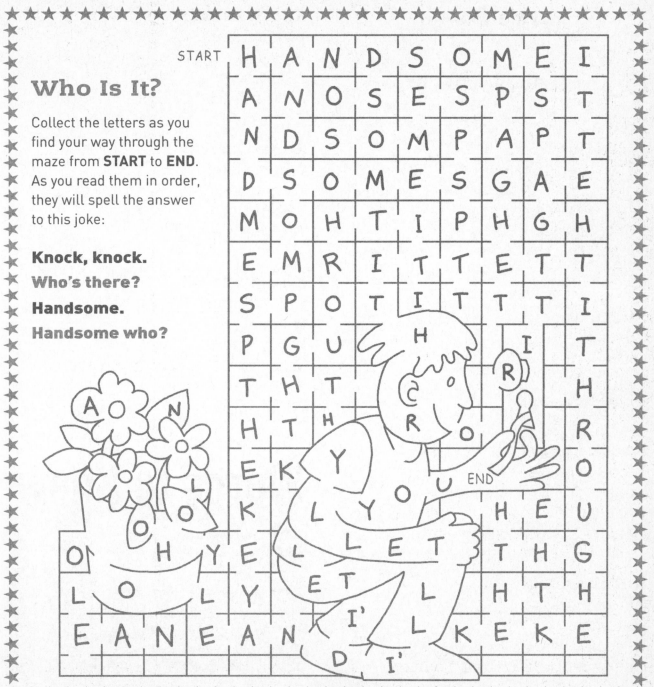

START

What's So Funny

HA HA HA HA HA

Knock knock!

Who's there?
Blake.
Blake who?
Blake a leg!

Knock knock!
Who's there?
Olin.
Olin who?
Olin a day's work!

Knock knock!
Who's there?
Dana.
Dana who?
Dana talk with food in your mouth!

Knock knock!
Who's there?
One shoe.
One shoe who?
One shoe come over for a while?

Knock knock!
Who's there?
Alba.
Alba who?
Alba in the other room!

Knock knock!
Who's there?
Termites.
Termites who?
Termites the night!

Knock knock!
Who's there?
Mikey.
Mikey who?
Mikey won't work, can you open the door?

Words to Know

Side-splitting: Have you ever laughed so hard you thought you'd just bust? That's where the term "side-splitting" comes from. Side-splitting laughter is the type of laughter that takes over your whole body.

ONE TWO THREE O'CLOCK KNOCK

Knock knock!
Who's there?
Trixie.
Trixie who?
There are Trixie can't do
because we didn't train him!

Knock knock!
Who's there?
Nobel.
Nobel who?
Nobel, that's why I knocked!

Knock knock!
Who's there?
Chris.
Chris who?
Chris-mas time is just around the
corner!

Knock knock!
Who's there?
Orange.
Orange who?
Orange you happy?

Knock knock!
Who's there?
Amy.
Amy who?
Amy 'fraid I forgot the rest of the joke!

Knock knock!
Who's there?
Utica.
Utica who?
Utica long way!

What am I?

I am red with black dots, very small, and like to fly. I eat small tasty bugs and you usually find me resting comfortably on flowers in the summertime. People are always asking me to fly home. **What am I?**

A ladybug

155

Knock knock!
Who's there?
Soda.
Soda who?
Soda hole in your shirt!

Knock knock!
Who's there?
Tango.
Tango who?
Tango faster if you want!

Knock knock!
Who's there?
Maida.
Maida who?
Maida world be at your fingertips!

Knock knock!
Who's there?
Juneau.
Juneau who?
Juneau what time it is?

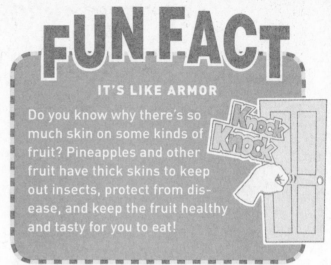

FUN FACT

IT'S LIKE ARMOR

Do you know why there's so much skin on some kinds of fruit? Pineapples and other fruit have thick skins to keep out insects, protect from disease, and keep the fruit healthy and tasty for you to eat!

Knock knock!
Who's there?
Wanda.
Wanda who?
Wanda bough breaks, the baby will fall!

Knock knock!
Who's there?
Doris.
Doris who?
Doris locked!

Knock knock!
Who's there?
Jamaica.
Jamaica who?
Jamaica mistake and no one ever forgets!

Mixed Up Endings

Collect all words with the same number above them and write
them on the line with the corresponding number below.
Now, rearrange the words to get the answer for each joke!

3. Swiss	1. here!	4. over!	2. somebody	1. echo	3. like
1. There's	6. can	5. Australia!	4. minute	6. You	5. I'm
4. Anita	2. Pecan	1. a	6. yodel?	3. sound	2. time!
2. else	4. think	3. You	4. to	5. Yes,	4. it
3. clock!	1. in	5. from	2. next	1. terrible	3. a

1. Knock, knock. Who's there? **Who.** Who who?

2. Knock, knock. Who's there? **Pecan.** Pecan who?

3. Knock, knock. Who's there? **Cook.** Cook who?

4. Knock, knock. Who's there? **Anita.** Anita who?

5. Knock, knock. Who's there? **Kangar.** Kangar who?

6. Knock, knock. Who's there? **Little old lady.** Little old lady who?

Knock knock!
Who's there?
Dinosaur.
Dinosaur who?
Dinosaur because she fell down!

Knock knock!
Who's there?
Fossil.
Fossil who?
Fossil last time, let me in!

Knock knock!
Who's there?
Virtue.
Virtue who?
Virtue get that nice sweater?

Words to Know

> **Funny bone:** Ever hear someone say they are going to tickle your funny bone? Well, they aren't actually going to tickle a bone in your body. They mean they are going to make you laugh. Your funny bone is your sense of humor.

Knock knock!
Who's there?
Tennis.
Tennis who?
Ten is five plus five!

Knock knock!
Who's there?
Wannetta.
Wannetta who?
Wannetta time, please!

Knock knock!
Who's there?
Brin.
Brin who?
Brin me some pie!

Knock knock!
Who's there?
Jack.
Jack who?
Jack your coat in the coatroom!

Knock knock!
Who's there?
Goose.
Goose who?
Goose see
   a doctor
   for that cough!

Knock knock!
Who's there?
Ben.
Ben who?
Ben waiting around for hours!

Knock knock!
Who's there?
Beryl.
Beryl who?
Beryl luck next time!

Knock knock!
Who's there?
Major.
Major who?
Major look!

Knock knock!
Who's there?
Wooden.
Wooden who?
Wooden you like to find out!

Knock knock!
Who's there?
Sam.
Sam who?
Sam person who told you the last
   knock-knock joke!

Knock knock!
Who's there?
Throne.
Throne who?
Throne out the garbage!

What's So Funny

Knock knock!
Who's there?
Gouda.
Gouda who?
Goudas can be!

159

TRY THIS

The Power of Your Hair

Turn on the water in the bathroom sink so just a thin stream of water flows out. Then, comb your hair about twenty times. Put the comb near the water, but not touching it. Watch as the water bends to reach the comb. This is because of the static electricity in your hair!

Knock knock!
Who's there?
Beth.
Beth who?
Beth time of my life!

Knock knock!
Who's there?
Accord.
Accord who?
Accord of wood for the fireplace!

Wendy's Here

Knock, knock.

Who's there?

Wendy.

Wendy who?

Wendy boxes are all colored in, you will see who it is!

Color Code:
B - BROWN   G - GREEN
P - PEACH   R - RED
K - BLACK   L - LIGHT BLUE

L	L	L	L	K	K	K	K	K	K	L	L	L	L
L	L	L	K	B	B	B	B	B	B	K	L	L	L
L	L	K	B	B	K	K	K	K	B	B	K	L	L
L	K	B	B	K	P	P	P	P	K	B	B	K	L
L	K	B	K	P	P	P	P	P	P	K	B	K	L
L	K	B	K	P	G	P	P	G	P	K	B	K	L
L	K	B	P	P	P	P	P	P	P	P	B	K	L
L	K	B	P	P	P	K	K	P	P	P	B	K	L
L	K	B	P	P	P	P	P	P	P	P	B	K	L
K	K	B	K	P	R	P	P	R	P	K	B	K	K
K	B	B	K	P	P	R	R	P	P	K	B	B	K
K	B	B	B	K	P	P	P	P	K	B	B	B	K
L	K	K	B	B	K	K	K	K	B	B	K	K	L
L	L	L	K	K	K	P	P	K	K	K	L	L	L
L	L	L	L	K	P	P	P	P	K	L	L	L	L

Knock knock!
Who's there?
Kentucky.
Kentucky who?
Kentucky you in at night!

Knock knock!
Who's there?
Goddess.
Goddess who?
Goddess stop this madness!

Knock knock!
Who's there?
Howard.
Howard who?
Howard I know?

Knock knock!
Who's there?
Colleen.
Colleen who?
Colleen up the kitchen
when you're done cookin'!

Knock knock!
Who's there?
Evan.
Evan who?
Evan-ly angels!

Knock knock!
Who's there?
Kip.
Kip who?
Kip looking till we find it!

Knock knock!
Who's there?
Hello.
Hello who?
Hel-lo can you go?

What am I?

I run over hills and around mountains. I jump over rivers and make my way through thick forests. You can't go anywhere without me, and if you step outside your door, I'll be waiting there. **What am I?**

The Road

Knock knock!
Who's there?
Swear.
Swear who?
Swear are we going?

Knock knock!
Who's there?
Ghana.
Ghana who?
Ghana go to town!

Knock knock!
Who's there?
Hyde.
Hyde who?
Hyde like to tell you another joke!

Words to Know

Palindrome: A word, sentence, or number that reads the same backward and forward. For example, the number 13531 is a palindrome. So is the name Bob.

Knock knock!
Who's there?
Faith.
Faith who?
Faith it, it's over!

Knock knock!
Who's there?
Vaughn.
Vaughn who?
Vaughn day we'll see each other
    again!

FUN FACT

DOWN DEEP

The deepest place on earth is located in the Pacific Ocean. It is called the Challenger Deep, and it's a very dark and cold place to be. The bottom of Challenger Deep is 35,813 feet below the surface of the water (that's almost 7 miles)! Hardly anything at all can live there!

Knock knock!
Who's there?
Teacher.
Teacher who?
Teacher some manners!

Knock knock!
Who's there?
Dali.
Dali who?
Dali in the window sure is pretty!

Knock knock!
Who's there?
Buck.
Buck who?
Buck stops here!

Knock knock!
Who's there?
Lemmie.
Lemmie who?
Lemmie tell you a story!

Knock knock!
Who's there?
Foster.
Foster who?
Foster than a speeding bullet!

Knock knock!
Who's there?
Ogre.
Ogre who?
Ogre take a long walk!

Knock knock!
Who's there?
Tree.
Tree who?
Tree plus tree is six!

Knock knock!
Who's there?
Alaska.
Alaska who?
Alaska once more and that's it!

What's So Funny

Knock knock!
Who's there?
Wade.
Wade who?
Wade up, I've got more knock-knock jokes!

Open the Door

Complete each of these seven knock-knock jokes by writing the name of one of the objects on this page into the blank spaces provided.

1. _____ your sister who I am!

2. _____ _____ like to know ?

3. _____ you come out and play?

4. _____ me! Who are you?

5. _____ you for inviting me over!

6. _____ see you when you open the door!

7. _____ by you?

Knock knock!
Who's there?
Don't chew.
Don't chew who?
Don't chew know?

Knock knock!
Who's there?
Monroe.
Monroe who?
Monroe your boat!

Words to Know

Absurd: Completely ridiculous or silly. For example, it is absurd to think that there is a man living on the moon.

Knock knock!
Who's there?
Glitter.
Glitter who?
Glitter bug!

Knock knock!
Who's there?
Weirdo.
Weirdo who?
Weirdo you think you're going?

TRY THIS

Make a Five-Headed Puppet

Spread your hand out on a piece of paper. Trace your hand and fingers onto the paper with a pencil. Glue some yarn on the tip of each finger tracing so it looks like hair. Then paste googly eyes on each of the five heads. Draw noses and mouths with crayons or colored pencils. Then cut out the whole hand tracing. Glue a Popsicle stick to the back of the paper hand and put on a puppet show.

Knock knock!
Who's there?
Island.
Island who?
Island on the house with my parachute!

165

KNOCK 'EM DEAD WITH KNOCK-KNOCKS

Knock knock!
Who's there?
Adair.
Adair who?
'Ad-air once,
   but now I'm bald!

Knock knock!
Who's there?
Heaven.
Heaven who?
Heaven you heard enough knock-
   knock jokes?

Knock knock!
Who's there?
Candace.
Candace who?
Candace be true?

Knock knock!
Who's there?
Habit.
Habit who?
Habit your way, I'll have it mine!

Knock knock!
Who's there?
Freeman.
Freeman who?
Free-man from his chains!

Knock knock!
Who's there?
Pecan.
Pecan who?
Pecan somebody else!

Knock knock!
Who's there?
Band.
Band who?
Band from going there!

What am I?

I look like a fish and I live in water. But I'm not really a fish. I'm a mammal. I'm incredibly smart and I always have a smile on my face. Sometimes you'll see me doing tricks at the aquarium. **What am I?**

A dolphin

TRY THIS

Taste Tests

Have you ever noticed that when you have a cold, you have less of an appetite? This is partly because we need our sense of smell to enjoy our food. With the help of a grownup, cut up a bunch of different vegetables, fruits, and cheeses with similar textures. One of you can be the taster, and the other will be the server. The server tells the taster to close his eyes and hold his nose. Then the server places a piece of food in the taster's mouth. The taster has to guess what the food is without using his sense of sight or smell. How easy do you think it will be to guess what you're eating?

Knock knock!
Who's there?
Fran.
Fran who?
Fran of mine is coming to town!

Knock knock!
Who's there?
Unit.
Unit who?
Unit me a sweater!

Knock knock!
Who's there?
Hugh.
Hugh who?
Hugh must have been a star!

Knock knock!
Who's there?
Klaus.
Klaus who?
Klaus the window!

Knock knock!
Who's there?
Amoeba.
Amoeba who?
Amoeba wrong, but I may be right!

Knock knock!
Who's there?
Chicken.
Chicken who?
Chicken to see if
    you're okay!

167

Knock knock!
Who's there?
Renata.
Renata who?
Renata jokes, I'll have
  to learn some more!

Knock knock!
Who's there?
Mia.
Mia who?
Mia pants are on fire!

Knock knock!
Who's there?
Chess.
Chess who?
Chess the way it is!

Knock knock!
Who's there?
Yuri.
Yuri who?
Yuri great pal!

Come and Get It!

Your mom is cooking dinner when, suddenly . . .

Knock, knock.

Who's there?

Gus.

Gus who?

To find the end of this mystery, start at the letter marked with a dot. As you spiral into the center, collect every other letter. Write them in order on the lines. When you reach the middle, head back out again, collecting all the letters that you skipped over the first time.

U E S N W N H I O G M T O G C O S D O I N R G.

_ _ _ '

_ _ _ _

_ _ _ _ _

_ _

_ _ _ _ _ _ !

Knock knock!
Who's there?
Pasta.
Pasta who?
Pasta potatoes please!

Knock knock!
Who's there?
Pasture.
Pasture who?
Pasture bedtime!

Knock knock!
Who's there?
Stu.
Stu who?
Stu you want to tell me something?

What's So Funny

Knock knock!
Who's there?
May.
May who?
Mayday Mayday!

HA HA HA HA HA

Knock knock!
Who's there?
Dwight.
Dwight who?
Dwight way is the best way!

Knock knock!
Who's there?
Colin.
Colin who?
Colin all kids!

Knock knock!
Who's there?
Alpaca.
Alpaca who?
Alpaca the suitcase before we go!

FUN FACT

HOT AND COLD

The Sahara Desert is the largest desert in the world. It gets so hot there during the day, it is almost impossible to go more than four hours without water. At night, though, it can get so cold, the temperature may drop below freezing!

Words to Know

Skit: A short and funny play. A class might write a skit for a school performance. Sometimes a show will be made up of a few different skits.

Knock knock!
Who's there?
Sweden.
Sweden who?
Sweden sour chicken!

Knock knock!
Who's there?
Hammond.
Hammond who?
Hammond eggs make a good
    breakfast!

Knock knock!
Who's there?
Canoe.
Canoe who?
Canoe tell
    me a story?

Knock knock!
Who's there?
Lana.
Lana who?
Lana the free, home of the brave!

Knock knock!
Who's there?
Nanny.
Nanny who?
Nanny one home?

Knock knock!
Who's there?
Waddle.
Waddle who?
Waddle you give me for my birthday?

FUN FACT

ARACHNO-WHAT?

Arachnophobia is the fear of spiders, but most of these creatures are nothing to be afraid of! Spiders are actually good to have around. Almost all of them are completely harmless, and they catch and eat pesky insects.

We Deliver!

It's fun to order takeout food and have it delivered. But it's even more fun if the delivery person has a yummy name! Choose from the middle initials and last names scattered down the right side of this page. Write them on the correct lines to create seven deliciously different delivery people who might come knock-knocking at your door to bring dinner!

1. Knock, knock. Who's there? Manilla. Manilla who?
   Manilla _____

2. Knock, knock. Who's there? Barbie. Barbie who?
   Barbie _____

3. Knock, knock. Who's there? Frank. Frank who?
   Frank _____

4. Knock, knock. Who's there? Hamen. Hamen who?
   Hamen _____

5. Knock, knock. Who's there? Roland. Roland who?
   Roland _____

6. Knock, knock. Who's there? Marsha. Marsha who?
   Marsha _____

7. Knock, knock. Who's there? Sultan. Sultan who?
   Sultan _____

N.

Pepper

Mallow

Butter

Scream

Q.

Beans

Chicken

I.   Eggs

Knock knock!
Who's there?
Lionel.
Lionel who?
Lionel get you nowhere!

Knock knock!
Who's there?
Rich.
Rich who?
Rich man is a poor man with money!

Knock knock!
Who's there?
Orson.
Orson who?
'Orson carriage!

Knock knock!
Who's there?
Dishes.
Dishes who?
Dishes the police,
 open the door!

Knock knock!
Who's there?
Spider.
Spider who?
I spider hiding in the yard!

Knock knock!
Who's there?
Aspen.
Aspen who?
A-spen around until I get dizzy!

Knock knock!
Who's there?
Holly.
Holly who?
Holly days are fun!

What am I?

I'm fast as can be, and built for speed. I've got huge claws, and my nest is grand. I live in high cliffs, in canyon walls, and even on city skyscrapers.
What am I?

A falcon

Knock knock!
Who's there?
Pest.
Pest who?
Pest wishes to you!

Knock knock!
Who's there?
April.
April who?
April showers bring May flowers!

Knock knock!
Who's there?
Bach.
Bach who?
Bach to the future!

What's So Funny

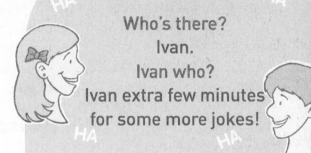

Knock knock!

Who's there?
Ivan.
Ivan who?
Ivan extra few minutes
for some more jokes!

Knock knock!
Who's there?
Heart.
Heart who?
Heart it through the grapevine!

Knock knock!
Who's there?
Telly.
Telly who?
Telly your brother to come home!

Knock knock!
Who's there?
Raisin.
Raisin who?
Raisin our hands
     before we speak!

Make a Rainbow

On a sunny day, get the garden hose and
then stand with your back to the sun.
Adjust the hose nozzle so it just lightly
mists water. Hold the hose up in front of
you, and then look closely. You will see a
rainbow in the mist.

173

Funny Friends

We've hidden the first half of fifteen knock-knock names in the grid. Look carefully as you highlight each name, and you'll find each person's last name, too. One is done for you! **HINT:** Middle initials are sometimes included. **EXTRA FUN:** Turn each name into a knock-knock joke!

LUKE	**ELLA**	**ALBIE**	**TOM**	**TIM**
PAT	**M. GLADYS**	**BABE**	**MATT**	**WANDA**
IMA	**HANK**	**MAURA**	**LEWIS**	**ABBY**

```
W  A  N  D  A  B.  F  R  E  N  Z  S  M.
M  B  A  L  B  I  E  C.  I  N  G  U  G
A  B  O  B.  S  O  M  S  R  A  S  L  L
U  I  T  O  M  A.  T  O  W  E  T  U  A
R  R  U  B  M  I  T  O  T  B  M  K  D
A  R  M  E  K  A  C  E.  T  A  P  E  Y
L  M  O  S  V  M  S  M  Z  M  Z  O  S
E  E  H  A  N  K  R.  C  H  I  F  U  F
S  L  L  R  A  B  R  A  B  S  O  T  R
S  L  T  B  A  B  E  E.  F  A  C  E  I
E  S  S  U  R  T  T  A  M  S  O  D
M  K  R  A  L  C  N.  S  I  W  E  L  A
A  B  B  Y  B  I  R  T  H  D  A  Y  Y
```

Words to Know

Parody: A play, sometimes a musical, that is meant to be very funny and often makes fun of something.

Knock knock!
Who's there?
Hacienda.
Hacienda who?
Hacienda the story!

Knock knock!
Who's there?
Whoville.
Whoville who?
Whoville answer the door ven I knock?

Knock knock!
Who's there?
Summer.
Summer who?
Summer time and the living is good!

Knock knock!
Who's there?
Dale.
Dale who?
Dale come if you invite them!

Knock knock!
Who's there?
Quiche.
Quiche who?
Quiche me, I love you!

Knock knock!
Who's there?
Root.
Root who?
Root for me at the game!

Knock knock!
Who's there?
Hiram.
Hiram who?
Hiram your best friend, don't you remember me?

Knock knock!
Who's there?
Phyllis.
Phyllis who?
Phyllis in on the details!

Knock knock!
Who's there?
Meter.
Meter who?
Meter in the lobby!

Words to Know

Guffaw: A loud burst of un-controllable laughter. If you're watching a movie that has many funny things happening, you might not be able to control your laughter. That's when you are likely to guffaw!

Knock knock!
Who's there?
Carrie.
Carrie who?
Carrie me home, I'm tired!

TRY THIS

Learn to See Around Corners!

Find a ruler, some tape, and a small mirror. Carefully tape the mirror to the ruler, making sure not to cover up the mirror with the tape. Stand to one side of a door and hold the ruler outside the doorway, so that the mirror is at the farther end. If you move the mirror around, you will be able to see different things in the room through the mirror!

Knock knock!
Who's there?
Rhoda.
Rhoda who?
Rhoda donkey at the zoo!

Knock knock!
Who's there?
Rozette.
Rozette who?
Rozette a bug,
    now she feels sick!

KNOCK-KNOCK YOURSELF SILLY

Knock knock!
Who's there?
Olive.
Olive who?
Olive you too!

Knock knock!
Who's there?
Lima bean.
Lima bean who?
Lima bean working on the railroad!

Knock knock!
Who's there?
Dee.
Dee who?
Dee-licious!

Knock knock!
Who's there?
Lisbon.
Lisbon who?
Lisbon to the movies twice this week!

Knock knock!
Who's there?
Cher.
Cher who?
Cher would be nice to see you again!

Knock knock!
Who's there?
Hive.
Hive who?
Hive got my eye on you!

Knock knock!
Who's there?
Stuart.
Stuart who?
Stuart up and serve it while it's hot!

FUN FACT

PENGUIN PAIRS

Male and female penguins have a very interesting way of courting each other. If a male penguin is interested in a female penguin, he may offer her small pebbles as a gift. If she accepts, he knows he has won her heart.

What am I?

I can be found in marshes, swamps, lakes, and ponds. I am famous in the South. I can grow up to 13 feet long, and as an adult I may weigh up to 500 pounds. I catch my food by clamping my jaws shut over them. **What am I?**

An alligator

Knock knock!
Who's there?
Isaac.
Isaac who?
Isaac-ly who you think it is!

Knock knock!
Who's there?
Vine.
Vine who?
Vine-derful news!

Knock knock!
Who's there?
Roxanne.
Roxanne who?
Roxanne sand are at the beach!

Knock knock!
Who's there?
Anita.
Anita who?
Anita good rest!

Knock knock!
Who's there?
Tonto.
Tonto who?
Tonto get ready for school!

Knock knock!
Who's there?
Chair.
Chair who?
Chair your secrets with me!

Knock knock!
Who's there?
Cedar.
Cedar who?
Cedar plane flying in the air!

Ho, Ho, Ho

The answer to this joke is missing the letters a, e, i, o, and u. Can you fit them in the proper blanks?

Knock, knock.

Beta.

Who's there?

Beta who?

_h, y__ b_t_ w_tch __t,

y__ b_t_ n_t cry,

y__ b_t_ n_t p__t,

_'m t_ll_ng y__ why —

S_nt_ Cl__s _s c_m_ng

t_ t_wn!

Knock knock!
Who's there?
Grant.
Grant who?
Grant me a wish!

Knock knock!
Who's there?
Babbit.
Babbit who?
Babbit in the garden
   ate our lettuce!

Knock knock!
Who's there?
Luke.
Luke who?
Luke through the
   peephole and
   you'll see!

Knock knock!
Who's there?
Sole.
Sole who?
'Sole new day!

Yesterday and Today

Collect some old photos of grandparents or other older relatives. Now get some pictures of you and your friends. Put the new photos next to the old photos to see how different things are today. What kind of clothes did the people in the old photos wear? Are there other differences you can detect?

Knock knock!
Who's there?
Iguana.
Iguana who?
Iguana tell you something!

Knock knock!
Who's there?
Diploma.
Diploma who?
Diploma is coming to fix the pipes!

Knock knock!
Who's there?
Chelsea.
Chelsea who?
Chel-sea you later!

Knock knock!
Who's there?
Fruit.
Fruit who?
Fruit of all evil!

Knock knock!
Who's there?
Utah.
Utah who?
Utah-king to me?

Knock knock!
Who's there?
Sabina.
Sabina who?
Sabina long time since I told you a
   knock-knock joke!

Knock knock!
Who's there?
Bolivia.
Bolivia who?
Bolivia me, I know what I'm talking
   about!

Knock knock!
Who's there?
Watson.
Watson who?
Wats-on the radio?

Knock knock!
Who's there?
Latin.
Latin who?
Latin me through the door is a
   good idea!

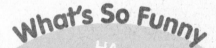

What's So Funny

Knock knock!

Who's there?
Peace.
Peace who?
Peace and carrots!

Words to Know

Vaudeville: A staged performance including a lot of different types of acts. There could be singing, dancing, comedy, acrobats, and even animal tricks. Everyone loves a good vaudeville show!

Knock knock!
Who's there?
Ike.
Ike who?
Ike could dance all night!

Knock knock!
Who's there?
Chicken.
Chicken who?
Chicken' out the situation!

Aye, Aye, Captain

First, figure out what word each letter and picture puzzle represents. Then, number the words in the proper order to create the answer to this joke:

Knock, knock.

Who's there?

Fire engine.

Fire engine who?

YAWNING FOR AIR

Yawning when you're tired is actually a wake-up call for the brain. Your brain needs lots of oxygen, which is carried in your bloodstream to all parts of your body. When you're tired, your heart pumps more slowly. This means oxygen gets to your brain slowly. When you yawn, your brain gets the oxygen a lot faster. That makes your brain happy!

Knock knock!
Who's there?
Ken.
Ken who?
Ken you tell me something new?

Knock knock!
Who's there?
Banana.
Banana who?
Banana split, so ice creamed!

Knock knock!
Who's there?
Galway.
Galway who?
Galway or else!

Knock knock!
Who's there?
U-8.
U-8 who?
U-8 my candy bar!

Knock knock!
Who's there?
Harry.
Harry who?
Harry-planes fly overhead!

Knock knock!
Who's there?
Eliza.
Eliza who?
Eliza when he doesn't want anyone to
    know the truth!

What am I?

I can eat a thousand flying insects in one night. My favorite place to live is very close to others like me. I can hang out upside down all day long. One of the best things about me is that I fly around at night and I don't need the light. **What am I?**

An bat

183

Where in the World?

Use each of the place names from around the world to complete one of the jokes below. Be careful—there are more names than you need.
EXTRA FUN: Turn each of the place names into a knock-knock!

1. _____ questions, you give the answers!

2. _____ matter? Cat got your tongue?

3. _____ to the party!

4. _____ lots of wood with my chain saw!

5. _____ come out and play?

6. _____ me very happy!

7. _____ go home now!

8. _____ ride my bike?

9. _____ a puppy for Christmas!

10. _____ have it, I don't want it!

"Calcutta hole in this paper."

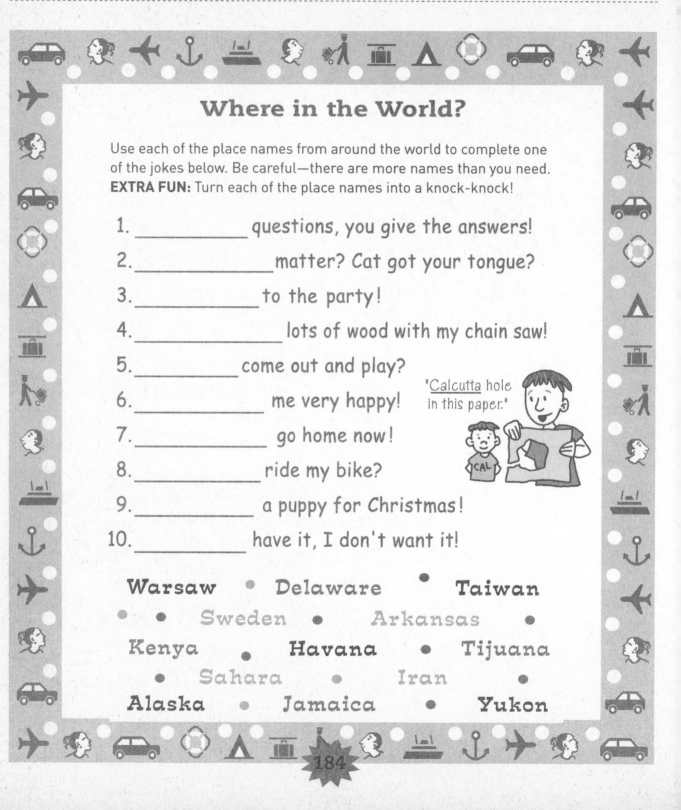

Warsaw • Delaware • **Taiwan**
• Sweden • Arkansas •
Kenya • **Havana** • Tijuana
• Sahara • Iran •
Alaska • Jamaica • **Yukon**

Knock knock!
Who's there?
Daryl.
Daryl who?
Daryl only be one chance!

Knock knock!
Who's there?
Tom.
Tom who?
Tom-ah-toes are yummy!

TRY THIS

Make Your Own Rain Catcher

Tape a ruler to the inside of a coffee can or small jar. Then set the jar outside the next time it rains. After the rain ends, you can measure how many of inches of rain have fallen during the rainstorm!

Knock knock!
Who's there?
Barry.
Barry who?
Barry sorry for the mix-up!

Knock knock!
Who's there?
Guava.
Guava who?
Guava good time!

Knock knock!
Who's there?
Ada.
Ada who?
Ada lot of candy
    and now I have a
    tummy ache!

Knock knock!
Who's there?
Minotaur.
Minotaur who?
Minotaur ready, we'll go!

Knock knock!
Who's there?
Vera.
Vera who?
Vera you going for dinner?

Knock knock!
Who's there?
Czar.
Czar who?
Czar-y about spilling the drink!

Knock knock!
Who's there?
Randy.
Randy who?
Ran-dy track twice!

Knock knock!
Who's there?
Waddle.
Waddle who?
Waddle you give me?

Words to Know

Spoof: A light and playful way of making fun of something. You might see a television show, a movie, or a play that's a spoof, or even read a story that spoofs something or someone.

Knock knock!
Who's there?
Illegals.
Illegals who?
Ill-egals stay in the nest till they're old enough to fly!

Knock knock!
Who's there?
Fission.
Fission who?
Fission for trout!

What's So Funny

Knock knock!
Who's there?
Wheelbarrow.
Wheelbarrow who?
Wheel-barrow the car and go for a ride!

HA HA HA HA HA

Knock knock!
Who's there?
Beehive.
Beehive who?
Beehive yourself or you'll get in trouble!

Knock knock!
Who's there?
Gwen.
Gwen who?
Gwen are we leaving?

Knock knock!
Who's there?
Thurston.
Thurston who?
Thurston for a milkshake!

Knock knock!
Who's there?
Honey.
Honey who?
Honey way home we'll stop for ice
    cream!

What am I?

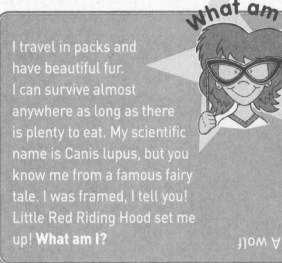

I travel in packs and have beautiful fur. I can survive almost anywhere as long as there is plenty to eat. My scientific name is Canis lupus, but you know me from a famous fairy tale. I was framed, I tell you! Little Red Riding Hood set me up! **What am I?**

A wolf

Knock knock!
Who's there?
Carl.
Carl who?
Carl get you there faster!

Knock knock!
Who's there?
Warner.
Warner who?
Warner lift to school?

Knock knock!
Who's there?
Farrah.
Farrah who?
Farrah 'nough!

What's So Funny

HA HA HA HA HA

Knock knock!
Who's there?
China.
China who?
**China tell you
something!**

A KNOCK HERE, A KNOCK THERE

Knock knock!
Who's there?
Egg.
Egg who?
Eggstremely cold!

Knock knock!
Who's there?
Andy.
Andy who?
He did it once, Andy did it again!

Knock knock!
Who's there?
Minnie.
Minnie who?
Minnie more miles to go!

Knock knock!
Who's there?
Eiffel.
Eiffel who?
Eiffel sick!

Knock knock!
Who's there?
Sybil.
Sybil who?
Sybil-ization!

Knock knock!
Who's there?
Curry.
Curry who?
Curry the package home!

Invent Your Own Animals

Look through some old magazines to see how many animal pictures you can find. Cut out the legs of a dog, the ears of a cat, the face of a chicken, the body of a giraffe, or whatever parts you want from the other animals that you see. Make your own combinations of the cut-outs, and come up with as many "new" animals as you can. Then give them all funny names, like "dogachickiraffe"! Now make up a story about where these types of creatures can be found, what they like to eat, and what strange habits they have!

Words to Know

Gag: A prank or joke that makes people laugh. Sometimes a comedian will have a running gag in the show (that means the same gag will be repeated over and over again). Running gags can also be part of television shows, movies, and plays.

Knock knock!
Who's there?
Duke.
Duke who?
Duke you come here often?

Knock knock!
Who's there?
Gladys.
Gladys who?
Gladys lunch time, I'm starved!

Knock knock!
Who's there?
Newark.
Newark who?
Newark for you when you finish the old work!

Knock knock!
Who's there?
Ears.
Ears who?
Ears looking at you, kid!

Knock knock!
Who's there?
Aretha.
Aretha who?
Aretha flowers for the door!

Knock knock!
Who's there?
Gecko.
Gecko who?
Gecko-ing or you'll be late!

Knock knock!
Who's there?
Grape.
Grape who?
Grape pie, can I have some more!

189

Knock knock!
Who's there?
Lacey.
Lacey who?
Lacey days of summer!

Knock knock!
Who's there?
Wafer.
Wafer who?
Wafer the bus!

Knock knock!
Who's there?
Enid.
Enid who?
Enid to take a nap!

What am I?

I look like a star in the sky but I live at the bottom of the sea. I'm tough on the outside and I've got a great talent: If I lose an arm I can easily grow a new one back! **What am I?**

A starfish

Knock knock!
Who's there?
Carrie.
Carrie who?
Carrie these boxes, they're not heavy!

Knock knock!
Who's there?
Tommy.
Tommy who?
My Tommy hurts from too much pie!

Knock knock!
Who's there?
Doughnut.
Doughnut who?
Doughnut be scared, it's only a joke!

FUN FACT

FREEZE FRAME

When you sneeze, all of your body functions stop—even your heart stops pumping for a moment. Whenever you sneeze, air rushes through your body at a rate of 100 miles per hour. And it's impossible to sneeze with your eyes open!

Do I Know You?

The letters in each column go in the squares directly below them, but not in the same order! Black squares are for punctuation and the spaces between the words. When you have correctly filled in the grid, you will have a silly conversation between two people on opposite sides of a door!

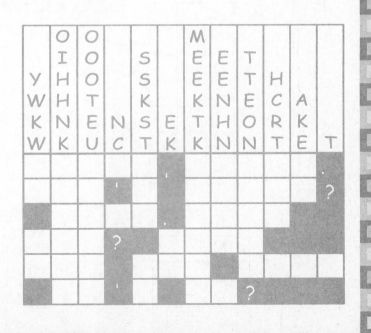

Who's there?

Hey! Open the door!

Don't Forget to Brush

See if you can fit all the words into their proper place in the grid. When you are finished, read down the center column to get the answer to this joke:

Knock, knock.

Who's there?

Tuba.

Tuba who?

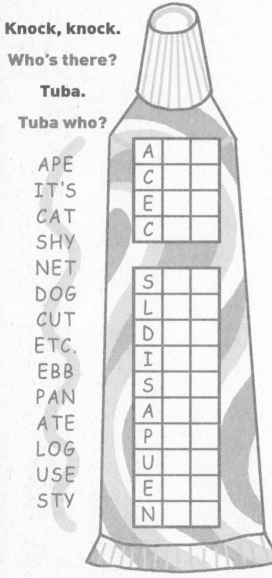

APE
IT'S
CAT
SHY
NET
DOG
CUT
ETC.
EBB
PAN
ATE
LOG
USE
STY

Knock knock!
Who's there?
Honeydew.
Honeydew who?
Honeydew-nuts are yummy!

Knock knock!
Who's there?
Congo.
Congo who?
Congo out, I'm grounded!

Knock knock!
Who's there?
Woodstock.
Woodstock who?
Woodstock up on food if I were you!

Knock knock!
Who's there?
Lorraine.
Lorraine who?
Lorraine is falling and I'm getting
    soaked!

Knock knock!
Who's there?
Daisy.
Daisy who?
Daisy goes to school, nights he sleeps!

Knock knock!
Who's there?
Bored.
Bored who?
Bored of education!

Knock knock!
Who's there?
Fresno.
Fresno who?
Fresno fun when he's angry!

Knock knock!
Who's there?
Beezer.
Beezer who?
Beezer black
    and yellow!

A Neighborhood Scrapbook

Go on a nature walk in your neighbor-
hood. See how many different types of
flowers and animals you can identify.
When you get home, look for pictures of
the flowers and animals in magazines.
Cut out some of these. Then paste the
pictures onto construction paper. Punch
holes in the construction paper and tie
the pages together with a ribbon.

What am I?

I live in the forest and I make loud noises with my beak when I find a tree with lots of tasty bugs in it. You can't mistake my sound. You may know my uncle—he's a funny cartoon character named Woody. **What am I?**

A woodpecker

Knock knock!
Who's there?
Seville.
Seville who?
Seville you come to the dance?

Knock knock!
Who's there?
Topeka.
Topeka who?
Topeka apples you
    have to go to the orchard!

Knock knock!
Who's there?
Hominy.
Hominy who?
Hominy times do I have to tell you?

Knock knock!
Who's there?
Tarzan.
Tarzan who?
Tarzan stripes!

Knock knock!
Who's there?
Moose.
Moose who?
Moose have been a long night!

Knock knock!
Who's there?
Disk.
Disk who?
Disk is a holdup,
    put your hands in the air!

Words to Know

Whimsical: Light or funny. Many things are whimsical. For example, knock-knock jokes are pretty whimsical! Stage-acting with a lot of clowning around is pretty whimsical too.

Knock knock!
Who's there?
Malcolm.
Malcolm who?
Malcolm it took you so long to answer the door?

Knock knock!
Who's there?
Walrus.
Walrus who?
Why do you walrus ask so many questions?

Knock knock!
Who's there?
Les.
Les who?
Les-sons to be learned!

Knock knock!
Who's there?
Garden.
Garden who?
Garden the secret treasure!

Knock knock!
Who's there?
Value.
Value who?
Value come to the park with me?

Knock knock!
Who's there?
Iona.
Iona who?
Iona TV set!

Knock knock!
Who's there?
Dozen.
Dozen who?
Dozen anyone know who I am?

What's So Funny

HA
HA
HA
HA
HA

Knock knock!
Who's there?
Burden.
Burden who?
Burden the tree is singing!

FUN FACT

JUST FOUR

There are thousands of words in the English language, but there are only four that end with "dous." Can you guess them? They are tremendous, horrendous, stupendous, and hazardous.

Knock knock!
Who's there?
Disguise.
Disguise who?
Disguise the limit!

Knock knock!
Who's there?
Arf.
Arf who?
Arf-a-got!

Knock knock!
Who's there?
Oil.
Oil who?
Oil we do is tell knock-knock jokes!

Knock knock!
Who's there?
Hallways.
Hallways who?
Hallways running off somewhere!

Knock knock!
Who's there?
Irish.
Irish who?
I-rish I had lots of money!

Knock knock!
Who's there?
Tibet.
Tibet who?
Early Tibet,
    early to rise!

Knock knock!
Who's there?
Rex.
Rex who?
Rex-taurant's just down the road!

Part Three

RIDDLES & BRAIN TEASERS

YOU MAY HAVE COME TO know riddles and brain teasers as a great way to get a good laugh, or maybe to challenge a friend. You may even like to challenge yourself with these riddles. But did you know that thousands of years ago, people just like you were interested in a good riddle or puzzle, too?

Some were interested for different reasons than others, depending on their needs. For instance, one of the first uses for a riddle was to "secretly" carry a message from one person to another—a quiz of sorts that only you knew the answer to, and hopefully the person on the other end would be smart enough to solve or figure out. Unfortunately, not everyone was. For example, one of the most famous riddles of all time was that of Samson from the Bible. As a challenge, Samson tried to trick the Philistines with a riddle about honey. Frustrated and angry, the people decided to solve the riddle of Samson's strength instead. When they discovered the answer, they removed his hair, took away his strength, and defeated him.

Many of the words or expressions in our world are forms of these earlier riddles and brain teasers. Take your name, for example. Did you know that your name has a hidden meaning? The stories behind both our first and last names are usually more than meet the eye. Entire books have been written to explain the original meanings behind any first name. Last names are usually easier to guess, as people used to "sneak" what they did for a living into their last name, such as Smith (for blacksmith or goldsmith) and Wagoner. Or, they would use their father's name and then add the word "son" on the end, as in Johnson and Peterson. And middle names? Well, they hid your family lineage by using your mother's maiden name for your middle name.

Puzzling maybe, but there's more: Do you know which famous author secretly fooled a great number of readers by using his last name spelled backward? Actually, his last name was Geisel, and when he wrote it backward, it became Lesieg . . . but he became famous through his middle name. Do you know what it was? Suess! Authors aren't the only tricksters. Artists and actors, musicians and entertainers also like to challenge us to try to figure out the sometimes-tough riddle of who they are. Or better yet, who they were.

Almost everyone loves a good mystery or puzzle, and puzzles are a fun way of exercising your brain and testing your friends' skills as well. Best of all, riddles and brain teasers are there to be enjoyed. So, prepare to be tricked, tested, riddled, and teased until you can't take any more—and have fun!

TIME FOR SCHOOL

Words to Know

Brain Teaser: A question or test used to tease and entertain our brains. Some types of brain teasers also stimulate our funny bones. These popular little puzzles or mysteries have been around for a long time.

Why do scissors cut in a line?
They can't stand to wait.

What did Mary tell her little lamb?
Ewe cannot be at school.

Where do elementary school teachers like to go sailing?
Out on the AB seas.

Why couldn't O go to the game?
Because it was too busy minding its Ps and Qs.

How did all the school supplies find their way out of the classroom?
They used the compass.

Which grade keeps the best time?
"Second" grade.

The school janitor has **100 keys** on his ring and can't remember which key opens the front door. What are the odds that he'll find it the first time? **Bonus:** What if he tries 2 keys?

1 in 100. Bonus: The odds are twice as good!

When Johnny **Falls** brought his plant to school for an experiment, nothing he tried could make it grow. Do you know why? **Hint:** His name is part of the clue.

It was fake ("false")

On Tuesday, little **Tommy** was asked to write I AM SORRY FOR WHAT I DID **50** times on a sheet of paper. The last time he was in trouble, he had to write it out **100** times. What do you think about his two offenses?

What he did on Tuesday was only half as bad as what he did the last time

Do you know which letter of the alphabet comes before **R? L? A?**

Q, K, nothing

199

TRY THIS

Count Me Crazy

Can you count backward from 100 by 6's? It would go like this: 100, 94, 88, 82, 76, 70, 64, 58, 52, 46, 40, 34, 28, 22, 16, 10, 4. Now, try counting backward by 5's, only this time see if you can count backward while walking backward! Careful now, you should be somewhere safe and in the open for this one!

If Carter Elementary School has **2** front doors, **2** back doors, **3** bathroom doors, and **7** classroom doors, how many doors are there "in" the school?

15, counting the indoors

When **Maddy** started school, she was **5** years old. Now that she is in third grade, she is only **6**. How can that be? **Hint:** Maddy's birthday is in February.

Maddy's birthday is on February 29 (it comes only once every 4 years, in a leap year)

What is a wizard's favorite subject?
Spell-ing.

Why is a ruler the most stubborn of your school supplies?
Because it's very narrow-minded.

Why was the English book following the math book around?
He was studying him.

Why did the pair of safety scissors fail her cutting test?
She didn't get the point.

When the police officers arrived at the scene of the crime, how did they know that the numbers, not the letters, were innocent?
It just didn't add up.

Words to Know

Riddle: A question or event of puzzling nature that requires you to think of an answer. Some riddles are a type of joke. Other riddles are really challenging.

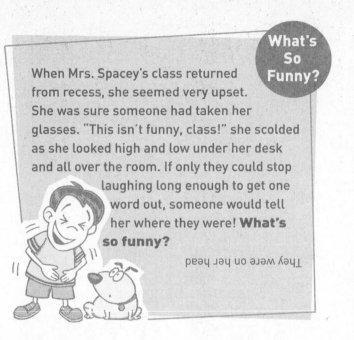

What's So Funny?

When Mrs. Spacey's class returned from recess, she seemed very upset. She was sure someone had taken her glasses. "This isn't funny, class!" she scolded as she looked high and low under her desk and all over the room. If only they could stop laughing long enough to get one word out, someone would tell her where they were! **What's so funny?**

They were on her head

For an entire week the students in **Mr. Wilson's** science class participated in an experiment to see how many hairs you lose from your head each day. After **1 week** of brushing, the average was around **100** hairs per day. Yet Mr. Wilson's brush was clean. Do you know why?

He was bald

Jennifer's teacher has **17** students in her class. When a new student arrived, she had to change the tables in her room. She used to have **2** medium tables, seating **5**, and **1** large table, seating **7**. Now, if she can also get small tables seating **3**, which tables will she need and how many of them?

Either 3 medium tables and 1 small, or 1 large, 1 medium, and 2 small

During recess, **Alexia** and her friends like to make up codes. Her favorite code uses the letter of the alphabet that comes right after the letter that it actually stands for. Using her code, can you figure out what she wrote in this message?

J MPWF CSBJO UFBTFST

I LOVE BRAIN TEASERS

FUN FACT

BRAIN POWER

The brain is a mass of tissue located inside your head. Your brain serves as central command control. It's the center of your nervous system and regulates your thoughts, emotions, and the functions of your body.

Why why did did the the history history teacher teacher say say every every thing thing twice twice?
Because history repeats itself.

What is a snake's favorite part of school?
Recessssssss!

Do you know why the chalk was always yawning?
It was "board."

What will you never find at the end of class?
The head of the class.

Which insect does the best in English class?
The spelling bee.

What do you call a group of strange numbers?
Odd.

There are **30** students in Jake's class. Fifteen of the students have brown hair, **10** of them are blond, and **5** have red hair. If all of the brown-haired students and half of the blonde-haired students have brown eyes, and all of the rest of them have green eyes, how many more students have **brown** eyes than **green**?

Ten more

"Well," said **Mrs. Ray**. "I see **5** people wore ponytails to school today." "Don't you mean **4**, Mrs. Ray?" asked Hannah. Why does Hannah think there are only **4**?

She has forgotten to count herself

Toby likes to climb up the slide at recess. Every time he climbs up **5** feet, he slides back down **2**. How many times does he need to climb up for him to reach 9 feet?

3 times

Rhyme—No Reason

Do you know how many letters in the alphabet rhyme with the letter B? Eight—C, D, E, G, P, T, V, and Z. Now try making a list of words for your family or friends to try to find a rhyme for. If you want to try an experiment on them, give them 2 sets of lists to try to memorize. One set has 8 words that rhyme, while the other has 8 that do not. Which list will be easier for them to remember?

Bad Band

Begin by writing as many answers as you can under the clues. Then, enter each letter into its numbered box in the answer grid (one has been done for you). Continue working back and forth between the clues and the grid. When you are finished, you will have the answer to the following riddle:

Why was the music teacher so angry during class each day?

1 E	2 F	3 H	4 F	5 A U	6 B	7 E		8 F	9 G	10 D
	11 E	12 C	13 C	14 G	15 G	16 A N	17 I	18 C		
19 F	20 C	21 D	22 H		23 B	24 H	25 I	26 H	27 B	28 D
	29 B	30 I	31 F	32 I	33 G	34 C	35 E			
36 H	37 B	38 D	39 D	40 A S !						

A. The center of our solar system

$\underset{40}{S} \ \underset{5}{U} \ \underset{16}{N}$

B. Covered with soap

$\overline{6} \ \overline{37} \ \overline{23} \ \overline{29} \ \overline{27}$

C. Melodies

$\overline{12} \ \overline{13} \ \overline{34} \ \overline{20} \ \overline{18}$

D. Many of these make a forest

$\overline{38} \ \overline{21} \ \overline{10} \ \overline{39} \ \overline{28}$

E. Pleads

$\overline{1} \ \overline{7} \ \overline{35} \ \overline{11}$

F. Your skin will do this on a hot day

$\overline{31} \ \overline{19} \ \overline{2} \ \overline{4} \ \overline{8}$

G. To put out of sight

$\overline{9} \ \overline{33} \ \overline{14} \ \overline{15}$

H. Opposite of dirty

$\overline{3} \ \overline{24} \ \overline{22} \ \overline{26} \ \overline{36}$

I. How you hit a fly

$\overline{32} \ \overline{25} \ \overline{30} \ \overline{17}$

On the playground, **Travis** sees an amazing swing set with **20** swings. While he watches his friends swing, he realizes that as the first swing swings **forward**, the second one swings **back**, the third one swings **forward**, and so on. Which way is the eleventh one swinging?

Forward

For **Erin's** birthday, her mother brought cookies to school. Erin's class has **17** students and **1** teacher, but **3** children were sick that day and **1** went to the dentist. If her mother brought **30** cookies, how many **cookies** did everyone receive?

2 (2 for each child, 2 for the teacher, and 2 for Erin's mother)

TRY THIS

Writing Riddles and Brain Teasers

You can write brain teasers and riddles backward, by taking the punchline, or answer, and adding a question to the beginning of it. For example, using the phrase "This is the pits!" you can add the question, "What did one cherry say to the other when he knew it was the end?"

Shelby has a box of **32** crayons. All of her friends have boxes of **8** crayons. If she shares her crayons so that she and all **5** of her friends have an equal number of colors, how many **crayons** will she give to each of her friends?

4 crayons

Who am I?

It's my job to ask the puzzling questions, and it's the contestant's job to pick the right answers and win the million dollars. Sometimes, the contestant chooses to phone a friend. **Who am I?**

The host of Who Wants to Be a Millionaire?

Ian likes math class. One day the teacher asks him if he can think of any way that **1 + 1** could equal **1**. Ian was stumped. But in a few minutes, he could think of several ways. Can **you** think of any?

1 person + 1 hamburger, 1 spider + 1 fly, 1 cat + 1 bowl of milk, and so on

A Sloppy Subject

Color in each letter below that appears four times. Collect the uncolored letters from left to right and top to bottom, and write them in the spaces. When you're finished, you'll have the answer to this riddle:

When should kids wear bibs in school?

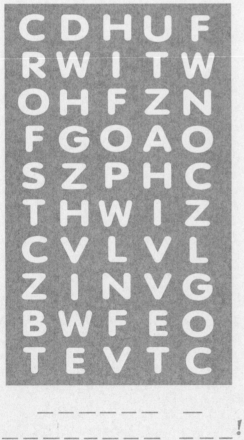

C	D	H	U	F
R	W	I	T	W
O	H	F	Z	N
F	G	O	A	O
S	Z	P	H	C
T	H	W	I	Z
C	V	L	V	L
Z	I	N	V	G
B	W	F	E	O
T	E	V	T	C

_ _ _ _ _ _ _ _

_ _ _ _ _ _ _ _ _ _!

What did one test say to the other?
My life is an open book.

Why did the capital letters have to stay away from the lowercase letters?
They couldn't see "I" to "i" (eye to eye).

How did the playground win the ball game?
The swing swung and the slide slid into home!

What does the alphabet do at the end of the day?
Catch a few more ZZZZZ's.

How did the tooth fairy do in school?
Fairy well.

Why did the fish have to leave school?
He was feeling "eel."

For **Robbie's** class party, the students played musical chairs. Each time the music stopped, Robbie moved over **3** chairs. There were **27** chairs in the circle. How many times did the **music stop** before Robbie was back in his own seat?

9 times

205

FUN FACT

WE'RE BRAINIACS

Our brains are made up of billions of cells. And although our brains are a larger part of our bodies compared to most other animals, size has little to do with intelligence. Studies have proven that someone with a small brain can actually be smarter than someone with a larger brain.

The monkey bars at **Bobby's** school have **11** bars. If Bobby starts with his right hand on the very first bar, and he skips every other bar as he swings across, while he is changing hands with every other swing, which of his hands will end up on bar **11**? Which one will end up on bar **5**?

His left hand will be on bar 11 and his right on bar 5

Each year **Mrs. Jones's** students bring her apples for the first day of class. Mrs. Jones likes to take the apples home and make pies out of them. If everyone in her class of **21** brings her an apple and it takes **7** apples to make a pie, how many **pies** can she make?

3 pies

What's the difference between **124** and **12**?

The number 4

When Bill added **5** and **5** together, his answer was an **X**. How can that be?

He was using Roman numerals: V + V = X

Color Me In!

206

Who am I?

I was one of the first doctors who started to understand the role of the brain in thinking. The Hippocratic Oath was named after me. **Who am I?**

Hippocrates

Did the math teacher know he would win the annual math contest?
He was counting on it.

Why was the calendar so scared?
His days were numbered.

What kind of school isn't in the front and isn't in the back?
A middle school.

What school did Sherlock Holmes attend?
Elementary, my dear Watson, elementary.

Where do teachers grow their flowers?
In the kinder-gardens.

Why did the computer teacher leave a trap in his room?
Because of the mouse problem.

The most exciting day at **Greenfield School** was the day that the magician came. Everyone could hardly wait for the amazing "pulling the rabbit out of the hat" trick. At the beginning of the show, **Merlin the Mystifying** placed the rabbit in the hat. At the end of the show, even Merlin was amazed. Not only did he pull 1 rabbit out of his hat—he pulled out **6 more!** How could that be?

The mother rabbit had 6 bunnies

Do You Know Your ZYX's?

Can you say the alphabet backward? Z, Y, X, W, V, U, T, S, R, Q, P, O, N, M, L, K, J, I, H, G, F, E, D, C, B, and A. How about an extra added twist? This time, try it while you are listening to music or TV at the same time. Concentration or the lack of it can affect how well we think and learn.

Beth has an unusual talent. She can walk backward for miles. Some days she even walks to school **backward**. If it takes her longer to get there, how much farther is it to **school**?

It isn't any farther—it just takes longer

What would happen if you **8** and **8**?

You'd get a very full stomach (ate and ate)

Math Class

Look at the fraction below each blank. Pick the shape that shows that fraction, using these rules:

• The white part of each shape is empty.
• The shaded part of each shape is full.

Write the letter of that shape on the line. When you are finished, you will have the answer to this riddle:

What do you get when you add 2 bananas, 1 apple, 15 grapes, and ¹/₂ melon?

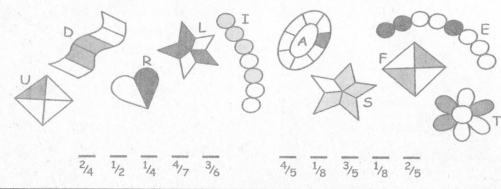

$$\frac{2}{4} \quad \frac{1}{2} \quad \frac{1}{4} \quad \frac{4}{7} \quad \frac{3}{6} \qquad \frac{4}{5} \quad \frac{1}{8} \quad \frac{3}{5} \quad \frac{1}{8} \quad \frac{2}{5}$$

Words to Know

Puzzle: A type of test or challenge sometimes used to confuse someone. Often puzzles are used for learning in school settings, such as language or math lessons. Other types of puzzles are actually objects or games.

In **Mrs. Sharpe's** class, each student has **1** writing instrument, either a pen or a pencil. If there are **21** students in her class and **1/3** use a pen, how many **pencils** are there in class?

14 pencils

As **Elizabeth** wrote the date on her paper, she realized it read **04-04-04**. All three numbers were the same! How many more **years** can this happen in a row?

8 more, until 12-12-12

What did the paper say to the scissors when they kept poking him?
Cut it out!

What did the numbers call the new room in their house?
Their addition.

Why do rabbits do so well in school?
They like to multiply.

What do you get when you put 2 500-pound elephants on a teeter-totter?
A broken teeter-totter!

Why did everyone think their teacher was so special?
She had a lot of "class."

What do you call numerals that don't feel anything?
"Numb"ers.

Why didn't the pencil do well on his test?
He wasn't very sharp.

IT'S A ZOO

Just for fun, **Cassie** taught her cat Freddie sign language. One day the cat tapped on the window (a sign for **"bird"**), tapped his tail on the wall (a sign for **"mouse"**), and jumped into the tub to swim (a sign for **"fish"**). What was Freddie trying to tell Cassie?

"I'm hungry."

When the **circus** comes to town Bobby always goes to see it. His favorite part is when the elephants build a pyramid. "Can you believe it?" asks the announcer. "A record **21 ELEPHANTS**!" Amazed, Bobby starts counting: 1 on top, 2 below it, 3 more below them, and so on. If the announcer is right, how many elephants will be on the **bottom** row?

6 elephants

Words to Know

Joke: A joke is an act or statement that causes laughter. Funny riddles are a type of joke.

What do you call 2 half rabbits put together?
A rabbit "whole."

What do you call a really strange ant-eater?
An "odd-vark."

Why did the stallion need a cough drop?
He was hoarse.

What Beatles song do fish everywhere love?
"Twist and Trout."

What do you get when you cross Sir Lancelot with a horse?
A "knight-mare."

What did one cat call the other when he wouldn't play fair?
Cheetah!

FUN FACT

TICKLE ME FUN

Did you know it is impossible for you to tickle yourself? It's true; one of the things needed in tickling is the element of surprise—not expecting to be tickled. Not sure? Try it for yourself.

What is **bald** but has its head covered?

The bald eagle

Which one of these **does not belong** to the set? Lion, tiger, elephant, and polar bear.

The elephant, because he has no fur

When a small **campground** was robbed last week, the police brought the only witness in for a line-up. All of the **animals** were brought in and placed in a line. When it came time for the witness to point out the bandit, she said she couldn't be sure which one had done it, because the robber looked like he was wearing a **mask**. Do you know who it was?

The raccoon

One night **Tommy** had a bad dream. There was a bull chasing him all around the arena, but just as the **bull** was about to ram him, Tommy got away. Do you know how?

He woke up

Which one of these **does not belong** in the group—shark, whale, and swordfish?

The whale, because it's a mammal

Egg is to **chicken** as acorn is to what?

A tree

TRY THIS

An Anagram of Your Own

Have you ever tried to make your own anagrams? An anagram is a word or phrase formed by recording the letters of another word or phrase, like "late" and "tale." How many anagrams can you and your friends come up with?

Loop the Zoo!

Find the path through the zoo that takes Zack to three of his favorite animals. Along the way, collect the letters that spell out three different answers to this riddle: What goes black, white, black, white, black, white?

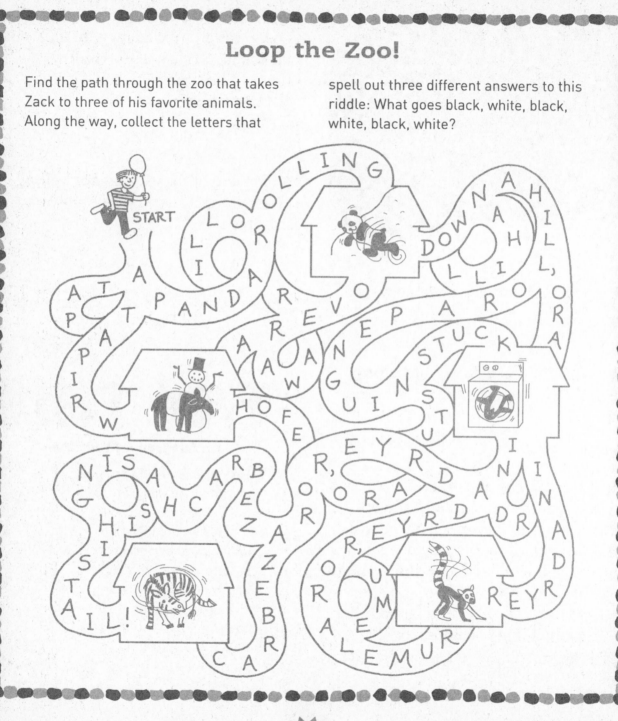

Where does a mother robin keep her money?
In a nest egg.

What do cows do for fun?
They go to the "moo-vies."

How do sheep go to sleep?
They count people.

Why was the cow so excited when a horse moved in next door?
He had never had a "neigh-bor" before.

What was the last thing the frog did before he jumped?
He croaked.

What time is it when you sit on your cat?
Time to get a new one.

Words to Know

Pun: A pun is a play on words using two meanings of the same word or two words that sound the same but are spelled differently. For example, the word "sew" in the following joke: "Why do I have to?" the little sewing machine asked his mother. "Because I said SEW!" she replied.

Andrew has amazing pets. His dogs and cats would get along, but they **eat** each other's food. How does Andrew keep this from happening?

He feeds the dogs during the day, while the cats are sleeping; he feeds the cats during the night, while the dogs are asleep

Take a look at the following sentence: **"Ants** busily crawl, doing everything **fast."** What's special about it?

The words are in alphabetical order by first letter

Fish swim and **birds** fly, but does it ever happen the other way around? Do birds ever **swim** and do fish ever **fly**? Can you think of any examples?

Penguins swim; flying fish can fly for short periods of time

What do horses have at night?
"Night-mares."

What do you call 2 insects that raise their young?
"Pair-ants."

Why did the fox sell his fur?
Because he "pelt" like it.

Why does the duck walk everywhere he goes?
Because he can't drive.

Why shouldn't you make a tired canine tell the truth?
Because you're supposed to let sleeping dogs lie.

Do possums really hang upside down from trees all night?
It's a "possum-bility."

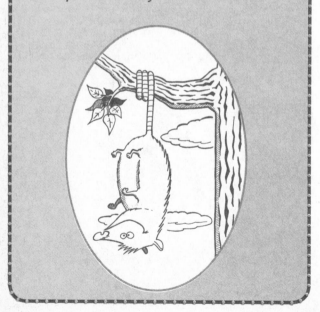

AN APRIL 1 TRADITION

Are you an April Fool? Being foolish is a tradition given to us long ago. Back then, the New Year was celebrated from March 21 to April 1. When it was decided the New Year should start on January 1, anyone who celebrated the old date became an April Fool.

One day, **cows** from the Busy "B" ranch and cows from the Lazy "1" ranch got all mixed up. The ranch **cowboys** were confused. How can they tell the cows **apart** in order to separate them?

Most cows are branded, so they should look for a "B" or a "1" brand on each cow

When the **circus** came to town, everyone was surprised—even the lion tamer, as he discovered **7** new lion cubs in the lion cage. Before long, everyone agreed it would be best to separate the feisty **cubs**. But how? Then the ringmaster had an idea: "I know a way you can place **3** large rings to make **7** sections, one for each cub." Do you know how to do that?

Place the first 2 rings so that one slightly overlaps the other—that's 3 sections; then, place the third ring in the center of the 2, to make 7 sections

Who am I?

I work all day turning letters to help our contestants try to solve a riddle. Not only do they have a "wheely" good time, but they also have a chance to win a "fortune." **Who am I?**

Vanna White from Wheel of Fortune

What do you get when you wake a sleeping bear?
Trouble!

What are three words you never say to a raccoon?
Coonskin cap.

What do you call a really picky cat?
A "paw-ticular" feline.

How can you tell when a polar bear is moving?
There's a "fur sale" sign in the yard.

What do you give to a 500-pound alligator when he knocks at your door?
Anything he wants.

How do fish finish their floors?
They "carp it."

Say What?

On each line, add the first and last letter to complete the name of the animal that is suggested by what that animal is saying. Then, read DOWN the shaded column to answer this riddle:

What is it that camels have that no other animals have?

_RA_	"I'm grouchy!"
AND	"Where's the bamboo?"
_U_	"I'll grow up to be a big bear!"
ONKE	"Got a banana?"
_RO_	"-odile is the last part of my name!"
YEN	"Ha, Ha, Ha!"
_OR_	"You won't like me in your apple!"
NAK	"What'ssssss up?"
_W_	"Whoooo's there?"
_AT_	"Turn out the light! We like the dark!"

Take the Laughing Test

How do you think you would do on a laughing test? To try the challenge, record someone laughing, then play back the tape to see if you can keep from laughing yourself. They say laughter is contagious. Can you come up with laughing tests of your own?

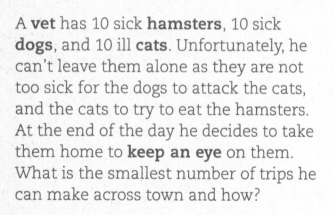

A **vet** has 10 sick **hamsters**, 10 sick **dogs**, and 10 ill **cats**. Unfortunately, he can't leave them alone as they are not too sick for the dogs to attack the cats, and the cats to try to eat the hamsters. At the end of the day he decides to take them home to **keep an eye** on them. What is the smallest number of trips he can make across town and how?

2: On the first trip he takes the cats and on the second trip he takes the dogs and the hamsters

What do **stripes, mane, tail,** and **hooves** have in common?

They're all traits of a zebra

Which **creature** doesn't belong—**wasp, bee, spider, or ant**?

The spider—it's an arthropod, not an insect

Birds and fish are to **worms** as cats and snakes are to **what**?

Mice—birds and fish eat worms; cats and snakes eat mice

What do you call a sleeping baby goat?
A "kid napping."

What happens when you blend a reptile with a back street?
You get an "alley-gator."

What travels faster than the speed of dog?
A cat!

Why was the rabbit so excited about her engagement ring?
It was 5 carrots!

Why did they take Polly away?
She went crackers!

What did the giraffe say when he bent down to talk to the fish?
LONG time no sea.

Feel Better

A riddle and its answer were put into the large grid, and then cut into eight pieces. See if you can figure out where each piece goes, and write the letters in their proper places. When you have filled the grid in correctly, you will be able to read the puzzle from left to right, and top to bottom. **HINT:** The black boxes stand for the spaces between words.

When **Mini's** family pulled up at the motel, Mini, her parents, and **12** brothers and sisters poured out of the car. How **could** that happen?

Mini and her family are mice.

What do a **shark,** a **mouse,** and a **mole** have in common?

All of their babies are called "pups."

FUN FACT

A HUMAN SURVIVAL GUIDE

Over time people have studied how the human brain and body work together. One thing your brain knows is that you need at least 5 things to survive—water, food, oxygen, shelter, and clothing.

The minute **Rastus** laid eyes on the rattlesnake, it lunged at him, but it could not bite the **boy**. Can you guess **why?**

Rastus was at a zoo and the snake was behind glass

Where do hogs go when they need a loan?
To the piggy bank.

What did one mouse say to the other mouse who held the door open for him?
Why, that was very "mice" of you!

What did one python say to the other before they made a deal?
Let's "snake" on it.

Why did the cub get in trouble with his mother?
She caught him "lion."

Why couldn't the dog say, "Ahhh"?
Because the cat got his tongue.

What's So Funny?

When Ted arrived home one evening, he was startled by a bear in his yard! After his initial panic, he stopped and breathed a sigh of relief. The bear was no danger to him at all! **What's so funny?**

The bear was stuffed

218

TRAVEL THE WORLD

Words to Know

Enigma: An enigma is a phrase or question that is confusing or hard to understand. Enigmas or riddles have been used throughout time to test one's ability to solve a puzzle or mystery.

When the **storm** hit and the **plane** attempted to land, everyone in the air and on the ground was speechless. Yet somehow they **communicated** the directions to land. How?

They used signals

What do the **stop light, fire truck,** and **stop sign** have in common?

They're all red

When **Anna's** family decided to take a vacation, everyone wanted to go. So Anna, her **mom** and **dad**, her two **brothers**, their **Aunt** Lucille, their **Uncle** Ed, and **Grandma** rode the bus together all the way from New York to California and back again. How many **people** in all made the trip?

9, including the bus driver

How did the snow pile get across the sea?
It went a-drift.

What did the P. E. teacher ride in to the ball?
A coach.

How did the train engine know he was lost?
He was on the wrong side of the tracks.

How long does it take for a person to fly to Chicago?
People can't fly, silly!

What kind of water greets you?
An ocean wave.

What does a train say when it has a cold?
Ahhh Choo-Choo!

Who am I?

There was no mystery I could not solve. All I needed was a magnifying glass and my good friend. It's elementary, my dear. **Who am I?**

Sherlock Holmes

What do you call an imaginary yacht?
A dream boat.

How did the dentist get across the river?
With a "tooth ferry."

How do you fasten a railroad track together?
With a railroad tie.

What do you call an angry ship?
A steamed boat.

When does a truck sleep?
When it gets "tire-d."

What is the opposite of a put-down?
A pick-up.

When **Juan's** plane left the ground it was **2 P.M.** After flying for **2** hours, it landed—but the clocks at the airport showed that it was *still* **2 P.M.** How can this be?

The airplane flew through 2 time zones

If **three** friends moved to the same town, and one lived on **E-X** Avenue, while another lived on **E-Y** Road, where does the third one live?

E-Z Street

What **doesn't** belong? Snow skis, Jet Ski, bus, motorcycle.

The Jet Ski—it's the only one that doesn't travel on land

FUN FACT

LAUGHING OUT LOUD

Did you know that the older you get, the less you laugh? Babies laugh on and off all day long, while someone who is older may laugh only once a day. Now, make sure you don't miss your chance to laugh your head off!

Do you know what a watch does on vacation?
Time travel.

What did the space travelers eat on their flight?
Astro-nuts.

What's the last thing you see when a train goes by?
Its tracks.

Why wouldn't the police officer cross the road?
Because the light wasn't green.

Why did the army sergeant's car die?
Because its "tank" was empty.

What do accountants ride in?
A "tax-i."

Ike the famous bike rider pedaled for hours on his bike only to find that he was right back where he started. **What's so funny?**

He was on his exercise bike at the gym.

What **doesn't belong** in this list? Pen, paper, spatula, notebook.

spatula

Joey and his sister **Hannah** like to play "I Spy" when they travel in the car. They decide that this time the first person who "spies" the most legs on the trip wins! Joey sees 2 **deer**, 11 cows, 2 **cats**, and a spider. Hannah sees 1 turkey, 7 **cows**, 3 sheep, and 4 **cats**. Who won?

Joey with 68 to Hannah's 58

Words to Know

Amusement: What people do or use in order to entertain themselves or someone else. Silly or fun things are used to amuse people every day.

The class was really **puzzled** when the teacher asked them: "When can you see through the **desert**?" Do you know?

When it is heated to almost 3,000 degrees and the sand becomes glass

Funny Flight

"I just flew home from Paris, and..."

First, figure out what word each picture puzzle represents. Then put the words in the proper order to finish what this silly traveler is saying. Write the numbers in the upper left-hand corner of each picture.

What did the thief get when he stole the tram?
Bus-ted!

What does an elephant always take on safari?
His trunk.

What do girl scouts put on their S'mores when they camp at the swamp?
"Marsh"mallows.

Where does dinnerware go on vacation?
To China.

As **Mrs. Rockefeller** was leaving the airport, she found herself accidentally trapped in the revolving **glass doors**. She had no luggage, no tools, and nobody was around. She eventually made a **hole** and escaped. How? **Hint: Her name.**

She cut a hole in the glass with her diamond ring

No matter how long the new department **store clerk** walked down the stairs, he could never seem to reach the basement. **Why?**

He was walking down the "up" escalator

Where in the World?

First unscramble the names of eight different places around the world. Then match each one to a riddle to discover eight popular vacation spots!

1. Where do fish go on vacation?
2. Where do songbirds go on vacation?
3. Where do zombies go on vacation?
4. Where do Thanksgiving birds go on vacation?
5. Where do geometry teachers go on vacation?
6. Where do locksmiths go on vacation?

nliFnad   *hTe ranCay nsIlsad*

eruTky   *ehT edaD aSe*

auCb   *heT arlFoid seKy*

Who am I?

I am the brains behind Garfield's intelligent tricks. I also try to help Odie think of ways to get back at him. I have been "drawn" to fun for years.
Who am I?

Jim Davis

Sydney and Sadie are cousins. One day, Sydney and Sadie went on vacation to Japan. Sadie's flight took 7 hours while Sydney's took 33. Both flights were nonstop and Sydney and Sadie both left home at the same time from the same city in California. How can this be?

Sadie's plane flew west; Sydney's plane flew east

If flying to California takes **1½** hours, and flying to Texas takes **2**, and flying to Hawaii takes **twice as long** as a trip to both places, how long is your flight to Hawaii?

7 hours

What **vehicle** travels over the **ground** at speeds much **faster** than a car but can also go through mountains?

A train

Where do skydivers put their laundry?
In the "para-chute."

What did the child say to the captain when their boat hit rough waters?
I can't steer this, "canoe"?

Where do restless travelers like to go?
To Rome.

What place do worms like to visit the most?
The Big Apple.

What is one way to save money when you go to the lake?
Buy a "sale boat."

TRY THIS

Stare Me Down

Have you ever tried having a stare down contest? It's fun and easy. All you need is a friend and a lot of concentration. While sitting straight across from your friend, your challenge is to see who can stare into the other person's eyes the longest without blinking or laughing. It's that easy . . . or is it?

Why did the plant get lost on its trip?
It took the wrong "root."

How does a baby beetle get around?
In a buggy.

What do you call it when a highway stumbles?
A road trip.

How does milk travel around?
In a "car ton."

What does a skunk's car run on?
Fumes.

How does Robin Hood get from here to there?
In an "arrow plane."

If April showers bring May flowers, what do May flowers bring?

Pilgrims

What can **travel** all over the world, without anyone **seeing** it?

The wind

What do the **words** yield, walk, merge, and slow have in **common?**

They're all street signs

FUN FACT

A HYPO WHAT?

The hypothalamus gland in your brain is the reason you can laugh or find some things funny. It also controls your other emotions. One other interesting thing the hypothalamus does is remind your brain to stay awake.

The Hungry Traveler

The following riddle is missing 12 important letters! See if you can fit the letters from the box into the correct blanks. To create an ending that fits this silly story, unscramble the letters in the second box, and fit them into the blanks. **HINT:** You will use some of the letters more than once!

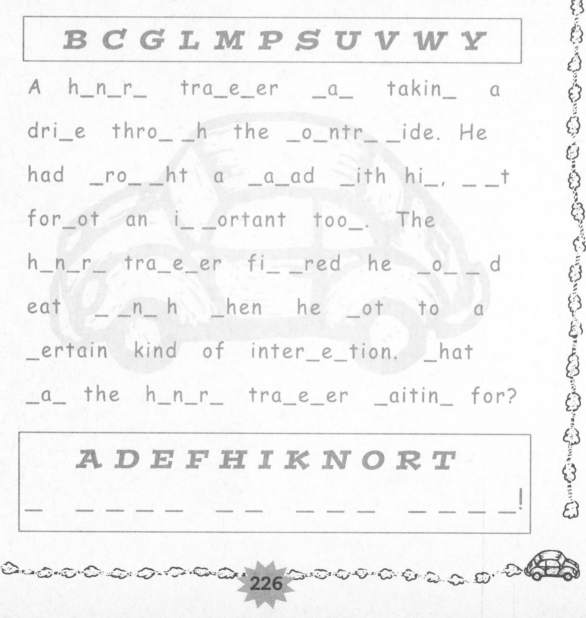

B C G L M P S U V W Y

A h_n_r_ tra_e_er _a_ takin_ a dri_e thro_ _h the _o_ntr_ _ide. He had _ro_ _ht a _a_ad _ith hi_, _ _t for_ot an i_ _ortant too_. The h_n_r_ tra_e_er fi_ _red he _o_ _d eat _ _n_h _hen he _ot to a _ertain kind of inter_e_tion. _hat _a_ the h_n_r_ tra_e_er _aitin_ for?

A D E F H I K N O R T

_ _ _ _ _ _ _ _ _ _ _ _ _ _ _ _ _!

Car, tricycle, scooter, and wheelbarrow. What is **special** about this group?

Their order—4 wheels, 3 wheels, 2 wheels, and 1

When **Bartholomew** went to the beach, he found an item that was strong enough to hold a **rock**, but unable to hold **water**. Do you know what this mystery **item** was?

A sieve

Write Your Own Comic Strip

If you like to read the "funny pages" or comics in the newspaper, you know a picture or comic can make you laugh. But have you ever tried to make your own comic strip? Learning how to draw or make comics can be a lot of fun. Try it on a rainy day—or try it today!

Why did the motorcycle stop by the side of the road?
It was "two tire-d" to go on.

What did the mother river name her baby?
Brook.

How do stones get where they are going?
They rock-it.

What do puppies like to ride in?
Waggins.

What do you get when you cross 2 curlers with 2 butter knives?
A pair of roller-blades.

When the night **guards** found a tourist unconscious on the ground, they were unsure of who he was or whom to **contact**. Eventually, at the hospital, they "developed" a plan. **What was it?**

They processed the film from his camera

Who am I?

Some say the way that I solved the biggest escape puzzle of all time was simply magic. I like to think it was because I used my brain. **Who am I?**

Harry Houdini

FOOD AND DRINK

Words to Know

Conundrum: A conundrum is a riddle that has a pun (or something with two different meanings) for the answer. Here's an example: Why was the letter B in a boat? He was going out to C. But there's another meaning to "conundrum"—it could also be a dilemma or a problem that cannot be solved.

When is a riddle not a riddle?
When you put a "G" in front of it (griddle).

What do you call really scared pasta?
Chicken noodles.

What can rise without ever sleeping?
Bread.

If your dog's down, what's your cat?
Catsup.

Why did the coffee cup go down to the police station?
To report that he had been mugged.

How did the police officers help him?
They showed him several mug shots.

What's the next word?
Dirt, worm, bird, _____.

Cat (it's a food chain)

Once upon a time, a little girl dressed in **blue** went to her grandmother's **Swiss cottage**. Why?

She was hungry for some cheese

When **Sara** invited some friends over to watch a movie, her parents decided to order **pizza** for all of them. When the delivery came, there were **2** large pizzas and **1** small one. If a large pizza serves **8** people and a small pizza serves **4**, how many friends were at Sara's house?

7 friends (20 servings minus 3 for Sara and her parents)

FUN FACT

WHAT'S YOUR IQ?

Your IQ or Intelligence Quotient is arrived at by measuring your chronological age with your mental age. The average score is around 100. The score of a genius will average around 40 to 50 points higher.

TRY THIS

Writing on the Wall

Over time researchers have found that no two people have the same handwriting, just like no two people have the same fingerprints. If you study a few samples of other people's handwriting, you may also discover that handwriting can sometimes reveal personality traits. For example, those who separate their letters may be artistic and independent, while those whose letters are very close together might enjoy some company.

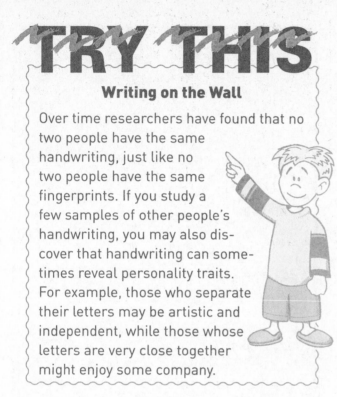

When there was a knock at the **door**, a man who could not **see** and could not **hear** somehow knew that someone had left him apple pie outside. **How did he know?**

He could smell it

Jill left a solid object on the **floor** of her room for 3 hours. In those 3 hours, no one had touched it, and yet it completely **disappeared** on its own. What was the object?

An ice cube

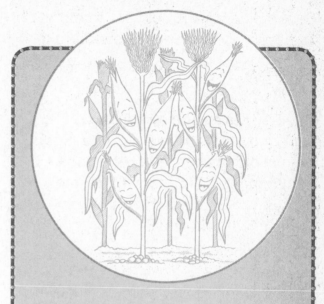

What do you call a giggling field of corn?
Laughing stalks.

What does Count Dracula use to cut his food?
A "stake" knife.

What kind of food is sick all the time?
Wheat germ.

When 2 eggs were placed in a blender, the first egg asked, "What's going on here?" What did the second egg say?
"Beats me."

How does bread get up in the morning?
It rises.

Why do melons rarely marry?
They "cantaloupe" (can't elope).

Cucumbers, carrots, onions, tomatoes, and peas—which one **doesn't** belong?

Tomatoes, because they are fruit

One day **Katherine** decided to make a picture out of **food**, just for fun. First she used strawberries, then oranges, then lemons, then kiwis, then blueberries, and then another fruit. What did she use **last** and **why?**

Purple grapes—she was making a fruity rainbow

Let's Play Charades

One sure way to get everyone laughing is to start up a game of charades. The next time you get together with family or friends, try acting out one of these: Fun house mirrors, riding a rollercoaster, buying new shoes, shopping for groceries, and running a race. Can you think of any other fun charades?

What do trees eat their ice cream out of?
Pinecones.

Why did the knife cross the road?
Because there was a fork in it.

What do you call a little potato?
Small fry.

What do you get when a bunch of grapes tries to cross a highway?
A traffic jam.

How does a cucumber know when it's in trouble?
It's in a pickle.

What drink always comes to your rescue?
Lemon-aide.

What type of **food** can contain all of the **food groups?**

Pizza!

Frosting, platter, candles, and sprinkles—what's **missing?**

Birthday cake

Frightened Food

Use a colored marker to highlight each of the 30 foods stuffed into this letter grid. The words can go sideways, up and down, diagonal, and even backward! After you have found them all, collect the unused letters from TOP to BOTTOM and LEFT to RIGHT, and write them in order on the blank spaces provided. When you're finished, you'll have the answer to this riddle:

EXTRA FUN: Use three different colors of highlight markers to show your answers!

APPLE
BEET
BLINTZ
BREAD
BROWNIES
CAKE
CARROT
CHEESE
CLAM
EGG
HAMBURGER
HOTDOG
JELLY
KIWI
MILK
ORANGE
PEA
PEANUT BUTTER
PEAR
PEPPER
PIE
PIZZA
PLUM
PORK
RADISH
SALAD
SPAGHETTI
TUNA FISH
TURKEY
YAM

What has bread on both sides and is easy to frighten?

S	P	A	G	H	E	T	T	I	E	I	P
E	G	N	A	R	O	U	A	P	P	L	E
A	B	C	S	E	I	N	W	O	R	B	A
C	L	A	M	P	Y	A	M	R	C	E	N
H	I	K	R	L	I	F	K	K	C	E	U
K	N	E	A	U	M	I	L	K	C	T	T
A	T	E	E	M	W	S	A	L	A	D	B
P	Z	U	P	I	H	H	J	G	R	C	U
E	N	Z	R	S	D	S	E	O	R	H	T
P	A	N	I	K	A	D	L	D	O	E	T
P	W	D	I	P	E	C	L	T	T	E	E
E	A	G	G	E	R	Y	Y	O	H	S	R
R	E	G	R	U	B	M	A	H	P	E	A

_ _ _ _ _ _ _ _ _ _ _ _ _ _ _ _ !

Every night when **Pop** came home, as he opened his door a light came **on**, and as he closed it, the light went **off**. **Why?**

Pop was a soda, and his home was the refrigerator!

What's going on here?

Cup	Plate
Fork	Knife
Spoon	Napkin
Glass	Saucer

The second word in each pair begins with the same letter as the last letter of the first word

Daniel took a piece of **bread**, and on top of that he placed a slice of **tomato**. Next, he added a piece of **lettuce**, a slice of **meat**, and a piece of **cheese**. Do you know what he made?

A food pyramid

Good Home Cookin'

Start at the letter marked with a dot. As you spiral into the center of the shell, collect every other letter. Write them in order on the lines below. When you reach the middle, head back out again, collecting all the letters that you skipped over the first time. Write these letters in order on the lines. When you are finished, you will have the answer to this riddle:

Where does a snail like to eat lunch?

_____ _____ _____ _____   _____ _____ _____ _____ _____ _____!

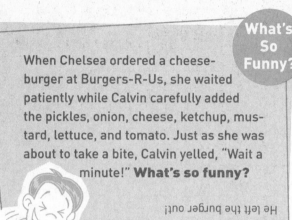

What's So Funny?

When Chelsea ordered a cheese-burger at Burgers-R-Us, she waited patiently while Calvin carefully added the pickles, onion, cheese, ketchup, mustard, lettuce, and tomato. Just as she was about to take a bite, Calvin yelled, "Wait a minute!" **What's so funny?**

He left the burger out!

What's a pig's favorite way to cook?
Bakin' (bacon).

What did the potato call his son?
Chip.

What does a hog do in the sun?
Roast.

What do mugs build their homes out of?
"Cup boards."

Why were the cups and the forks all alone?
Because the dish ran away with the spoon.

What did the syrup call her sweetheart?
Honey.

In **cooking** class the teacher asked for volunteers. Each volunteer had to answer a question. When it was **Amy's** turn, the teacher asked her what the difference was between **freezing** and **boiling**. Amy used the examples of ice cubes and hot cocoa. Although her teacher thought those were good examples, it wasn't the answer she was looking for. **Do you know the answer?**

180 degrees

When **Ben** and his father went to the grocery store, his father asked him if he could find **4 foods** in the store that had holes in them but that were still whole. Ben found more than 4. **How many** can you think of?

Doughnuts, macaroni, bagels, olives, crackers, and Swiss cheese are just a few possible answers

Who am I?

"To be or not to be" is my hint of who I am. I could also mention Romeo and Juliet. I am well known for my plays as well as my poems. **Who am I?**

William Shakespeare

Second Helping

Place each of the seven-letter words into the boxes in alphabetical order, starting with the top row and working your way to the bottom.

When you're finished, read down the third column to get the answer to this riddle:

What food tastes better before it is cooked?

For a second helping of laughs, read down the fourth column to get the answer to this riddle:

What did the teddy bear say after eating a really big meal?

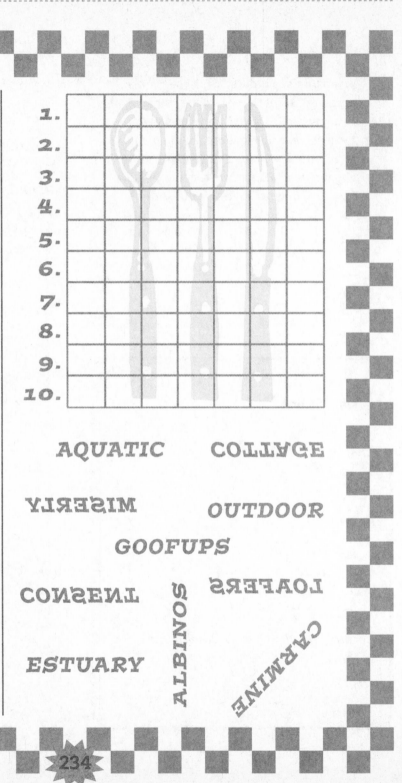

1.
2.
3.
4.
5.
6.
7.
8.
9.
10.

AQUATIC   COLLAGE

MISERLY   OUTDOOR

GOOFUPS

CONSENT   LOAFERS

ALBINOS

ESTUARY   CARMINE

When **Ozzy** and his friend **Owen** went to tour their local greenhouse, the florist had a mystery for them to solve. "When is a **flower** not a flower?" the florist asked. Do you know the answer?

When it's flour

What is a **liquid** outside your fridge and a **solid** inside your fridge?

Flavored gelatin

Now I See It, Now You Don't

The way the brain sees things is not always the same from one person to the next. Some people don't see color the same way as others. One way to check for color blindness is to find 4 socks, each one with a different shade of green. Can you tell the difference between the 4 colors? People who are color-blind cannot see the minor differences in the color.

What do comic book characters like to eat?
Superhero sandwiches.

What did the other groceries say when the sausage brought the salami to the party?
Well, he's bratwurst (brought worse).

Why were the windows "shuttering"?
Because they heard the homeowners say it was "curtains" for them!

What do you call a naughty glove?
A bad mitten.

When the builder had to climb onto the roof, did he pick the first thing he saw (the scaffolding) or the second thing?
He chose the ladder (latter).

What do cherubs serve at their parties?
Angel food cake.

Who's going to make the salad?
Let us (lettuce)!

What bear can grow 10 times its own size overnight?
A gummy bear in water.

Why wouldn't the apple join the other fruits in the salad?
She didn't find it as a-peel-ing.

Did you hear that the ice cream parlor closed?
Yeah, I heard that the sundaes wouldn't work on weekdays, the ice cream bars went nuts, and the bananas split.

FUN FACT

SILLY "SCIENCE"

The study of the shape of your head is called phrenology. For years people thought the way that your head was shaped determined your talents, gifts, or traits. Luckily, this notion was eventually disproved.

When **Ed's** mother called out, "Ed, supper is ready!" **4 people** came. Who were they?

Four generations of Eds—Ed I, Ed II, Ed III, and Ed IV

It goes in **fast**, but comes out **slow**—and yet, the amount is the same. **What can this be?**

A funnel

Every day a strange man walked past several **grapevines** growing on a fence. One very **hot** day the owner asked the strange man what he had done with his grapes. "I did not take your grapes," replied the strange man, "I am innocent!" The strange man was telling the **truth**, yet the grapes were gone. Can you solve the **mystery?**

The owner's grapes had turned to raisins in the hot sun

ACTING SILLY

TRY THIS

Front to Back—and Back Again

Have you ever tried to write a palindrome? Palindromes are words or phrases that read the same both forward and backward. "Dad" is a good example. Another is "Madam, I'm Adam." How many palindromes can you think of?

How did **Sonny** know his son would be home **soon**?

He added another O

What do you get when you put **.14** and **3** together? The answer is as easy as **pie** . . .

3.14

One night as the **children** were walking past the Parch house, a thick **fog** set in. Cold and scared, the children moved on down the street. Then as **quickly** as it had appeared, the fog ended, and there was no other fog anywhere in sight. **How can that be?**

It was Halloween and the "fog" came from dry ice

What do kindergarten teachers eat for lunch?
Alphabet soup.

How do you make a riddle stop?
You take away its "r" and "d" (idle).

What did the PE teacher name his son?
Gym (Jim).

Why couldn't the geometry teacher solve her own problems?
She didn't have the right angle.

Why did all the letters have to stay after school?
They were caught making "alpha bets."

What did the sleeping pines do?
They knotted off.

You never write on what paper?
Toilet paper.

What happens if you stand when you sleep?
You dream "up" things.

What is the difference between being a fool and being foolish?
4 letters (a & ish).

What is something only two brains can have?
A brain baby.

How many chickens does it take to make a pillow?
None, chickens can't sew!

Where does little bear keep his things at school?
In his cubby.

What do you call just one nap?
A sleep.

FUN FACT

DOUBLE-SIDED

Did you know that your brain has two sides? The left side of the brain is in charge of things like art and picturing things in your head. The right side is in charge of things like speech, math, and language. Sometimes one side is stronger than the other. Which is your stronger side?

If Sheldon sells **shells** by the shore, and Dora drums drums by the **door**, then who sits on **sofas** on Saturdays? Is it Julie, Laura, Sophie, or Erin?

Sophie (because her name begins with "s").

Tightrope, trapeze, water slide, and cannon—which one **doesn't** belong in this group?

The water slide (it belongs at a swimming pool, not a circus)

Words to Know

Tongue Twister: A word or phrase that is hard to repeat quickly due to the repetition of multiple consonants within the words.

"Silly **Sally** sings songs as silly Sammy somersaults." Can you say this **5 times** fast? Can you make up your own **tongue twister?**

Comic Contest

These four people have entered into a comic contest. Count the number of not-quite-normal things you can see about each contestant's costume and pet. For example, contestant number 1 is wearing a "baseball" cap. The winner has the most comic accessories! Make your lists in the spaces below.

Brains of Jell-O

Do you know anyone who's so silly, it's like he's got a brain full of Jell-O? Now you can make one yourself. Take a batch of cookie dough and press it down in a bowl, making two big dents (for brain lobes) in it. Cover your dough mold with plastic wrap, making sure it's completely protected, and then pour prepared liquid Jell-O inside. Refrigerate your Jell-O brain for several hours. When the Jell-O hardens, you can move it from the cookie mold to a platter, and use the cookie dough to make brain cookies to go with the Jell-O.

For **Daddy's** birthday, Victoria helped Mommy bake a birthday **cake**. When Mommy walked away for a moment, she told Victoria, "Don't forget to put in the **flour**." So she did. When Mommy came back, she couldn't stop **laughing**. What did she find?

There was a daisy in the mixing bowl

Silly Sally can turn around **25** times in **2** minutes. If she wants to break the town record of **37** minutes of spinning, how many **times** will she need to **spin**?

475 times

What's the **missing word** in the last pair? Little lightning bugs, small snails, mini mice, ___ turtles.

Tiny

Ever since **Dan** got dressed this morning, he's had the strangest feeling that he's going the **wrong way**. Do you know why?

His clothes are on backward

What has 10 fingers on each hand?
A pair of gloves.

Who is the only person the tooth fairy won't visit at night?
Count Dracula.

What would the Count say if she did?
"Fang you" very much.

Why couldn't the jester get his medicine bottle open?
It was "fool" proof.

What did Pinocchio say when he was asked if he was lying?
Who nose?

How much sleep did the insomniac get?
Nod a wink.

Who am I?

Many still believe I had the greatest mind of all time. My theory of relativity was the beginning of many new inventions that we have today. Science was my favorite subject. **Who am I?**

Albert Einstein

What is a woodpecker's favorite dessert?
"Tap-ioca" pudding.

What object in space is never hungry?
The full moon.

What does Cyclops drink out of?
Eye glasses.

What type of fishing do the Three Billy Goats Gruff like to do?
Trolling.

What did the mother bolt say to her baby when she tucked him in bed?
Sleep tight.

What's the difference between April 1st and April 2nd?
One day.

When **Nate** told his mother that he could turn an open bottle filled with water **upside down** and the water would not pour out, she said, "I'll believe it when I see it." And she did. What did Nate do in order **to keep** the water in the bottle?

The bottle was in a tub of water and he never raised it higher than the opening of the bottle.

One day Backward **Betty** decided to try a mud bath like the stars take. The nearest **mud puddle** she could find was in the neighbor's driveway. As Betty began to bathe, something seemed strange. **What was wrong?**

It wasn't mud—it was cement

FUN FACT

SIZING UP YOUR BRAIN

In the past, some experts wondered if the size of your brain decided how smart you could be. Now they know that it's not really true. But here's another fact—did you know that the size of your head compared with your body changes considerably as you grow? At birth, your head is ¼ of your body size. By the time you're an adult, your body catches up and your head is only 1/10 of your body.

Color Us In!

"**Jack** and **Jill** went down a hill to fetch a pail of dirt. Jill fell down and broke her foot, and Jack came tumbling after. What's **wrong** with this story?

Everything is backward

When it was finally **Mr. Smiley's** turn at the Laughs-R-on-Us booth, they told him he had better take his **turn** now, as they were about to run out. So what did Mr. Smiley get?

The last laugh

Silly Sally

Can you guess what Silly Sally likes? Take a look at the following clues:

Silly Sally likes...

...noodles, but not ravioli

...meatballs, but not hotdogs

...trees, but not bushes

...riddles, but not jokes

EXTRA FUN: The picture of Silly Sally shows several things that Sally likes. Can you figure out what they are, and why?

I may be silly, but I am not strange!

Silly Slogans

Write each numbered word in the correct box. Now, rearrange
the words to finish the silly slogan for each business!

1. a	3. in	5. look	4. bright	3. cuts!	1. deal!
4. a	6. looking	3. ...are	1. ...want	6. sale!	3. all
2. ...knead	3. short	6. a	3. know	5. ...want	6. yard
6. for	1. good	3. the	6. ...are	3. a	2. dough!
3. we	5. to	4. idea!	3. hurry —	4. ...need	5. better!

1. Top Card Playing Company
"Come see us when you...

2. B&B Baking and Loan
"Come see us when you...

3. Al's Barber Shop
"Come see us when you...

4. Larry's Lightbulbs
"Come see us when you...

5. Elegant Eyewear
"Come see us when you...

6. Good Deal Real Estate
"Come see us when you...

243

Why was the King of Hearts so upset?
Because his Ace was in the hole.

What do you call it when 5 royal cards get together?
A full house.

When the scientist didn't like Frankenstein's attitude, what did he do about it?
He "changed" his mind.

Why was the garbage man so sad?
He was down in the dumps.

Why was the cowboy so tired?
Because his giddy-up-and-go gotty-up-and-went!

What do you get when you drop a 500-pound potato off the top of a skyscraper?
500 pounds of s-mashed potatoes.

What do you call a really cold puppy?
A chili dog.

Clarence the **clown** took off his big shoes, curly wig, baggy pants, polka-dotted tie, all of his makeup, suspenders, and his gloves. On the way to his trailer, a little **girl** stopped to say, "You're a clown, aren't you?" **How did she know?**

He forgot to take off his red nose!

Some days **Jack** felt really **up**, and some days Jack felt really **down. Why?**

He's a Jack-in-the-box

If **Lilly** licks a lollipop while watching 3 30-minute cartoons and she only **licks** halfway through her **lolly**, how long will it take to finish it?

90 more minutes

Who am I?

I liked to make people laugh and I would use anything I could think of—songs, poems, stories, art, and cartoons. I wrote several fun and silly books for children, like *Where the Sidewalk Ends.* **Who am I?**

Shel Silverstein

Words to Know

Memory: Ability to store information in your brain. Without your memory, you could never remember your brother's birthday or where you put your favorite book. And did you know that memory is one of the things required for laughter?

What type of print will you never find in a newspaper?
A footprint.

What can adult teeth have?
Baby teeth.

How do clouds make other clouds get out of their way?
They use their foghorns.

How can you tie something so you will always remember it?
With a "forget-me knot."

What did one "Most Wanted" poster say to the other?
I've been framed!

Every once in a while, the workers at the **perfume** factory smell a horrible, strong **skunk** smell. **Why is this?**

Some perfumes are made from the smelly spray that comes from skunks.

What **object** can go **up** and come **down** all by **itself?**

A helium balloon—when you blow it up it goes up, but in a few days it comes back down.

What **two** things combine to look like a miniature **tornado?**

A bathtub drain and water.

What's So Funny?

Jordan has some very silly dreams. One night he dreamt that he was a clown and when he woke up his nose *was* a little red. The next time he dreamed he was a king, only to find when he woke up that his comforter was around him like a robe. But tonight's dream had to be the silliest of all! Jordan dreamt he was sleepwalking! **What's so funny?**

When he woke up he was in the yard!

245

CROSSING OVER

FUN FACT

USE YOUR HEAD!

Everyone has a *pons* (meaning "bridge"). Your pons is a part of your brain that is in charge of many things, like sorting all of the information you take in to decide what is important enough to think about.

Do you know how to get a riddle really upset?
Take away its d's and you'll "rile" it.

What do you get when you cross 40 robbers with a herd of sheep?
Ali Baa Baa and 40 thieves.

Why did the math teacher cross the road?
Because he had "2."

Who wrote the book 1001 Crosswords?
Chris Cross.

What do you get if you cross a movie theater with a palm reader?
Show-'n'-tell.

Why did the playground cross the road?
To get to the other slide.

When **Geoffrey** wrote a paper about crossing the English Channel for English class, he left out the **crossing** part. Because of this, no one could read his paper. **Why?**

He didn't cross his t's

How can 6 **toothpicks** have only 6 **points?**

When you make 2 triangles out of them

Who am I?

I was a powerful Egyptian queen, known for my beauty, intelligence, and power. Unfortunately, it all came to an end because of a Roman general. **Who am I?**

Cleopatra

When **Maggie** and **Annette** found 2 nails on the ground, one **lying** across the other, Maggie bet Annette she couldn't get them apart without **touching** them. Maggie lost the bet. How did Annette manage to do the **trick?**

She used 2 magnets

If a train going **40 miles** an hour reaches a railroad crossing in **40 minutes**, how long will it take a train going **20 miles** an hour to reach it?

80 minutes

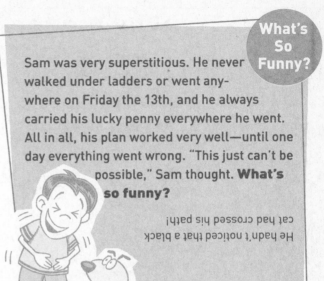

What's So Funny?

Sam was very superstitious. He never walked under ladders or went anywhere on Friday the 13th, and he always carried his lucky penny everywhere he went. All in all, his plan worked very well—until one day everything went wrong. "This just can't be possible," Sam thought. **What's so funny?**

He hadn't noticed that a black cat had crossed his path!

Cross Plumber

Cross out the letters that appear more than three times in the letter grid. Collect the remaining letters from left to right and top to bottom, and write them in order on the blank lines. When you are finished, you will discover the answer to this riddle:

What do you get when you cross a plumber with a jeweler?

___ ___ ___ ___ ___

___ ___ ___ ___ ___ ___ ___

___ ___ ___ ___ ___ ___ !

A	C	S	R	L			
M	F	Y	I	P	Q	C	
L	N	K	Z	S	J	Z	G	Q
A	W	C	V		Q	V	F	M
M	S	C	R		K	Y	K	O
Z	U	S		L	N	S
D	F	M		Z	C	M
W	Q	J		T	J	C
K	C	H	M		Q	S	Q	E
M	V	B	Q		Z	A	W	L
J	Y	C	T	K	S	H	Q	T
P	P	V	Z	U	Y	M
B	W	F	S	P

Why Did the Lion . . .

Find your way from **START** to **END**, collecting the letters. When you read them in order, you will discover the answer to this riddle:

Why did the lion cross the grassland?

Words to Know

ESP: Extrasensory perception is the believed ability to have a type of sixth sense. Someone who claims to be able to read your mind or know your thoughts is said to have ESP.

What do you get when you cross a snowman with a pickup full of carrots?
Frozen food in a delivery truck!

What do you get when you cross an automobile with music?
Cartoons (car tunes).

What time is it when you cross an alarm clock with a skunk?
Time to go!

Why did the cheater have 2 X's on his head?
He had been double-crossed.

Why did the fish cross the road?
Because he was already "caught" in the middle.

Why did the fertilizer cross the road?
Because the grass wasn't greener on the other side!

As **Cami** began crossing the railroad tracks, she realized a **train** would be there soon. She saw no train, heard no sound, but knew it just the same. **How did she know?**

She could feel the vibration on the tracks

As **Rhonda** saw the "walk" sign light up, she started to cross the **street**. Instantly, several cars screeched to a halt inches from her. **Why?**

She was looking at the sign for the other direction

Testing for ESP

Do you or someone you know have ESP? One test for ESP that you can try on your friends is to make a few cards with circles, wavy lines, or dots on them. After you have shown them the cards, look at one of the cards and ask your friend to sense which one you are looking at. You can take turns testing each other to see who does best.

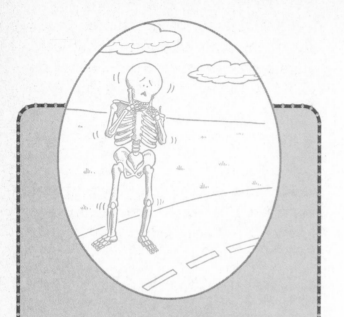

Why wouldn't the first skeleton cross the road?
No guts!

Why did the second skeleton cross it?
No brains!

And why didn't the third skeleton cross it?
He just didn't have the heart to!

Why wouldn't the rooster cross the road?
He was too much of a chicken.

Where does an X always sit?
In the cross section.

Why did the bee cross the road?
He wanted to see his "honey."

In science class, **Amanda** learned that when you put salt on a **slug**, something very horrible happens. **Do you know what?**

The slug melts

When **Lila** told her mother she would come straight home after **school**, her mother knew it wasn't true. **How?**

She saw that Lila's fingers were crossed

"I **spin**, yet I am never dizzy. I have clouds, but have no **rain**. As I cross the **land**, you cannot see how deadly I am." **What is it?**

A dust storm

FUN FACT

A RIDDLE OF A NAME

"Rumpelstiltskin" is a well-known fairy tale, maybe because it was part of the famed Brothers Grimm collection of fairy tales. In the tale, Rumpelstiltskin tells the Queen that she has to guess his name, or he will take her firstborn child. Do you remember how the Queen solved this riddle?

Hinky Pinkies

The answer to each Hinky Pinky riddle is two rhyming words of two syllables each. Write the answers into the numbered grid. **EXTRA**

FUN: When you're finished, read down the shaded column to find the answer to one more Hinky Pinky:

What do you get when you cross a monster with someone who works at your school?

What do you get when you cross...

1. ...a sticky candy with a hot breakfast drink?
2. ...a comic book action hero with a detective?
3. ...a lawyer with a large bird of prey?
4. ...a South American pack animal with a serious play?
5. ...a baby cat with a winter handwarmer?
6. ...a comedian with a rabbit?
7. ...a werewolf with Tinkerbell?
8. ...a molecule with a violin?
9. ...a tired person with a pointy tent?
10. ...a king with a small hunting dog?
11. ...a mad scientist with a white and yellow flower?
12. ...a large tropical bird with an orange vegetable?
13. ...a hot pepper with a boy named William?
14. ...a field of daisies with a generator?
15. ...a reptile with a magical man?

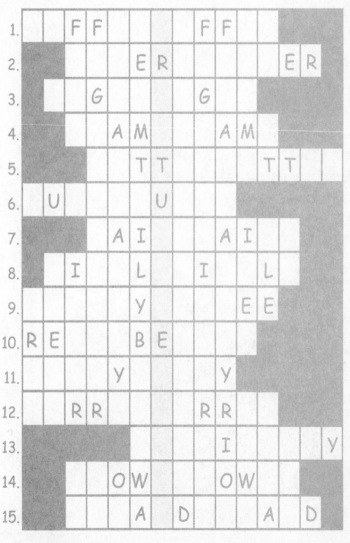

Which pair of the following **words**, crossed exactly in the middle like a **crossword**, will join at the same **letter**? Party, money, stand, brunt, flash, salad.

Stand and flash

Crossing what two things creates a lot of **foam** and so may be used to simulate a **volcano?**

Baking soda and vinegar

Mr. Wilson pulls up to a pedestrian crossing, but no one is there. Can he go on? The answer is no! **Why?** Hint: Is there something else that is stopping him?

Yes—the light is still red

FUN FACT

CRAZY TALK

Did you know that between your left brain and your right brain you have a corpus callosum that allows the two sides of your brain to "talk"? The corpus callosum lets you hear something on one side of your brain and then picture it with the other side.

Who am I?

I had a theory or idea that man may have started out as a chimpanzee or ape and then slowly changed or evolved into what he is today. **Who am I?**

Charles Darwin

Why did the Martians keep bringing more men?
They needed "Xtra terrestrials."

Why did the bank teller cross the road?
He didn't have any cents.

Why did the rhino swim to the other side of the river?
He wanted to get his "point" across.

Why did the squirrel cross the busy road?
I guess we'll never know!

What did the Troll warn the Three Billy Goats Gruff?
Don't cross me!

Why did the electrician light up?
His wires were crossed.

What do you get when you cross an ape with a magician?
Hairy Houdini (Harry Houdini).

How did George Washington and Huck Finn cross the river?
George chopped down the cherry tree and Huck made a raft out of it.

Why did the owl cross the road?
Whooooo cares?

Why did the book cross the road?
It was looking for cover.

How did the pharmacist get all of his medicine across the road?
He "drug" it.

Why did the nail cross the road?
He was bent on it.

Words to Know

Rebus: A kind of puzzle in which a picture represents a word or part of a word. Sometimes a rebus will be used in a storybook to introduce new words, or in a game to challenge the guesser to solve the picture puzzle.

TRY THIS

Tell a Story in Pictures

You can make a rebus of your own by writing a short story or retelling a familiar one using pictures that you draw in the place of some of the words. An example could be the story of Goldilocks and the Three Bears. You could substitute a picture of a bear each time the word "bear" appears.

What is a **cross** between *star* and *led*?

Star-t-led

How did **Peter** get across the Nottafoot River without a **boat?**

He walked—it was only 11 inches deep

When **Xavier** would turn in his homework, his **teacher** knew which paper was his, even though he always forgot to sign his name. **How did she know?**

He always did the Xtra credit

253

What do angry quilters make?
Cross stitches.

Why did the rope cross the road?
Why "knot"?

Why didn't the crossword get the answer?
He was too puzzled!

What can you find at the intersections in church?
Look for "cross" walks.

Why did the letters cross the road?
It was EZ.

How do roads talk?
They use "sign" language.

Who am I?

I grew up in Pennsylvania telling funny stories and making people laugh. My big break came when I told a few jokes on TV. I am a very well-known comedian and had a family TV show named after me. **Who am I?**

Bill Cosby

When the **water** ran across the floor of the pool house, no one panicked. **Why?**

They were hosing off the floor

When the **plane** crossed the sky at a weird angle, the control tower knew there was trouble and called for help. The plane's **radio** was out and the pilot was too far away to signal. How did the tower learn of the **problem?**

The pilot was a sky writer

Otto was really confused when he received a letter from his eye **doctor** that read: "Tsn't tt about ttme you came tn for a vtstt?" **What was wrong?**

Otto's i's were crossed because he was cross-eyed!

Words to Know

Comedy: A type of amusement that relies on humor to entertain people. Funny stories and actions are often used in a comedy routine.

254

PERFECTLY AT HOME

Katherine's room is too far away from the bathroom to hear whether someone is using the **shower**. And yet, Katherine knew that her mom had taken a shower this morning. **What tipped her off?**

The shower was still wet

What do the **words** "end," "multiplication," "kitchen," and "coffee" have in common? **Hint:** They are all adjectives for one noun.

They are all a kind of table

Daniel filled a bathtub up to 1 inch from the top. No more **water** was put in it, but it still overflowed. **How can that be?**

He got in

Words to Know

Teasing: Teasing is bothering, annoying, or taunting others by making fun of them. Some teasing is just for fun—nothing to get offended about—but sometimes teasing becomes mean and should be stopped.

Who am I?

You may have laughed at the troubles of poor old Charlie Brown, a cartoon character I created. I drew and wrote about Charlie and all the rest of the "Peanuts" gang to make others laugh. **Who am I?**

Charles Schulz

Why did the poltergeist try to scare the gambler out of his house?
I don't know, but he didn't have a ghost of a chance.

What do builders write on?
Construction paper.

Why did the actor get fired?
Because he brought the house down.

What did the old block name his son?
Chip.

Why did the plug-in have to stay home?
She was grounded.

Why did the cow and the moon have to eat out all the time?
Because their dishes ran away with their spoons!

Why did the hammer get into trouble?
Because he hit the nail on the head!

Where do roses sleep?
In a flower bed.

How did the window know which bugs were good?
She screened them.

How many sides does a house have?
Two—an "in" side and an "out" side.

What kind of dance did the porch learn?
The two-step.

Why did the bee have to stay home?
It had hives.

TRY THIS

Tommy's Tennis Tongue Twister

Try this tongue twister: Tommy tied 20 tiny tennis shoes. After you say that 5 times fast, how about making up a few of your own to try on your family and friends? Here's a hint to making new tongue twister—pick a consonant (in the case of this tongue twister, it's "t") and then try to come up with a bunch of words with that consonant.

Color Me In!

FUN FACT

TWIST AND SHOUT!

Tongue twisters have been entertaining people—tying up their tongues—for years. Many tongue twisters have made their way into children's books and collections. A good tongue twister is almost impossible to say quickly.

"The **longer** it goes, the **shorter** it grows." What is it?

A burning candle

What's So Funny?

One day, while Goldilocks was on her way to the Three Bears' house, she got distracted. Eventually, she remembered where she was going and arrived at the cottage in the woods, just as the bears were leaving for their walk. As Goldie opened the door, she gasped! **What's so funny?**

The bears had already eaten!

Bob and **Bill** decided to build a tree house. They've got a tree with a trunk that's **15 feet** tall, so they decided to build stairs that go up the tree. Unfortunately, all they have are **6 boards**. How far apart do Bob and Bill need to nail the **6 boards** so that the stairs are evenly spread out?

2.5 feet from the center of each board

Half a House?

Seems like the builder only finished half of this very fancy house. Can you complete the job? Draw the other half of the house, copying the first half square by square.

Next, figure out what letter goes in each box, below. When you are finished, you will get the answer to this riddle:

What kind of house does every house builder know how to build?

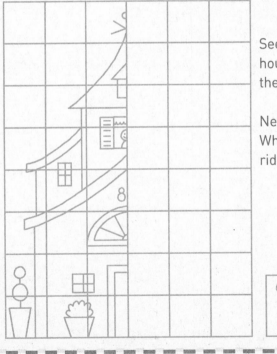

C-2	H+6	J-5	Z-3	K+4	S-5	B+3

TRY THIS

Dream, Dream, Dream

You can try to figure out what you or someone else's dreams might mean. If you look in a dream encyclopedia or dream interpretation book, you will see what some people believe are the meanings or clues behind the things you may dream about—for example, falling can symbolize a loss. Of course, in order to interpret your dreams, you first have to try to remember them when you wake up.

Bathtub, toilet, shower—what's **missing** from this group?

Sink

As **Barry's** mom walked through the house she saw a bag of **candy** in the entryway and a wrapper in the dining room. By the time she reached the **kitchen**, she knew Barry didn't like the candy very much. **How did she know?**

He had spit the candy out in the trash can

Why did it take the ant so long to get home?
It was "uphill" all the way.

What do pans like to eat?
Pot pies.

Why didn't the china hutch like to be teased?
He could "dish" it out, but he couldn't take it.

What state covers more ground than any other?
Floor-ida!

Why did General Custer sit in his chair all the time?
Because he had made his last stand.

Why did the chicken run out of the house screaming?
It couldn't take being "coop-ed" up in the house!

Marissa is writing a school report on her computer at home. The other night, a **virus** invaded her computer and her report got all jumbled. Can you tell what this **sentence** was and what the report was about? **Here is the sentence:** Sometimesth eyli keto eatho lesincl othing,es peciallyth ingsma deofwo ol.

The sentence is, "Sometimes they like to eat holes in clothing, especially things made of wool." The report was about moths.

Mr. Axeman the carpenter asked his assistant **Woody** if he knew the three things that make a pen different from a pencil. **Do you know?**

The three things are the letters "c," "i," and "l"

What did the windows do when they saw the storm coming?
They shuttered!

What did all the king's horses and all the king's men say when Humpty Dumpty fell off the wall?
He was a good egg!

What do 24 hours do at night?
Call it a day.

Why couldn't the chair be fixed?
It would cost an arm and a leg.

How did the tools get the truth out of the wood?
They drilled it.

Why didn't the window have any money?
It was broke.

Who am I?

I wear a striped shirt and big glasses, and I'm a part of many puzzle books. You can try to find me in pictures, where I may be skiing on a mountain full of people or hiding out in a gigantic shopping mall. **Who am I?**

Waldo from *Where's Waldo?*

Which Window?

Roberto lives in a big, old house that has been turned into a bunch of apartments. Use the clues below to figure out which window is his.

- The window to the right of Roberto's has a plant on the windowsill.
- The window above Roberto's has no shade.

- Roberto's window has curtains that his mom made for him.
- Roberto's window does not have a shutter.

EXTRA FUN: Read the letters in the windows from bottom to top, and right to left, and you will find the answer to this riddle:

Which side of a house gets the most rain?

260

Fun House

Can you find 24 funny things in this living room? When you're finished, see if you can figure out what's so funny about the answer to this riddle:

What kind of house weighs the least?

A LIGHTHOUSE!

FUN FACT

EGO MANIA

Did you know you have an "ego"? Your ego is your "self." Many believe it is the main force behind your personality—it's who you really are.

How do you make a **house** using only **6 nails?**

Take 4 nails and lay them out in a square, head to point; then put the other 2 on top of the square to make the triangle roof.

When **Breanna** went to **Brittney's** house, she had planned to be there for breakfast and lunch. To make things simpler they had **brunch**. What did they end up missing?

E, a, k, f, a, s, t, and l

When an **ice sculptor** left his house on Wednesday, he had **4** beautiful swans in the freezer. Yet when he returned on Sunday, **they were gone!** No one broke in and there is a logical answer. What could have happened?

He left the freezer door open

How does Rover stay out of the dog-house?
He buries the evidence.

What do bathrooms in outer space have?
Meteor showers.

Why did the porch tell the steps to knock it off?
They kept "stair-ing"!

What do homes wear when it gets cold out?
House coats.

What does every floor of the house have to have before bed?
Bedtime stories.

What do you call a hat that follows you everywhere you go?
A stalking cap!

Why didn't the outside of the house understand what was so funny?
It was an "inside" joke.

What did the swingset say to the sandbox when the teeter-totter arrived?
Wow! Did you SEE what I SAW?

How can you tell when a toilet's not well?
It's flushed.

What's an envelope's favorite part of the house?
The "seal-ing."

Why did the colander have to go to the doctor?
It was a little strained!

Why couldn't the ball player ever go home?
He was out in "left" field.

I invented a test that used 10 different inkblots. These images helped psychologists try to understand how a patient thinks by what the person felt he or she was seeing in the blots. **Who am I?**

Who am I?

Hermann Rorschach

Mrs. Smith lives in a 20-story apartment building. She lives on the **15th** floor, and yet she never passes by the **13th** floor. What's the explanation?

Because 13 is thought to be an unlucky number, some apartment buildings don't have a 13th floor

Jasmine's dining room table has enough room for only **6** people, yet every night **8** eat there. **How can that be?**

There are 6 human family members plus the dog and the cat—they eat under the table

One night **2 burglars** broke into the Joneses' house. As soon as they were inside, they heard a **voice**. The burglars got scared and left. No one was home, **so whom did they hear?**

The announcer on the radio, which Sally Jones had forgotten to turn off

Words to Know

Dream: A group of thoughts, images, and feelings that you experience during the REM (rapid eye movement) portion of your sleep. Another type of dreaming is daydreaming—imagining something while you are awake.

Every time **Clarence** went into the house, something went wrong, very wrong. Clarence would **gain** weight only to instantly **lose** it again. Once he even swore he was shrinking. But the next day he felt taller than ever. **Why?**

Clarence went to a fun house with distorting mirrors.

Liza lives in a grey house, while **Lisa** lives in a house that's gray. **What's the difference?**

The spelling of "grey" and "gray."

Inkblot Tests

To create your own inkblot guessing game or test, you will need 10 blots. To make them, all you need are 10 pieces of paper folded once and then opened. Pour a little bit of paint on one side of the paper. Then, refold the paper, pressing gently on the blot. Open the paper again and let the paint dry. Now all you need is someone to test. Start by asking, "When you look at this picture, what do you see?"

How did the tools get from the house to the tool store?
The compass gave directions, while the screwdriver drove.

When the princess arrived at the castle and found the new labyrinth, how did she feel?
A maze-d!

What does Sir Galahad turn on when he gets scared at night?
A knight light.

In **Centerville**, it normally takes **2 days** to send a letter from one house to another—**1 day** to mail it, and **1** to have it delivered. But Mrs. Smith always receives her mail the same day it is sent. **How can that be?**

She married the postman!

How could the **carpenter** know how tall to make his door just by using his **hands?**

He could cut the door according to his arm span, because your arm span is the same as your height.

LET'S PLAY SPORTS

What's So Funny?

Keep Pedaling!
Lance Pedlin is a famous biker who can pedal for hours on his bike. One day, he got on and started pedaling, and he kept going and going, but when he was done, he was still where he started.
What's so funny?

He was on his exercise bike

What happens when a clumsy football player plays ball?
A field trip.

Why did the racecar driver jump into the pool?
He wanted to put in a few laps.

Why did the golfer have to buy new shoes?
He had a "hole in one."

What did the high diver wear to his wedding?
A "swim" suit.

What does Dracula take with him when he goes to a ball game?
His bat.

What do dolphins wear to the beach?
Swim fins.

Words to Know

Sense: The ability to see, smell, hear, touch, and taste all of the things that you come in contact with are made possible by your 5 senses. Your brain relies on the senses to perceive the outside world.

TRY THIS

It's Not Funny to Me!

No two people have exactly the same sense of humor. If you want to see this for yourself, you can conduct a little experiment. Find yourself 5 jokes and 5 volunteers. Read each joke separately to your volunteers, then write down who laughed at which ones. When you are done, you can chart your results and compare them. What did you discover?

If there are **9** players on a **baseball** team and **11** players on a **football** team, how many **swimmers** are there on the swim team?

Any number—swim teams vary in number of teammates

The **mountain** climbers had almost reached the top of the cliff when their rope began to fray. For each inch they moved, **2** strands would break. The climbers had **49** inches to go, with a **100**-ply rope. **Will they make it?**

Yes

When is **8** not twice as much as **4**?

When you're trying on shoes

Amanda is an excellent swimmer. She can hold her breath for **2** minutes. She can also swim **300** yards in half an hour. So, can Amanda swim **25** yards without coming up for air?

No, she would only be able to go 20 yards

What did one twine say to the other right before he fell into a hole?
JUMP, ROPE!

Why did the tennis players get into so much trouble?
They were making a lot of "racket."

Where do basketball players settle their arguments?
In "court."

How do swimmers get where they are going?
In car "pools."

What sport did Little Red Riding Hood play best?
"Basket" ball.

What sport is after "nine"?
Ten-nis.

Night Games

Start with the number 1 and connect all the dots in order.

Which animals are always invited to night baseball games?

What sports item hangs upside down from its toes?
A baseball "bat."

What sport makes a lot of people "jumpy"?
Trampolining.

What is a baseball player's favorite part of the playground?
The slide.

What do catchers wear when it gets cold out?
Their gloves.

What did the photographer say to the badminton rackets?
Watch the birdie!

What kind of shoes do woodpeckers dance in?
Tap shoes.

FUN FACT

CALLING YOUR CONSCIENCE

Did you know that there is a part of you that is very aware of what is going on around you all the time? It is called your conscience. Your conscious mind remembers and can recall different things that have happened to you.

If the pitching machine at **Sports World** shoots out **1** ball every **10** seconds while you are trying to hit it, how long will it take to empty the machine of its **90** balls?

15 minutes

John works in sports every day, yet he never goes home sore or tired or sweaty. **How can this be?**

He's the scorekeeper.

Do you see a **pattern** here? Number of **catchers** on a baseball team, number of **teams** in a game, number of **strikes** before an out, number of **bases** in a diamond.

1, 2, 3, 4

Who am I?

I am the one who helped "Little Red" solve the riddle of my identity, by showing her what big teeth I have. **Who am I?**

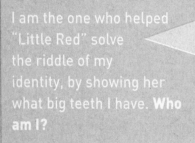

The Wolf

Where do bad gymnasts go?
Behind parallel bars!

How did the archer get to the contest?
He followed the arrows.

Why do athletes need so much money?
Because of the "tro-fees."

How do monarchs swim?
They do the butterfly stroke.

What is a washing machine's favorite pastime?
Cycling.

What did the desperate golfer eat?
His sand-wedge.

Overcoming Any Obstacle

Have you ever made a silly object obstacle course? You and your friends will have fun trying to see who can complete the course the fastest. Your course can include writing the first letter of your name in a plate of whipped cream, walking 20 steps with a tennis ball between your knees, and popping a balloon by sitting on it, as well as any other silly things you can think of. And the winner of the silly course gets a silly prize!

When **Eve** ran track she was covered in sweat, yet by the time she was ready to go **home**, her skin was dry. **Why?**

The sweat evaporated

When the school **rowing team** left the dock, they paddled for **15** minutes, then turned around. **Ten** minutes later they returned. How come it took them **5** minutes less to come back?

The wind was against them going out and with them coming back

hOops!

Fill in the answers to the clues, putting one letter in each numbered space. Then transfer the letters to the boxes that have the same numbers. When all the boxes are filled in correctly, you will have the answer to the riddle!

A. ___ ___ ___   Easily frighened; timid
    10 2   7

B. ___ ___ ___ ___ ___   Woman on her wedding day
   20 9 19 17 3

C. ___ ___ ___   What a spider builds
   13 8 21

D. ___ ___ ___ ___ ___   One thickness of something
    5 11 15 23 18

E. ___ ___   Short nickname for father
    4 14

F. ___ ___ ___ ___ ___   Place in a barn for a horse
   16 1   6 12 22

Why is a basketball court often wet?

| 1 | 2 | 3 | | 4 | 5 | 6 | 7 | 8 | 9 | 10 |

| 11 | 12 | 13 | 14 | 15 | 16 | | 17 | 18 | 19 | 20 | 21 | 22 | 23 | !

When **Tina** the tennis pro returned all of the balls that came to her, none came back to her. **Why?**

She wasn't playing with another person—she was using a ball machine.

When **Skip** brought his new track shoes home, he realized the store clerk had put the wrong **laces** in the box. These laces were only half as long as they needed to be. **What did Skip do?**

He skipped every other hole when he laced them

Which one of these **does not** belong? Helmet, goalie, touchdown, quarterback.

Goalie—the rest relate to football

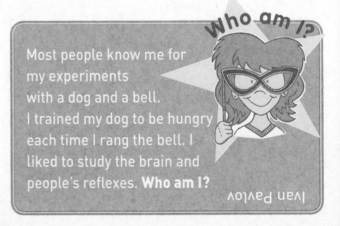

Most people know me for my experiments with a dog and a bell. I trained my dog to be hungry each time I rang the bell. I liked to study the brain and people's reflexes. **Who am I?**

Ivan Pavlov

UNDERNEATH THE CONSCIOUS

Your conscious mind is composed of all that you remember and have knowledge of. But there is another part of your mind, called your subconscious. The subconscious may store information without your remembering it.

When **Kyle** fell out of the boat, everyone waited for his return. After **20** minutes, he still did not come up for air. **Why?**

He was scuba diving

"I dive but use no **water**,
I **fly** but have no wings,
I land but have no **wheels**."
Who is it?

A skydiver

Balls of Fun

There are many sports that have their own special ball to use. Can you unscramble the names of ten of these sports? When you're finished, find your way through the maze of balls!

EXTRA FUN: Can you think of 10 more sports that use balls?

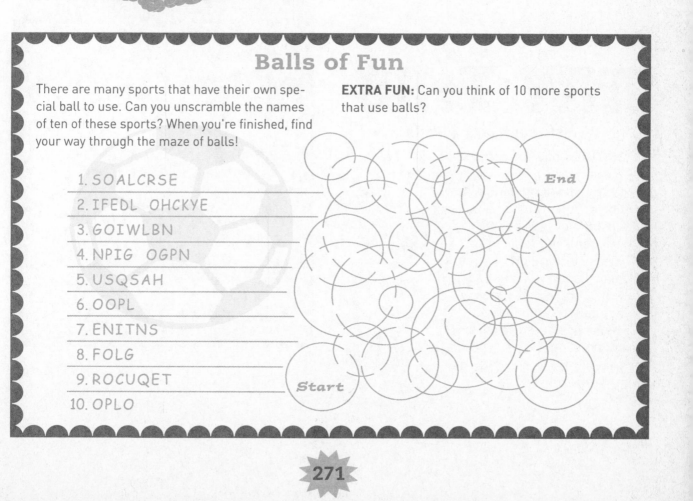

1. SOALCRSE
2. IFEDL OHCKYE
3. GOIWLBN
4. NPIG OGPN
5. USQSAH
6. OOPL
7. ENITNS
8. FOLG
9. ROCUQET
10. OPLO

Start

End

271

What do these **words** have in **common?** Hole, hazard, slice, wood.

They are all golf terms

What do these **things** have in **common?** Diamond, slide, innings, umpire.

They are all baseball terms

In what **sport** are you doing better as your score is getting **lower?**

Golf

Words to Know

IQ: IQ or Intelligence Quotient is a measure of one's ability to think. An IQ test allows people to measure genius as well as normal thinking ability.

TRY THIS

Test Your Reading Skills

You know how to read, but can you read upside down? Don't worry, you don't have to be hanging upside down. Just flip the book upside down and see if you can keep reading. Is it easy or difficult? As you may discover, it's not easy! But, who knows, you may actually be able to read faster upside down than right side up!

What did the mountain climber tell her stinky boots to do?
Take a hike!

Where do all the sports shirts come from?
Jersey.

What did the hockey player ask the puck right before the game?
Want to "stick" around for a while?

Why don't rockets play football?
They prefer liftoffs to touchdowns.

What is a dish's favorite pastime?
"Bowl-ing."

272

What did one sports shoe say to the other?
Nothing, they were tongue-tied.

What comes after a ball?
B ball.

What do baby basketballs do?
Dribble.

What sport hurts the most?
Paddleball.

What was Jack and Jill's best sporting event?
Downhill racing.

Where do 4 woods hang out?
At a golf "club."

What is a fly swatter's favorite sport?
Squash

First base ball game day. What should come **next**?

Day off! First base, baseball, ball game, game day, day off!

"I have a **tongue**, but cannot speak. I have a **toe**, but have no feet."
What is it?

A shoe

Who am I?

When Belle tried to solve the mystery of her missing father, she found a new mystery in me. She was a beauty, and she transformed me into a beautiful person as well.
Who am I?

The Beast from *Beauty and the Beast!*

273

ALL IN THE FAMILY

TRY THIS

A Matter of Symmetry

Being symmetrical means that your right side and left side are mirror images of each other. The human body is symmetrical because we have 2 eyes, 2 arms, and 2 legs, and they are very much alike. But do they act the same? For example, most people have one hand that they prefer writing with. But what if you tried writing with a hand you don't normally use? If you can do most things with both hands, you are what they call "ambidextrous."

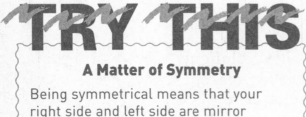

If **two** twins were both to **marry** and they both had twins, and then their **twins** had twins, **how many** twins would there be?

14 twins

Every year **Dillon** gets older, he gets a dollar more for his birthday. How much **money** will he have when he is **10**?

$55

What type of father has no sole?
The barefoot type.

What did Samuel Wilson become when he married an aunt?
Uncle Sam.

If you can't tell your Grandpa something, what do you do?
Telegram (tell a Gram)!

Which one of Mother Earth's children warms her heart the most?
Her "sun"!

What did the Old Woman Who Lived in a Shoe need more than anything else?
A break!

What does your mother's sister become when she's nervous?
Aunt-sy.

Words to Know

Humor: Something that is designed to be comical or amusing. Jokes and comedy are said to be humorous, because they can make us laugh.

Who am I?

It was my job to solve the riddle of the missing girl who lost her glass slipper. The only way to solve the problem was to try the shoe on every foot in the kingdom. **Who am I?**

The Prince from Cinderella

Let's say that in the **Wilkins family**, X = red hair, and Y = brown hair, and Z = blonde hair. If there are **2 times more** X's than Y's or Z's, what are the odds of the **fifth** child having **blonde** hair?

1 in 4

What was the piano's father's father?
His "grand" pa.

What do you call it when your sister demands to enter?
In-Sis-ting.

Who takes care of baby moths?
Their moth-er.

Where do apples search for their roots?
In their family tree.

What does a little doe call her mother?
Mommy deer.

What do you call a ladder's kid?
Its step child.

FUN FACT

JUST WHAT THE DOCTOR ORDERED

Some say laughter is the best medicine, and that may very well be true. Without laughter or happiness you may become sad or depressed. To snap out of it, it's possible that all you need is a good laugh.

Words to Know

Sarcasm: Humorous comments made with an ironic tone. People may use sarcasm to make a negative point.

What is a family of kittens after they are 13 days old?
2 weeks old.

Why was Old Mother Hubbard so scared of her cupboards?
They were "bear."

What did Peter Peter Pumpkin Eater's wife sell?
Shells by the seashore.

What did King Tut call his mother?
Mummy.

Who had the angriest child in history?
Dolly Madison ("mad is son").

What is small, buzzes, and lives by the water?
Bay bees (babies).

Identical twins **Cindy** and **Wendy** took a long walk in the forest. After a while they decided to play **hide and seek**. Cindy quickly found Wendy . . . or so she thought. Soon, it turned out that Cindy had actually found *herself*. **How could this be?**

She saw her own reflection in the water

When **David** called a family of **ducks** over to feed them, his voice echoed throughout the **hills**. But when the ducks called back, David only heard one reply. **Why?**

A duck's quack doesn't echo

What's So Funny?

One day, Wendy told her mother that she wasn't sure why, but it seemed like suddenly her whole world had turned upside down. Everyone was frowning and nothing was as it was supposed to be. Not even gravity. **What's so funny?**

She was standing on her head

Who were the Wrong Sisters' siblings?
The Wright Brothers.

How many kids did Daniel's uncle have?
None, his aunt had all of them.

How did the baby cabbage know he was winning?
He was a "head" of the game.

What kind of family reunions do puzzles have?
They gave "get (it) togethers."

What did the fishing poles always wish for?
A "reel" family.

What do track stars call their family members?
Relay-tions.

As a cartoonist and movie producer, I wanted to share my "world" with you. I hope that you could see it wasn't such a small world, after all. Someday you may "land" at one of my amusement parks. **Who am I?**

Who am I?

Walt Disney

Big Brothers

Mr. and Mrs. Wood have a large family. They have always been married to each other, and neither one has any children with anyone else. How is it possible, then, that one child in the Wood family has four brothers, while another child in the Wood family has five brothers?

The answer to this brain teaser is hidden in the letter grid. Use these clues to help figure it out:

- The answer starts in one of the four corners.
- You read the answer in logical order, one word after the other.
- You must add the punctuation.

D	L	I	H	C	X	I	S	E
R	O	B	E	H	T	F	O	V
E	Y	L	I	H	W	S	E	A
N	S	E	I	F	E	R	N	H
F	W	T	V	S	V	E	O	S
I	I	H	E	R	A	H	Y	D
V	L	E	B	E	H	T	N	O
E	L	G	R	H	L	O	A	O
B	H	I	O	T	L	R	L	W
O	A	R	L	W	I	B	R	E
Y	V	E	F	O	U	R	I	H
S	A	N	D	O	N	E	G	T

The Family Name Game

Miss Patti

Miss Frieda

Miss Fran

Miss Paula

Miss Carol

Miss Fiona

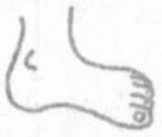

Miss Rachel

Miss Cathy

Mr. Peter

Mr. Sam

Mr. Burt

Mr. Carl

Mr. Patrick

hello

Mr. Walt

Mr. Brian

Mr. Paul

Some brides combine their old last name with their new husband's last name. See if you can make some familiar compound words by matching up the pictures that represent the last names of each bride and groom. Write each bride's new last name in the numbered boxes.

EXTRA FUN: The first seven names will criss-cross with name number eight!

8.
Mrs. Cathy

1. Mrs. Patti

2. Mrs. Frieda

3. Mrs. Fran

4. Mrs. Paula

5. Mrs. Carol

6. Mrs. Fiona

7. Mrs. Rachel

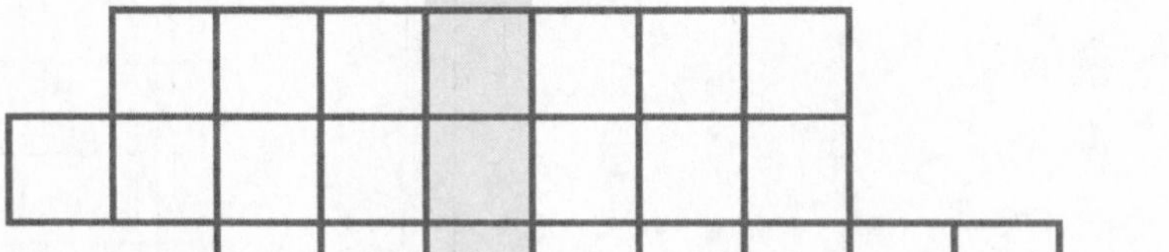

If 3 **sisters** have 3 **daughters** each, and each of their daughters has 3 daughters, how many **females** are in their family?

39 females

While **Cassie** and her mother were shopping, her mother asked if Cassie would bring her a **pair**. "A pair of what?" asked Cassie. "Just one pair," answered her mom. **What did she mean?**

She wanted a pear!

What were the Three Little Kittens who lost their mittens?
Cold.

What do suits have that no one else can have?
Family ties.

Why wouldn't Jack in the Beanstalk's mother let him watch football?
Because of the Giants.

Whom did the bug's uncle marry?
His "ant."

Why did they take Tina's cousin away 2 times?
Because he was twice removed.

What was the shredder's distant grandmother called?
Grate, grate, grate grandmother.

Amazing Mazes

Here's a fun trick to try while solving a maze puzzle. Take the paper with the maze and place it horizontally over a hard surface next to a vertical mirror. Now, can you get through the maze by looking at the mirror? Remember: You can't look at the maze itself—just at its reflection in the mirror.

Watch Out!

The letters in each column go in the squares directly below them, but not in the same order. Black squares are the spaces between words. When you have correctly filled in the grid, you will have a silly conversation between a worried mom and her daughter!

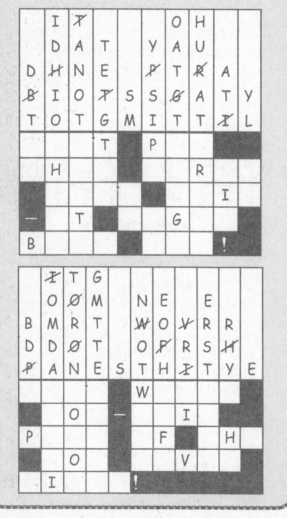

There are **11 children** in Mary's family. If there are **3** more **girls** than **boys**, how many boys and girls are there?

7 girls and 4 boys

How long will it take for the Tillman Triplets to eat **3 ice cream** cones, if it takes the Thompson Twins **10** minutes to eat **2**?

10 minutes, assuming they eat at the same speed

FUN FACT

A RUNNING MAZE

Human-sized mazes are known as labyrinths. In the old tales, people were challenged to pass through a labyrinth, and those who got lost starved to death or were attacked by a monster known as the Minotaur. Today, scientists use miniature labyrinths to experiment with mice and learn about their behavior.

It's **Norma's** twelfth birthday. This year, her family gave her a **boom box**. If every year before **were the same**, how many does she have?

One—every year is not the same!

When **Toby's** family entered the Yummyville **eating contest**, Toby was amazed when his little brother won the prize for swallowing over 1,000 items in **2 minutes**. **Do you know how he did it?**

Each item was a grain of rice

Hidden Family

Can you find the family member who is hiding in each one of these sentences?

1. **We had fun cleaning the garage!**
2. **The leprechaun told me where to find a pot of gold!**
3. **The music was so raucous, I needed to cover my ears!**
4. **Under the sofa there are many dustballs.**
5. **Did you read the same memo the rest of us read?**
6. **During a crisis, terrific people often show up to help!**
7. **The chicken broth erased the last symptoms of Brian's cold.**
8. **My friend in L.A. was happy to have me visit her!**

Why did the watch go visit its parents?
It wanted to have some family "time."

What do you get when you hook a bunch of yarn together?
A close "knit" family.

What does a wrestler say when he can't say "aunt"?
Uncle.

What do you call baby jellybeans?
Sweet.

What's the difference between a brother and a bother?
An "r."

What is your father if you take his favorite chair?
A mad dad.

What is the Trampoline family's favorite time of year for vacation?
The spring.

Someone in the **Steinbeck** family plays an instrument. Can you guess which instrument? **Here's a clue:** "I have no locks, but 88 keys."

The piano

If **Lisa's** family has **1** child every **2** years and Lisa, who's the oldest, is now **11**, how many children are in her family now?

6 children

Karl and **Kate** were both in the kitchen at **1:30** for a snack, yet neither one saw the other. **How can this be?**

Karl was there at 1:30 p.m. while Kate was there at 1:30 a.m.

TRY THIS

Optical Illusions

When your brain and eyes work together, sometimes they can play tricks on you. Some of these tricks are known as optical illusions. To try one optical illusion test, take 2 empty paper towel tubes and hold the end of each one up to your eyes. Keeping them straight, look through the tubes. Now, while you are still looking through them, move the ends that are farthest from your eyes together until they touch. What do you see?

Who am I?

It may "shock" you to know what I discovered—and some say I had an "electric" personality. To this day, I'm sometimes called one of the Founding Fathers, and my portrait appears on one of those green bills you use to pay for things. **Who am I?**

Benjamin Franklin

When the **Smith** family decided to move, everyone pitched in, including Sybil and her sister. If the girls can carry 2 **large** objects or 6 **small** ones each time, how many **trips** will it take to move 10 large objects and 16 small ones?

8 trips

If it takes **12** minutes for the **Gowen** family to wait for a ride on the roller coaster, and **5** minutes for everyone to get off it, how many minutes are spent screaming?

7 minutes

Jack has a lot of dishes to do. He has enough dishes to fill **4 sinks**, and it takes him **10 minutes** to wash one sinkful, **5** minutes to rinse it, and **5** minutes to dry. How much time would it save him if he waited and rinsed all the dishes at the end **(10 minutes total)**, and let them all air dry?

It would save him 30 minutes

When **Marty's** dad asked him if he had been taking out the **trash** like he was supposed to, he answered, "Yes, I look at the moon every night I go out." Of course his father knew this was a lie. **Why?**

The moon is not visible every night

Words to Know

Genius: Someone who is considered to be extremely intelligent. Most people believe that geniuses are born that way and that a person can't just be taught to become a genius.

ANSWERS

Hole In One • page 3

What did the witch use to
fix her broken jack-o'-lantern?

1. P_UPPY
2. J_U_MP
3. LU_M_P
4. HAP_P_Y
5. SHAR_K_
6. SM_I_LE

7. SA_N_D
8. SLOP_P_Y
9. S_A_D
10. _T_UNA
11. _C_HURCH
12. C_H_INA

She used a

**PUMPKIN
PATCH**

Picto-Laugh #1 • page 12

a spider walking
across a mirror

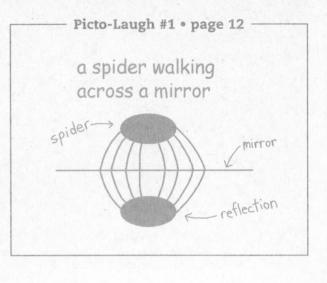

Why Oh Why? • page 7

Why did the chicken cross the playground?

| TO | GET | TO | THE | OTHER | SLIDE |

Write the answer here.

Say What? • page 13

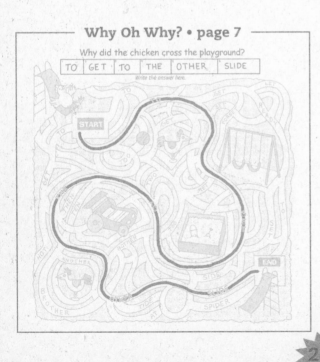

	T		A	U		T		F	I	N	H
H	E	O	W	T	S	N	A	R	Y	I	S	G
H	E		W	A	S		T	R	Y	I	N	G
	T	O		T	U	N	A		F	I	S	H

ANSWERS

Sounds Funny To Me • page 19

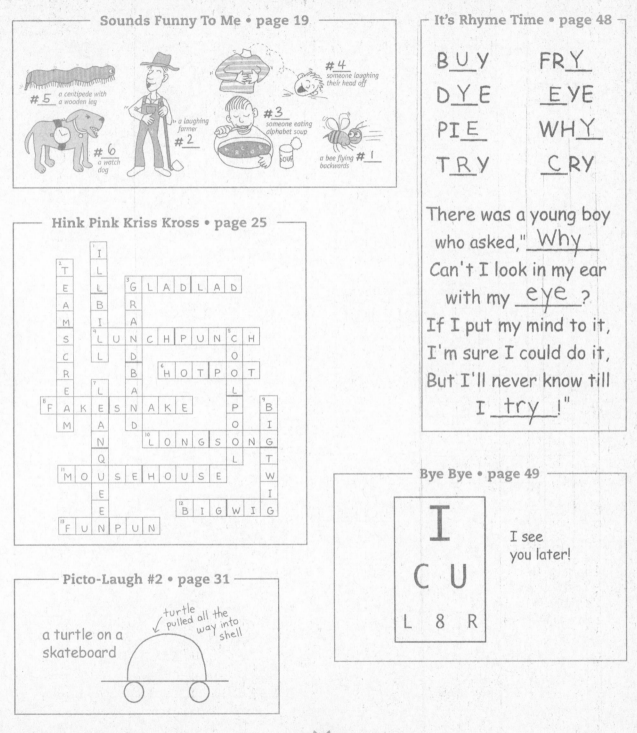

#5 a centipede with a wooden leg

#6 a watch dog

#2 a laughing farmer

#3 someone eating alphabet soup

#4 someone laughing their head off

a bee flying #1 backwards

It's Rhyme Time • page 48

B U Y   F R Y
D Y E   E Y E
P I E   W H Y
T R Y   C R Y

There was a young boy
who asked," Why
Can't I look in my ear
with my eye ?
If I put my mind to it,
I'm sure I could do it,
But I'll never know till
I try !"

Hink Pink Kriss Kross • page 25

(crossword grid)
GLADLAD
TEAMSCREE / ILLBIRLDBAD / GRAD / LANQUEEE
LUNCHPUNCH
HOTPOT
FAKESNAKE
LONGSONG
MOUSEHOUSE
BIGWIG
FUNPUN
(down words) SCHOOLPOOL / BIGTWIG

Bye Bye • page 49

I
C U
L 8 R

I see
you later!

Picto-Laugh #2 • page 31

a turtle on a
skateboard

turtle pulled all the way into shell

285

ANSWERS

Picto-Laugh #3 • page 52

aerial view of a person in a sombrero riding a bike without using their hands

handlebars
back tire
brim of Sombrero
peak of Sombrero

Love to Laugh • page 53

```
        G
  S N I C K E R
        G
    G   G
C H U C K L E
    F   E
    F
  C A C K L E
    W
```

Picto-Laugh #4 • page 54

aerial view of a person in a sombrero frying an egg in a pan

brim of sombrero
middle of sombrero
pan
egg white
egg yolk
handle of frying pan

It's Joke Time! • page 55

What time is it when five tigers are chasing you?

What time is it when you have a toothache?

What time is it when baseball teams have a tie score?

What time is the same backward or forward?

NOON!
5 after 1!
5 to 5!
2:30 (tooth-hurty)!

Picto-Laugh #5 • page 59

the blower of the world's biggest bubble gum bubble

bubble
legs and feet

Fill Me In • page 60

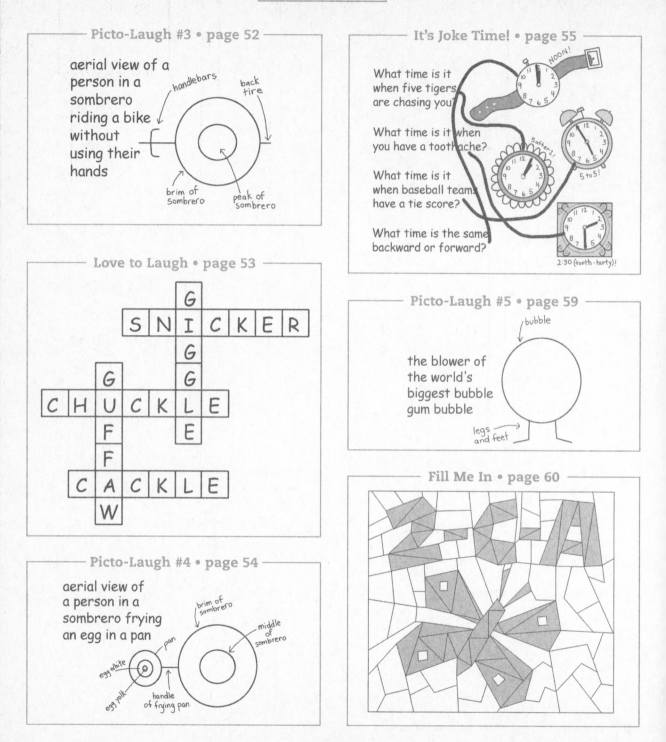

286

ANSWERS

Picto-Laugh #6 • page 66

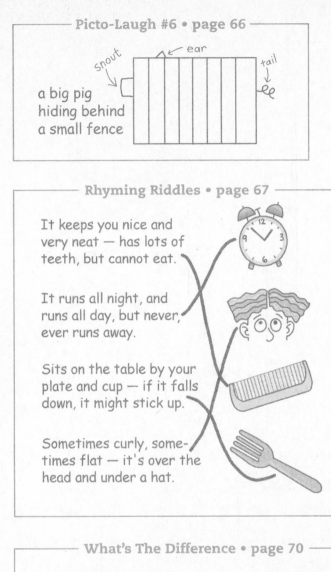

a big pig hiding behind a small fence

Rhyming Riddles • page 67

It keeps you nice and very neat — has lots of teeth, but cannot eat.

It runs all night, and runs all day, but never, ever runs away.

Sits on the table by your plate and cup — if it falls down, it might stick up.

Sometimes curly, sometimes flat — it's over the head and under a hat.

Quick Draw • page 72

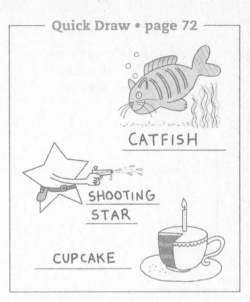

CATFISH

SHOOTING STAR

CUPCAKE

Oops! • page 82

OOPS! I'm stuck in the elevator door!

OOPS! My pigtails are too tight!

OOPS! I swallowed my spoon!

What's The Difference • page 70

1. One CATCHES DROPS, and the other DROPS CATCHES.

2. One is BAD MONEY, and the other is a MAD BUNNY.

3. One WATCHES CELLS, and the other SELLS WATCHES.

4. One is an EASY CHEATER, and the other is a CHEESY EATER.

5. One is a BAD SALAD, and the other is a SAD BALLAD.

6. One is a FIT BUNNY, and the other is only a BIT FUNNY.

ANSWERS

Picto-Laugh #7 • page 87

a boa constrictor that has just swallowed a Volkswagon Beetle

Two In One • page 92

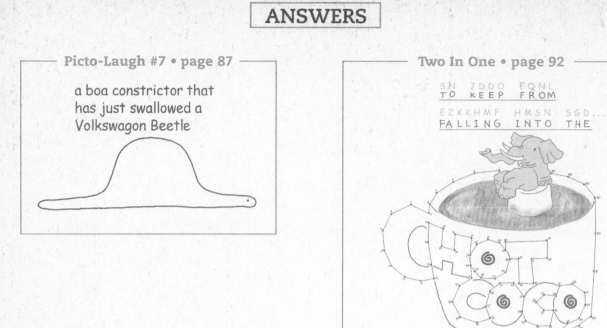

SN JDDO EQNL
TO KEEP FROM

EZKKHMF HMSN SGD...
FALLING INTO THE

Geo-Giggles • page 90

What did

DELAWARE (Dela wear) ?

She wore her

NEW JERSEY !

What did

TENNESSEE (Tennes see)?

She saw what

ARKANSAS (Arkan saw) !

What did

IDAHO (Ida hoe) ?

She hoed her

MARYLAND (merry land) !

Picto-Laugh #8 • page 91

a snake going up a flight of stairs

Elemorphant • page 93

ELEPHANT

1. ~~ELE~~PHANT   delete ELE
2. PHANT → P̶H̶ANT (E)   change H to E
3. PEAN̂T   add U

ELEPHANT

1. ELEPHAN̂T   add U
2. ELEP̶H̶ANUT (E)   change H to E
3. ~~ELE~~PEANUT   delete ELE

ANSWERS

Noah • page 99

SURPRISE   NOAH

DOESN'T   KNOW   YOU

EITHER

I Can't Hear You • page 102

Knocked to Pieces • page 101

K	N	O	C	K		K	N	O	C	K	
W	H	O	'	S		T	H	E	R	E	?
		L	U	K	E			L	U	K	E
	W	H	O	?			L	U	K	E	
W	H	O		I	T		I	S		B	E
F	O	R	E		Y	O	U		O	P	E
N		T	H	E		D	O	O	R	!	

Mix and Match • page 109

KNOCK, KNOCK.
Who's there?
BOO.
Boo who? ①

KNOCK, KNOCK.
Who's there?
CASH.
Cash who? ④

KNOCK, KNOCK.
Who's there?
COWS.
Cows who? ②

KNOCK, KNOCK.
Who's there?
ATCH.
Atch who? ⑤

KNOCK, KNOCK.
Who's there?
YOU.
You who? ⑥

KNOCK, KNOCK.
Who's there?
YA.
Ya who? ③

Say What? • page 102

ANSWER:
LENA
LITTLE
CLOSER
AND I
WILL
TELL YOU

Please Fix That • page 114

P	O	O	D	L	E	
L	I	T	T	L	E	
	O	I	L		O	N
	T	H	A	T		
D	O	O	R		–	
	I	T	'	S		
S	Q	U	E	A	K	Y

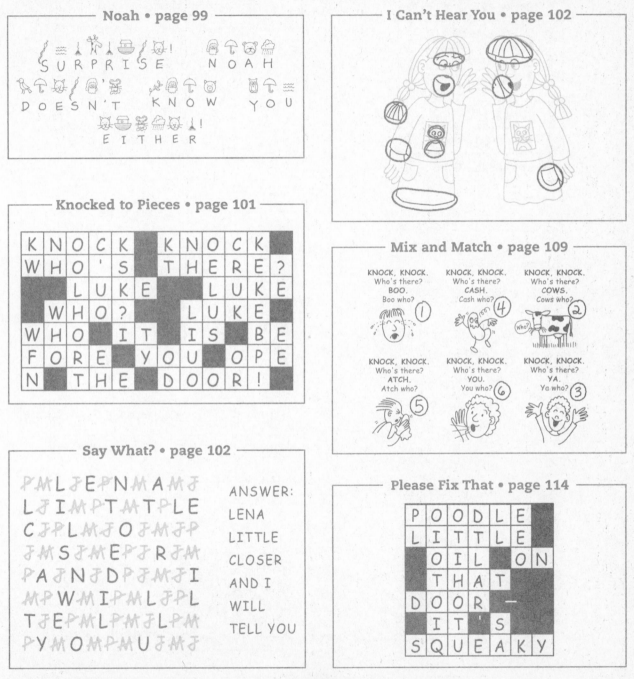

ANSWERS

Hidden Helper • page 117

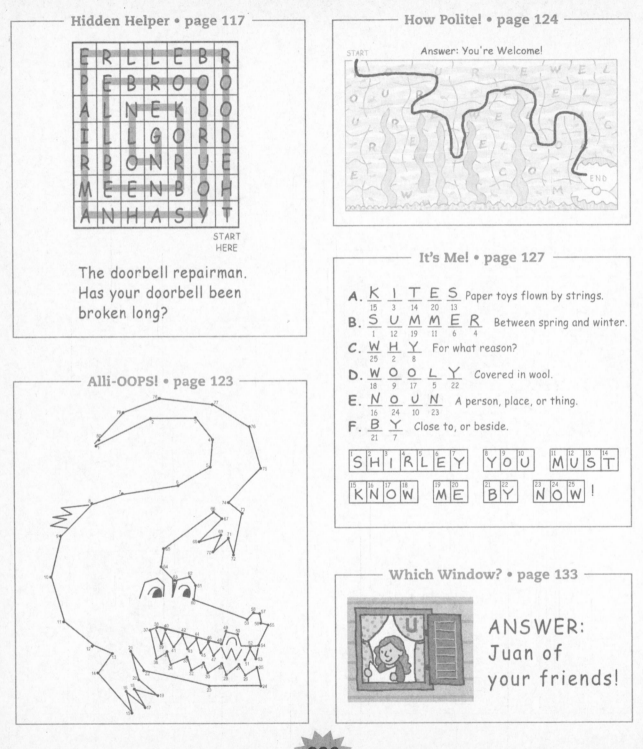

E	R	L	L	E	B	R
P	E	B	R	O	O	O
A	L	N	E	K	D	O
I	L	L	G	O	R	D
R	B	O	N	R	U	E
M	E	E	N	B	O	H
A	N	H	A	S	Y	T

START
HERE

The doorbell repairman.
Has your doorbell been
broken long?

How Polite! • page 124

START

Answer: You're Welcome!

END

Alli-OOPS! • page 123

It's Me! • page 127

A. <u>K I T E S</u> Paper toys flown by strings.
 15 3 14 20 13

B. <u>S U M M E R</u> Between spring and winter.
 1 12 19 11 6 4

C. <u>W H Y</u> For what reason?
 25 2 8

D. <u>W O O L Y</u> Covered in wool.
 18 9 17 5 22

E. <u>N O U N</u> A person, place, or thing.
 16 24 10 23

F. <u>B Y</u> Close to, or beside.
 21 7

¹S	²H	³I	⁴R	⁵L	⁶E	⁷Y		⁸Y	⁹O	¹⁰U		¹¹M	¹²U	¹³S	¹⁴T

¹⁵K	¹⁶N	¹⁷O	¹⁸W		¹⁹M	²⁰E		²¹B	²²Y		²³N	²⁴O	²⁵W	!

Which Window? • page 133

ANSWER:
Juan of
your friends!

290

ANSWERS

Half a Chance • page 138

E-4	Q-5	E+4	T-1	M+2	14
A	L	I	S	O	N

T+3	T-5	M+1	A+3	5	V-4	12	D-3	J+4	G-3
W	O	N	D	E	R	L	A	N	D

Rhyme Time • page 142

FLOCK

CLOCK

WINDSOCK

SHOCK

LOCK

DOCK

SOCK

SHAMROCK

BLOCK   AB

ROCK

Crazy Criss-Cross • page 145

```
D E L I G H T E D
      M E R R Y
      F I N E
E X C I T E D
  W O N D E R F U L
      P E R K Y
      C H E E R F U L
A W E S O M E
      S W E L L
F A N T A S T I C
      G R E A T
  E X C E L L E N T
H A P P Y
      G O O D
      S U N N Y
```

Knock Once • page 148

K	N	O	C	N	O	C	K
N	O	K	N	O	K	O	N
O	C	N	K	C	N	N	O
C	N	O	O	N	O	C	C
N	C	N	O	K	C	O	N
O	K	O	K	C	O	N	O
C	O	C	N	O	C	K	C
K	N	O	C	N	O	C	K

Who Is It? • page 153

START

Answer:
Handsome
spaghetti
through
the keyhole
and I'll
tell you!

Mixed Up Endings • page 157

1. **Knock, knock.** Who's there? **Who.** Who who?
There's a terrible echo in here!

2. **Knock, knock.** Who's there? **Pecan.** Pecan who?
Pecan somebody else next time!

3. **Knock, knock.** Who's there? **Cook.** Cook who?
You sound like a Swiss clock!

4. **Knock, knock.** Who's there? **Anita.** Anita who?
Anita minute to think it over!

5. **Knock, knock.** Who's there? **Kangar.** Kangar who?
Yes, I'm from Australia!

6. **Knock, knock.** Who's there? **Little old lady.** Little old lady who?
You can yodel?

ANSWERS

Wendy's Here • page 160

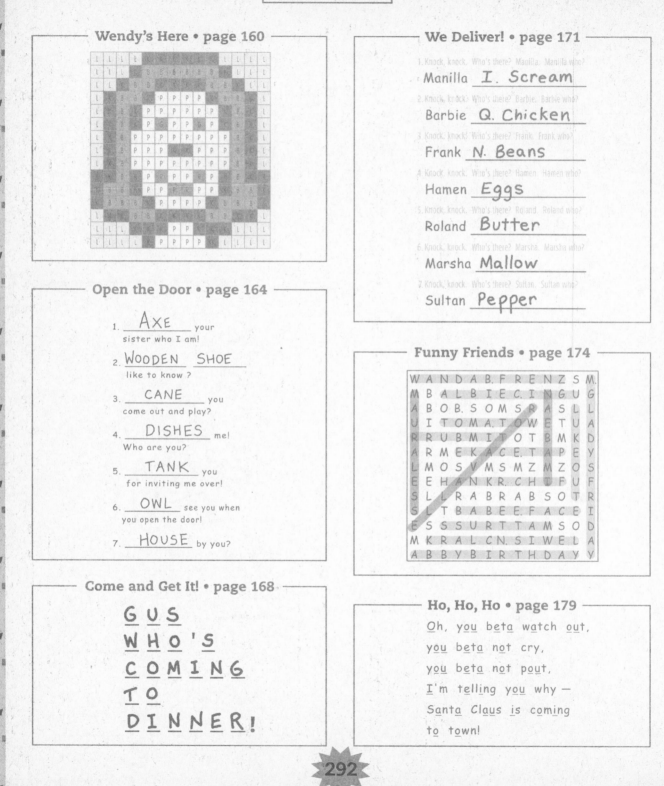

Open the Door • page 164

1. __AXE__ your sister who I am!
2. __WOODEN__ __SHOE__ like to know ?
3. __CANE__ you come out and play?
4. __DISHES__ me! Who are you?
5. __TANK__ you for inviting me over!
6. __OWL__ see you when you open the door!
7. __HOUSE__ by you?

Come and Get It! • page 168

G U S
W H O ' S
C O M I N G
T O
D I N N E R !

We Deliver! • page 171

1. Knock, knock. Who's there? Manilla. Manilla who?
Manilla __I. Scream__

2. Knock, knock. Who's there? Barbie. Barbie who?
Barbie __Q. Chicken__

3. Knock, knock. Who's there? Frank. Frank who?
Frank __N. Beans__

4. Knock, knock. Who's there? Hamen. Hamen who?
Hamen __Eggs__

5. Knock, knock. Who's there? Roland. Roland who?
Roland __Butter__

6. Knock, knock. Who's there? Marsha. Marsha who?
Marsha __Mallow__

7. Knock, knock. Who's there? Sultan. Sultan who?
Sultan __Pepper__

Funny Friends • page 174

```
W A N D A B . F R E N Z S M .
M B A L B I E C I N G U G
A B O B . S O M S R A S L L
U I T O M A . T O W E T U A
R R U B M I T O T B M K D
A R M E K A C E . T A P E Y
L M O S V M S M Z M Z O S
E E H A N K R . C H T F U F
S L L R A B R A B S O T R
S L T B A B E E . F A C E I
E S S U R T T A M S O D
M K R A L C N . S I W E L A
A B B Y B I R T H D A Y Y
```

Ho, Ho, Ho • page 179

Oh, you beta watch out,
you beta not cry,
you beta not pout,
I'm telling you why —
Santa Claus is coming
to town!

ANSWERS

Aye, Aye, Captain • page 182

Fire engine one and prepare for blast off!

Where in the World • page 184

1. __ALASKA__ questions, you give the answers!
2. __WARSAW__ matter? Cat got your tongue?
3. __IRAN__ to the party!
4. __ARKANSAS__ lots of wood with my chain saw!
5. __KENYA__ come out and play?
6. __JAMAICA__ me very happy!
7. __HAVANA__ go home now!
8. __TIJUANA__ ride my bike?
9. __TAIWAN__ a puppy for Christmas!
10. __YUKON__ have it, I don't want it!

Do I Know You? • page 191

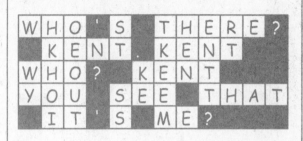

Don't Forget to Brush • page 192

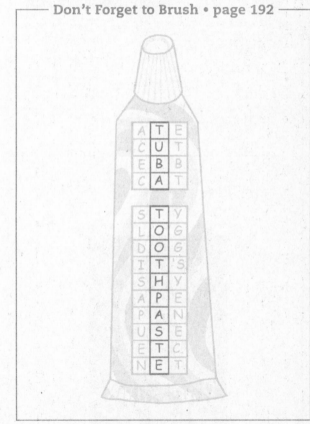

Do I Know You? • page 191

KNOCK, KNOCK.
WHO'S THERE?
HOOTIE.
HOOTIE WHO?
HOOTIE WHO
THINK YOU'RE
TALKING TO?

ANSWERS

Bad Band • page 203

Why was the music teacher so angry during class each day?

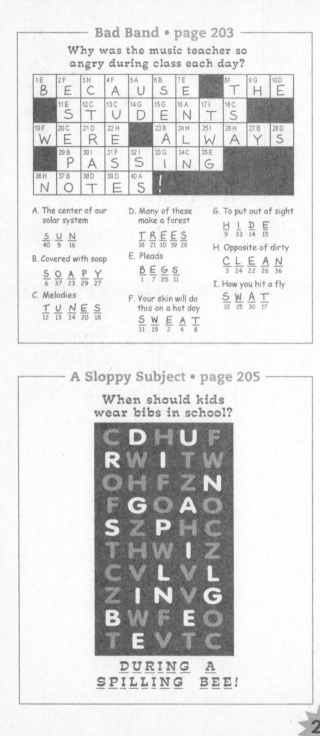

1E B	2F E	3H C	4F A	5A U	6B S	7E E		8F T	9G H	10D E
	11E S	12C T	13C U	14G D	15G E	16A N	17I T	18C S		
19F W	20C E	21D R	22H E			23B A	24H L	25I W	26H A	27B Y	28D S
		29B P	30I A	31F S	32I S	33G I	34C N	35E G		
36H N	37B O	38D T	39D E	40A S	!					

A. The center of our solar system
S U N
40 5 16

B. Covered with soap
S O A P Y
6 37 23 29 27

C. Melodies
T U N E S
12 13 34 20 18

D. Many of these make a forest
T R E E S
38 21 10 39 28

E. Pleads
B E G S
1 7 35 11

F. Your skin will do this on a hot day
S W E A T
31 19 2 4 8

G. To put out of sight
H I D E
9 33 14 15

H. Opposite of dirty
C L E A N
3 24 22 26 36

I. How you hit a fly
S W A T
32 25 30 17

A Sloppy Subject • page 205

When should kids wear bibs in school?

C D H U F
R W I T W
O H F Z N
F G O A O
S Z P H C
T H W I Z
C V L V L
Z I N V G
B W F E O
T E V T C

**D U R I N G   A
S P I L L I N G   B E E!**

Math Class • page 208

What do you get when you add 2 bananas, 1 apple, 15 grapes, and ½ melon?

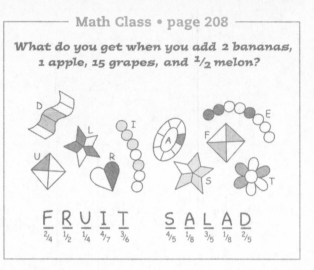

F R U I T
2/4 1/2 1/4 4/7 3/6

S A L A D
4/5 1/8 3/5 1/8 2/5

Loop the Zoo! • page 212

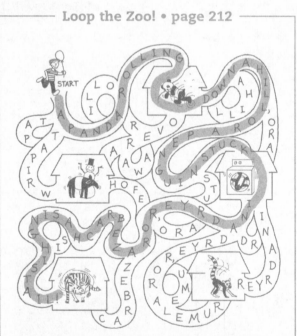

Answers: A panda rolling down a hill,
or a penguin stuck in a dryer,
or a zebra chasing his tail!

ANSWERS

Say What? • page 215

C<u>RA</u>B	"I'm grouchy!"
P<u>ANDA</u>	"Where's the bamboo?"
C<u>U</u>B	"I'll grow up to be a big bear!"
<u>M</u>ONKEY	"Got a banana?"
C<u>ROC</u>	"-odile is the last part of my name!"
<u>H</u>YENA	"Ha, Ha, Ha!"
<u>W</u>OR<u>M</u>	"You won't like me in your apple!"
<u>S</u>NAK<u>E</u>	"What'ssssss up?"
<u>OWL</u>	"Whoooo's there?"
<u>B</u>ATS	"Turn out the light! We like the dark!"

Feel Better • page 217

```
W H A T ' S   G R A Y   A N D
B R I N G S   F L O W E R S
T O   S I C K   A N I M A L
S   A T   T H E   Z O O ?   A
G E T - W E L L E P H A N T !
```

Funny Flight • page 222

"I just flew home from Paris, and..."

6 TIRED! ⊙ +D   3 ARMS   2 MY M+👁
5 SO (sounds like sew)   4 ARE R   1 BOY,

Where in the World • page 223

1. Where do fish go on vacation?
Finland

2. Where do songbirds go on vacation?
The Canary Islands

3. Where do zombies go on vacation?
The Dead Sea

4. Where do Thanksgiving birds go on vacation?
Turkey

5. Where do geometry teachers go on vacation?
Cuba

6. Where do locksmiths go on vacation?
The Florida Keys

The Hungry Traveler • page 226

A h<u>u</u>n<u>g</u>ry trav<u>e</u>l<u>e</u>r <u>wa</u>s taking a dri<u>ve</u> throu<u>g</u>h the <u>c</u>ountry <u>s</u>ide. He had b<u>r</u>ou<u>g</u>ht a <u>sa</u>l<u>a</u>d <u>w</u>ith him, <u>b</u>ut forgot an im<u>p</u>ortant too<u>l</u>. The h<u>u</u>n<u>g</u>ry trav<u>e</u>l<u>e</u>r fig<u>u</u>red he <u>c</u>ou<u>l</u>d eat <u>l</u>un<u>c</u>h <u>w</u>hen he got to a <u>c</u>ertain kind of inter<u>se</u>ction. What <u>wa</u>s the h<u>u</u>n<u>g</u>ry trav<u>e</u>l<u>e</u>r <u>w</u>aiting for?

<u>A FORK IN THE ROAD</u>!

Frightened Food • page 231

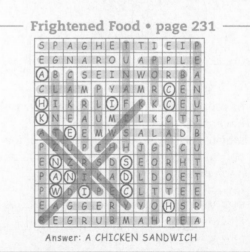

Answer: A CHICKEN SANDWICH

ANSWERS

Good Home Cookin' • page 232

Where does a snail like to eat lunch?

<u>IN A SLOW FOOD RESTAURANT!</u>

Second Helping • page 234

1. A L B I N O S
2. A Q U A T I C
3. C A R M I N E
4. C O N S E N T
5. C O T T A G E
6. E S T U A R Y
7. G O O F U P S
8. L O A F E R S
9. M I S E R L Y
10. O U T D O O R

Comic Contest • page 239

1. baseball cap, weather balloons, sweat-R (sweater), pet sheepdog
2. stocking cap, pet hot dog, blue (sad) jeans, pair of slippers (otherwise known as banana peels)
3. top hat, T-shirt, pet watchdog
4. THE WINNER! ski hat, rain coat, seeing i (eye) dog, bellbottom pants, elevator shoes

Silly Sally • page 242

Silly Sally like things that have double letters! Look at the picture of Silly Sally and you will see a balloon, a butterfly, glasses, earrings, mittens, buttons, a dress (covered with loops), boots, and a poodle!

Silly Slogans • page 243

1. **Top Card Playing Company**
   "Come see us when you... want a good deal!
2. **B&B Baking and Loan**
   "Come see us when you... knead dough!
3. **Al's Barber Shop**
   "Come see us when you... are in a hurry. We know all the short cuts!
4. **Larry's Lightbulbs**
   "Come see us when you... need a bright idea!
5. **Elegant Eyewear**
   "Come see us when you... want to look better!
6. **Good Deal Real Estate**
   "Come see us when you... are looking for a yard sale!

Cross Plumber • page 247

What do you get when you cross a plumber with a jeweler?

<u>A</u> <u>R</u>I<u>NG</u> <u>A</u>R<u>OU</u>N<u>D</u> <u>T</u>H<u>E</u> <u>B</u>A<u>T</u>H<u>T</u>U<u>B</u>!

ANSWERS

Why Did the Lion . . . • page 248

Answer: To get to the other pride!

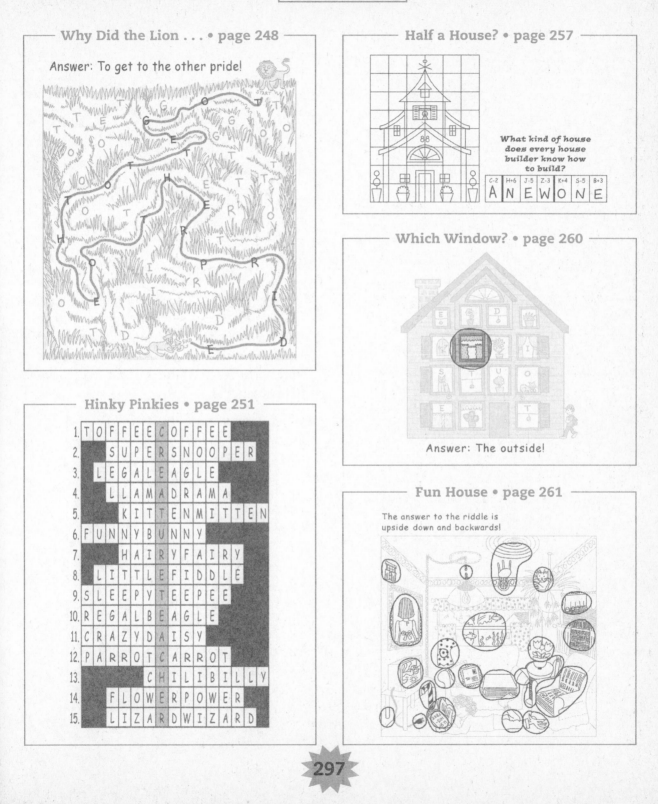

Hinky Pinkies • page 251

1. TOFFEE COFFEE
2. SUPER SNOOPER
3. LEGAL EAGLE
4. LLAMA DRAMA
5. KITTEN MITTEN
6. FUNNY BUNNY
7. HAIRY FAIRY
8. LITTLE FIDDLE
9. SLEEPY TEEPEE
10. REGAL BEAGLE
11. CRAZY DAISY
12. PARROT CARROT
13. CHILI BILLY
14. FLOWER POWER
15. LIZARD WIZARD

Half a House? • page 257

What kind of house does every house builder know how to build?

C-2	H+6	J-5	Z-3	K+4	S-5	B+3
A	N	E	W	O	N	E

Which Window? • page 260

Answer: The outside!

Fun House • page 261

The answer to the riddle is upside down and backwards!

ANSWERS

Night Games • page 267

Which animals are always invited to night baseball games?

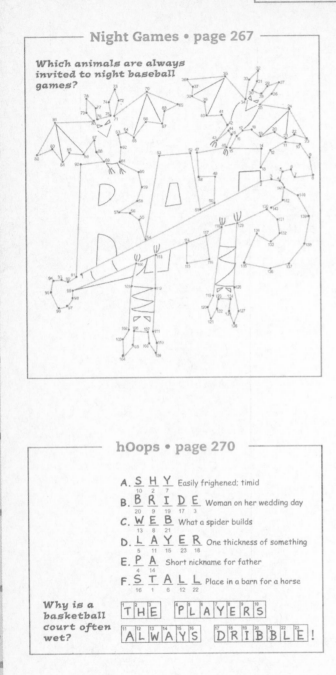

Balls of Fun • page 271

1. SOALCRSE LACROSSE
2. IFEDL OHCKYE FIELD HOCKEY
3. GOIWLBN BOWLING
4. NPIG OGPN PING PONG
5. USQSAH SQUASH
6. OOPL POOL (or POLO)
7. ENITNS TENNIS
8. FOLG GOLF
9. ROCUQET CROQUET
10. OPLO POLO (or POOL)

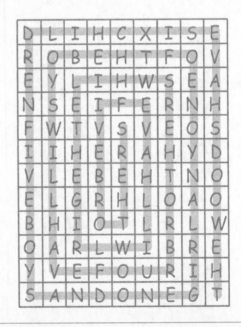

End

Start

Big Brothers • page 277

Starting in the lower righthand corner, going up, then spiraling around: The Woods have six children, five boys and one girl. Any one of the boys will have four brothers, while the girl will have five brothers.

D	L	I	H	C	X	I	S	E
R	O	B	E	H	T	F	O	V
E	Y	L	I	H	W	S	E	A
N	S	E	I	F	E	R	N	H
F	W	T	V	S	V	E	O	S
I	I	H	E	R	A	H	Y	D
V	L	E	B	E	H	T	N	O
E	L	G	R	H	L	O	A	O
B	H	I	O	T	L	R	L	W
O	A	R	L	W	I	B	R	E
Y	V	E	F	O	U	R	I	H
S	A	N	D	O	N	E	G	T

hOops • page 270

A. <u>S H Y</u> Easily frighened; timid
   10 2 7

B. <u>B R I D E</u> Woman on her wedding day
   20 9 19 17 3

C. <u>W E B</u> What a spider builds
   13 8 21

D. <u>L A Y E R</u> One thickness of something
   5 11 15 23 18

E. <u>P A</u> Short nickname for father
   4 14

F. <u>S T A L L</u> Place in a barn for a horse
   16 1 6 12 22

Why is a basketball court often wet?

¹T	²H	³E		⁴P	⁵L	⁶A	⁷Y	⁸E	⁹R	¹⁰S

| ¹¹A | ¹²L | ¹³W | ¹⁴A | ¹⁵Y | ¹⁶S | | ¹⁷D | ¹⁸R | ¹⁹I | ²⁰B | ²¹B | ²²L | ²³E | ! |

ANSWERS

The Family Name Game • page 278

8.
Mrs. Cathy

1. Mrs. Patti   P A N C A K E
2. Mrs. Frieda F L Y P A P E R
3. Mrs. Fran   F I R E W O O D
4. Mrs. Paula   P I G P E N
5. Mrs. Carol   C O O K B O O K
6. Mrs. Fiona   F O O T B A L L
7. Mrs. Rachel R A T T L E S N A K E

Watch Out! (1) • page 280

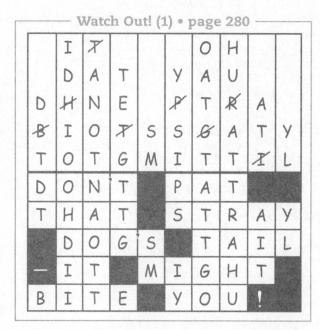

Watch Out! (2) • page 280

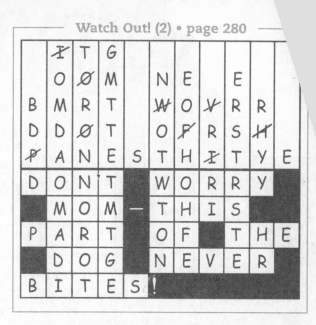

Hidden Family • page 281

1. We had f**un cle**aning the garage!
2. The leprech**aun t**old me where to find a pot of gold!
3. The music was so rau**cous, I n**eeded to cover my ears!
4. Under the so**fa ther**e are many dust-balls.
5. Did you read the same me**mo the re**st of us read?
6. During a cri**sis, ter**rific people often show up to help!
7. The chicken **broth er**ased the last symptoms of Brian's cold.
8. My friend **in L.A. w**as happy to have me visit her!

Have
EVERYTHING®
on Anything!

With **more than 19 million** copies sold, the Everything® series has become one of America's favorite resources for solving problems, learning new skills, and organizing lives. Our brand is not only recognizable—it's also welcomed.

The series is a hand-in-hand partner for people who are ready to tackle new subjects—like you!

For more information on the Everything® series, please visit *www.adamsmedia.com*

The Everything® list spans a wide range of subjects, with more than 500 titles covering 25 different categories:

Business	History	Reference
Careers	Home Improvement	Religion
Children's Storybooks	Everything Kids	Self-Help
Computers	Languages	Sports & Fitness
Cooking	Music	Travel
Crafts and Hobbies	New Age	Wedding
Education/Schools	Parenting	Writing
Games and Puzzles	Personal Finance	
Health	Pets	